Windows Debugging, Disassembling, Reversing

Practical Foundations: Training Course

Second Edition

Dmitry Vostokov
Software Diagnostics Services

Published by OpenTask, Republic of Ireland

Copyright © 2022 by Dmitry Vostokov

Copyright © 2022 by Software Diagnostics Services

All rights reserved. No part of this book may be reproduced, stored in a retrieval system, or transmitted, in any form or by any means, without the prior written permission of the publisher.

OpenTask books are available through booksellers and distributors worldwide. For further information or comments, send requests to press@opentask.com.

Product and company names mentioned in this book may be trademarks of their owners.

A CIP catalog record for this book is available from the British Library.

ISBN-13: 978-1-912636-35-8

Revision 2.5 (April 2022)

Summary of Contents

Contents 5

Preface to the Second Edition 15

Preface to the First Edition 16

Combined Preface from Original Editions 17

About the Author 18

Chapter x86.1: Memory, Registers, and Simple Arithmetic 19

Chapter x86.2: Debug and Release Binaries 33

Chapter x86.3: Number Representations 46

Chapter x86.4: Pointers 53

Chapter x86.5: Bytes, Words, and Double Words 68

Chapter x86.6: Pointers to Memory 73

Chapter x86.7: Logical Instructions and EIP 95

Chapter x86.8: Reconstructing a Program with Pointers 102

Chapter x86.9: Memory and Stacks 109

Chapter x86.10: Frame Pointer and Local Variables 128

Chapter x86.11: Function Parameters 141

Chapter x86.12: More Instructions 153

Chapter x86.13: Function Pointer Parameters 164

Chapter x86.14: Summary of Code Disassembly Patterns 170

Appendix x86: Using Docker Environment 174

Chapter x64.1: Memory, Registers, and Simple Arithmetic 176

Chapter x64.2: Debug and Release Binaries 191

Chapter x64.3: Number Representations 204

Chapter x64.4: Pointers 211

Chapter x64.5: Bytes, Words, and Double Words 229

Chapter x64.6: Pointers to Memory 235

Chapter x64.7: Logical Instructions and EIP 258

Chapter x64.8: Reconstructing a Program with Pointers 266

Chapter x64.9: Memory and Stacks 275

Chapter x64.10: Local Variables 295

Chapter x64.11: Function Parameters 305

Chapter x64.12: More Instructions 314

Chapter x64.13: Function Pointer Parameters 325

Chapter x64.14: Summary of Code Disassembly Patterns 329

Appendix x64: Using Docker Environment 335

Contents

Contents 5

Preface to the Second Edition 15

Preface to the First Edition 16

Combined Preface from Original Editions 17

About the Author 18

Chapter x86.1: Memory, Registers, and Simple Arithmetic 19

    Memory and Registers inside an Idealized Computer 19

    Memory and Registers inside Intel 32-bit PC 20

    "Arithmetic" Project: Memory Layout and Registers 21

    "Arithmetic" Project: A Computer Program 22

    "Arithmetic" Project: Assigning Numbers to Memory Locations 23

    Assigning Numbers to Registers 25

    "Arithmetic" Project: Adding Numbers to Memory Cells 26

    Incrementing/Decrementing Numbers in Memory and Registers 28

    Multiplying Numbers 30

    Multiplication and Registers 32

Chapter x86.2: Debug and Release Binaries 33

    "Arithmetic" Project: C/C++ Program 33

    Downloading and Configuring WinDbg Debugger 34

    WinDbg Disassembly Output – Debug Executable 36

    WinDbg Disassembly Output – Release Executable 45

Chapter x86.3: Number Representations 46

    Numbers and Their Representations 46

    Decimal Representation (Base Ten) 47

Ternary Representation (Base Three) 48

Binary Representation (Base Two) 49

Hexadecimal Representation (Base Sixteen) 50

Why are Hexadecimals Used? 51

Chapter x86.4: Pointers 53

A Definition 53

"Pointers" Project: Memory Layout and Registers 54

"Pointers" Project: Calculations 55

Using Pointers to Assign Numbers to Memory Cells 56

Adding Numbers Using Pointers 62

Multiplying Numbers Using Pointers 65

Chapter x86.5: Bytes, Words, and Double Words 68

Using Hexadecimal Numbers 68

Byte Granularity 69

Bit Granularity 70

Memory Layout 71

Chapter x86.6: Pointers to Memory 73

Pointers Revisited 73

Addressing Types 74

Registers Revisited 80

NULL Pointers 81

Invalid Pointers 82

Variables as Pointers 83

Pointer Initialization 84

Note: Initialized and Uninitialized Data 85

More Pseudo Notation 86

"MemoryPointers" Project: Memory Layout 87

Chapter x86.7: Logical Instructions and EIP 95

Instruction Format 95

Logical Shift Instructions 96

Logical Operations 97

Zeroing Memory or Registers 98

Instruction Pointer 99

Note: Code Section 100

Chapter x86.8: Reconstructing a Program with Pointers 102

Example of Disassembly Output: No Optimization 102

Reconstructing C/C++ Code: Part 1 104

Reconstructing C/C++ Code: Part 2 105

Reconstructing C/C++ Code: Part 3 106

Reconstructing C/C++ Code: C/C++ program 107

Example of Disassembly Output: Optimized Program 108

Chapter x86.9: Memory and Stacks 109

Stack: A Definition 109

Stack Implementation in Memory 110

Things to Remember 112

PUSH Instruction 113

POP instruction 114

Register Review 115

Application Memory Simplified 116

Stack Overflow 117

Jumps 119

Calls 121

- Call Stack 123
- Exploring Stack in WinDbg 125

Chapter x86.10: Frame Pointer and Local Variables 128

- Stack Usage 128
- Register Review 129
- Addressing Array Elements 130
- Stack Structure (No Function Parameters) 131
- Function Prolog 132
- Raw Stack (No Local Variables and Function Parameters) 133
- Function Epilog 135
- "Local Variables" Project 136
- Disassembly of Optimized Executable (Release Configuration) 139
- Advanced Topic: FPO 140

Chapter x86.11: Function Parameters 141

- "FunctionParameters" Project 141
- Stack Structure 142
- Stack Structure with FPO 144
- Function Prolog and Epilog 145
- Project Disassembled Code with Comments 146
- Release Build with FPO Enabled 149
- Cdecl Calling Convention 151
- Parameter Mismatch Problem 152

Chapter x86.12: More Instructions 153

- CPU Flags Register 153
- The Fastest Way to Fill Memory 154
- Testing for 0 156

TEST - Logical Compare 157

CMP – Compare Two Operands 158

TEST or CMP? 159

Conditional Jumps 160

The Structure of Registers 161

Function Return Value 162

Using Byte Registers 163

Chapter x86.13: Function Pointer Parameters 164

"FunctionPointerParameters" Project 164

Commented Disassembly 165

Dynamic Addressing of Local Variables 168

Chapter x86.14: Summary of Code Disassembly Patterns 170

Function Prolog/Epilog 170

Passing Parameters 171

LEA (Load Effective Address) 172

Accessing Parameters and Local Variables 173

Appendix x86: Using Docker Environment 174

Chapter x64.1: Memory, Registers, and Simple Arithmetic 176

Memory and Registers inside an Idealized Computer 176

Memory and Registers inside Intel 64-bit PC 177

"Arithmetic" Project: Memory Layout and Registers 178

"Arithmetic" Project: A Computer Program 179

"Arithmetic" Project: Assigning Numbers to Memory Locations 180

Assigning Numbers to Registers 182

"Arithmetic" Project: Adding Numbers to Memory Cells 183

Incrementing/Decrementing Numbers in Memory and Registers 186

Multiplying Numbers 189

Chapter x64.2: Debug and Release Binaries 191

"Arithmetic" Project: C/C++ Program 191

Downloading and Configuring WinDbg Debugger 192

WinDbg Disassembly Output – Debug Executable 194

WinDbg Disassembly Output – Release Executable 203

Chapter x64.3: Number Representations 204

Numbers and Their Representations 204

Decimal Representation (Base Ten) 205

Ternary Representation (Base Three) 206

Binary Representation (Base Two) 207

Hexadecimal Representation (Base Sixteen) 208

Why are Hexadecimals Used? 209

Chapter x64.4: Pointers 211

A Definition 211

"Pointers" Project: Memory Layout and Registers 212

"Pointers" Project: Calculations 213

Using Pointers to Assign Numbers to Memory Cells 214

Adding Numbers Using Pointers 221

Multiplying Numbers Using Pointers 225

Chapter x64.5: Bytes, Words, and Double Words 229

Using Hexadecimal Numbers 229

Byte Granularity 230

Bit Granularity 231

Memory Layout 233

Chapter x64.6: Pointers to Memory 235

- Pointers Revisited 235
- Addressing Types 236
- Registers Revisited 242
- NULL Pointers 243
- Invalid Pointers 244
- Variables as Pointers 245
- Pointer Initialization 246
- Note: Initialized and Uninitialized Data 247
- More Pseudo Notation 248
- "MemoryPointers" Project: Memory Layout 249

Chapter x64.7: Logical Instructions and EIP 258
- Instruction Format 258
- Logical Shift Instructions 259
- Logical Operations 260
- Zeroing Memory or Registers 261
- Instruction Pointer 262
- Note: Code Section 264

Chapter x64.8: Reconstructing a Program with Pointers 266
- Example of Disassembly Output: No Optimization 266
- Reconstructing C/C++ Code: Part 1 269
- Reconstructing C/C++ Code: Part 2 271
- Reconstructing C/C++ Code: Part 3 272
- Reconstructing C/C++ Code: C/C++ program 273
- Example of Disassembly Output: Optimized Program 274

Chapter x64.9: Memory and Stacks 275
- Stack: A Definition 275

Stack Implementation in Memory 276

Things to Remember 278

PUSH Instruction 279

POP instruction 280

Register Review 281

Application Memory Simplified 282

Stack Overflow 283

Jumps 285

Calls 287

Call Stack 289

Exploring Stack in WinDbg 291

Chapter x64.10: Local Variables 295

Stack Usage 295

Addressing Array Elements 296

Stack Structure (No Function Parameters) 297

Function Prolog 298

Function Epilog 299

"Local Variables" Project 300

Disassembly of Optimized Executable (Release Configuration) 304

Chapter x64.11: Function Parameters 305

"FunctionParameters" Project 305

Stack Structure 306

Function Prolog and Epilog 308

Project Disassembled Code with Comments 310

Parameter Mismatch Problem 313

Chapter x64.12: More Instructions 314

CPU Flags Register 314

The Fastest Way to Fill Memory 315

Testing for 0 317

TEST - Logical Compare 318

CMP – Compare Two Operands 319

TEST or CMP? 320

Conditional Jumps 321

The Structure of Registers 322

Function Return Value 323

Using Byte Registers 324

Chapter x64.13: Function Pointer Parameters 325

"FunctionPointerParameters" Project 325

Commented Disassembly 326

Chapter x64.14: Summary of Code Disassembly Patterns 329

Function Prolog/Epilog 329

Parameters and Local Variables 331

LEA (Load Effective Address) 333

Accessing Parameters and Local Variables 334

Appendix x64: Using Docker Environment 335

[This page intentionally left blank]

Preface to the Second Edition

Almost 5 years have passed since we published the first edition. Since then, we have also published "Practical Foundations of Linux Debugging, Disassembling, Reversing: Training Course" (ISBN-13: 978-1912636341) and "Practical Foundations of ARM64 Linux Debugging, Disassembling, Reversing: Training Course" (ISBN-13: 978-1912636372) books. At that time, we thought about revising our Windows course. Since then, Windows 11 appeared, and we also added Docker support for most of our Windows memory dump analysis courses. While working on the "Accelerated Windows Debugging 4" course (ISBN-13: 978-1912636532), we decided to make the second edition of Practical Foundations of Windows Debugging based on WinDbg from Windows 11 SDK and Visual Studio 2022 build tools and an optional Docker support for exercise environment. We also changed the ":=" operator to "<-" in our pseudo-code for Intel disassembly syntax flavor to align with our recent Linux Practical Foundations books, which use "->" in pseudo-code for x64 AT&T disassembly syntax flavor and "<-" in pseudo-code for ARM64 disassembly syntax. All sample projects were recompiled, and many diagrams were redone for the new edition to reflect changes in code generation. WinDbg syntax highlighting was also improved, including minor text improvements. There are also minor additions for C++11 and C++20.

This introductory training course can complement the more advanced course "Accelerated Disassembly, Reconstruction and Reversing: Training Course Transcript and WinDbg Practice Exercises with Memory Cell Diagrams, Revised Edition" (ISBN-13: 978-1908043757) from Software Diagnostics Services. It may also help with advanced exercises in "Accelerated Windows Memory Dump Analysis, Fifth Edition, Part 1, Revised, Process User Space: Training Course Transcript and WinDbg Practice Exercises with Notes" (ISBN-13: 978-1912636051) and "Accelerated Windows Memory Dump Analysis, Fifth Edition, Part 2, Revised, Kernel and Complete Spaces: Training Course Transcript and WinDbg Practice Exercises with Notes" (ISBN-13: 978-1912636082).

Since the first edition, we have also started adding additional social media links to our books' prefaces:

LinkedIn page:

https://www.linkedin.com/company/software-diagnostics-services

Twitter:

https://twitter.com/DumpAnalysis

Preface to the First Edition

This training course is a combined and reformatted version of the two previous books, "Windows Debugging: Practical Foundations" (ISBN: 978-1906717100 and 978-1906717674) and "x64 Windows Debugging: Practical Foundations" (ISBN: 978-1906717568 and 978-1906717926). The new format makes switching between and comparing x86 and x64 versions easy. The book also has a larger format similar to other training courses from Software Diagnostics Services, punctuation and code highlighting improvements, the output and screenshots from the latest WinDbg 10, and consistently uses WinDbg (X86) for 32-bit examples and WinDbg (X64) for 64-bit examples.

The book contains two separate sets of chapters and corresponding illustrations. They are named **Chapter x86.NN** and **Chapter x64.NN** respectively. There is some repetition of content due to the shared nature of x64 and x86 platforms. Both sets of chapters can be read independently. We included x86 chapters because many Windows applications are still 32-bit and executed in 32-bit compatibility mode on x64 Windows systems.

This introductory training course can complement the more advanced course "Accelerated Disassembly, Reconstruction and Reversing" (ISBN: 978-1908043672) from Software Diagnostics Services.

If you encounter any error, please contact us using this form:

https://www.patterndiagnostics.com/contact

Facebook page:

https://www.facebook.com/SoftwareDiagnosticsServices

Combined Preface from Original Editions

This book grew partially from original lectures I developed almost 12 years ago to train support and escalation engineers in debugging and crash dump analysis of memory dumps from Windows applications, services, and systems. At that time, when thinking about what material to deliver, I realized that a solid understanding of fundamentals like pointers is needed to analyze stack traces beyond **!analyze -v** and **lmv** WinDbg commands. Therefore, this book is not about bugs or debugging techniques but about background knowledge everyone needs to start experimenting with WinDbg and learn from practical experience and read other advanced debugging books. This body of knowledge is what the author of this book possessed before starting memory dump analysis using WinDbg 12 years ago, which resulted in the number one debugging bestseller: multi-volume Memory Dump Analysis Anthology. Now, in retrospection, I see these practical foundations as relevant and necessary to acquire for beginners as they were 12 years ago because operating systems internals, assembly language, and compiler architecture haven't changed in those years.

When writing the x86 version of this book, I realized that more practical examples were needed, and I recompiled every sample with Visual C++ Express Edition and provided detailed steps for WinDbg usage. I also recreated almost every illustration to fit and look better in the book format.

The appearance of AMD64 and Intel EM64T architectures and x64 Windows requires engineers to learn the new features of x64 architecture and assembly language. But, more importantly, they also need to forget old patterns of compiled code that persisted in reverse engineering literature for decades and adapt to the new ones. As a result, almost every illustration was recreated to reflect the x64 architecture, and almost every sample is provided with detailed steps for x64 WinDbg usage.

The book is useful for:

- Software technical support and escalation engineers
- Software engineers coming from managed code or Java background
- Software testers
- Engineers coming from non-Wintel environments
- Windows C/C++ software engineers without assembly language background
- Security researchers without assembly language background
- Beginners learning Windows software reverse engineering techniques

This book can also be used as an Intel assembly language and Windows debugging supplement for relevant undergraduate-level courses.

About the Author

Dmitry Vostokov is an internationally recognized expert, speaker, educator, scientist, inventor, and author. He is the founder of the pattern-oriented software diagnostics, forensics, and prognostics discipline (Systematic Software Diagnostics), and Software Diagnostics Institute (DA+TA: DumpAnalysis.org + TraceAnalysis.org). Vostokov has also authored more than 50 books on software diagnostics, anomaly detection and analysis, software and memory forensics, root cause analysis and problem solving, memory dump analysis, debugging, software trace and log analysis, reverse engineering, and malware analysis. He has over 25 years of experience in software architecture, design, development, and maintenance in various industries, including leadership, technical, and people management roles. Dmitry also founded Syndromatix, Anolog.io, BriteTrace, DiaThings, Logtellect, OpenTask Iterative and Incremental Publishing (OpenTask.com), Software Diagnostics Technology and Services (former Memory Dump Analysis Services) PatternDiagnostics.com, and Software Prognostics. In his spare time, he presents various topics on Debugging.TV and explores Software Narratology, its further development as Narratology of Things and Diagnostics of Things (DoT), Software Pathology, and Quantum Software Diagnostics. His current interest areas are theoretical software diagnostics and its mathematical and computer science foundations, application of formal logic, artificial intelligence, machine learning and data mining to diagnostics and anomaly detection, software diagnostics engineering and diagnostics-driven development, diagnostics workflow and interaction. Recent interest areas also include cloud native computing, security, automation, functional programming, and applications of category theory to software development and big data.

Chapter x86.1: Memory, Registers, and Simple Arithmetic

Memory and Registers inside an Idealized Computer

Computer memory consists of a sequence of memory cells, and each cell has a unique address (location). Every cell contains a "number". We refer to these "numbers" as contents at addresses (locations). Memory access is slower than arithmetic instructions, and there are so-called registers to speed up complex operations that require memory to store temporary results. We can also think about them as standalone memory cells. The name of a register is its address.

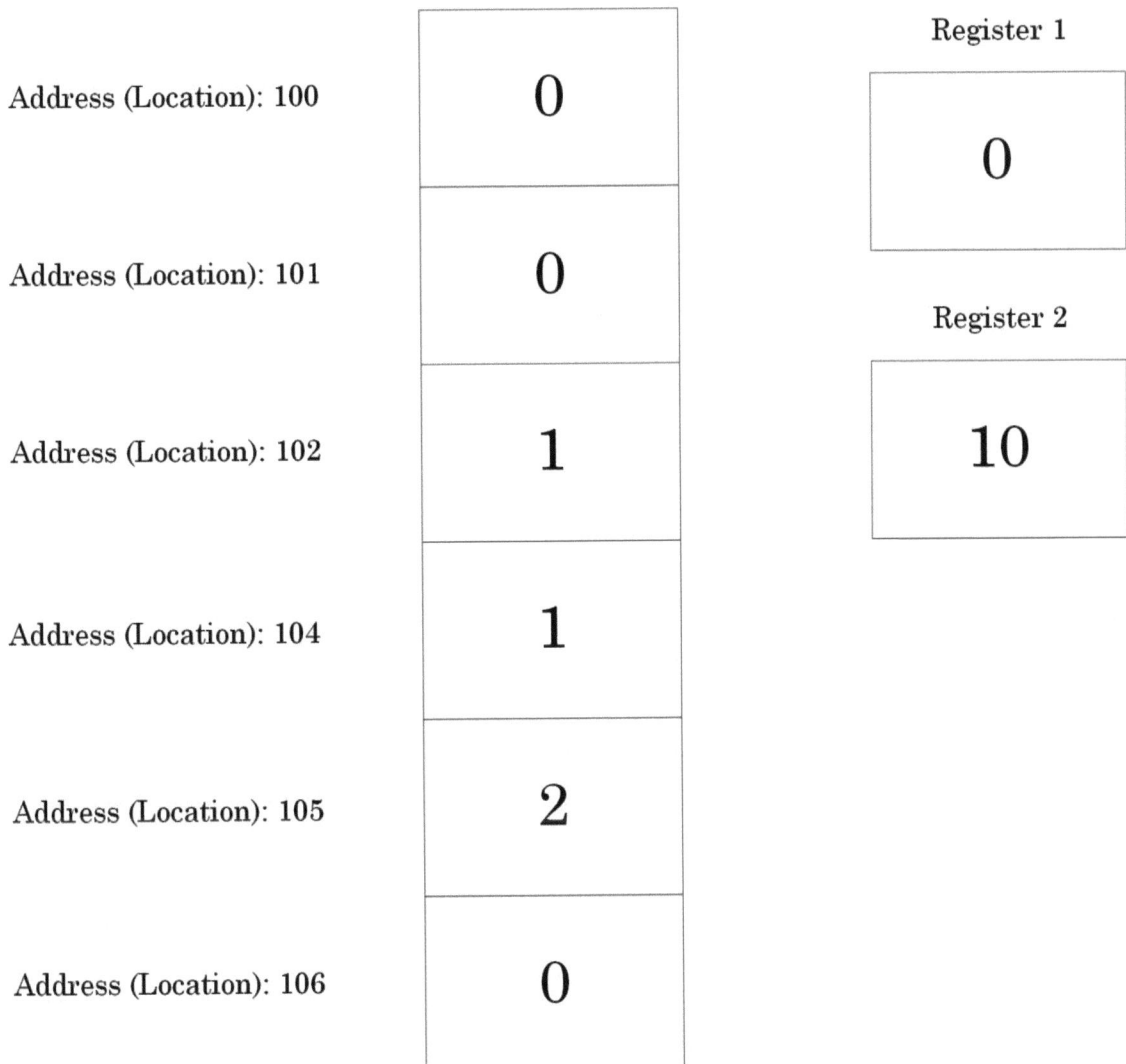

Picture x86.1.1

Memory and Registers inside Intel 32-bit PC

Here addresses for memory locations containing integer values usually differ by 4, and we also show 2 registers called EAX and EDX.

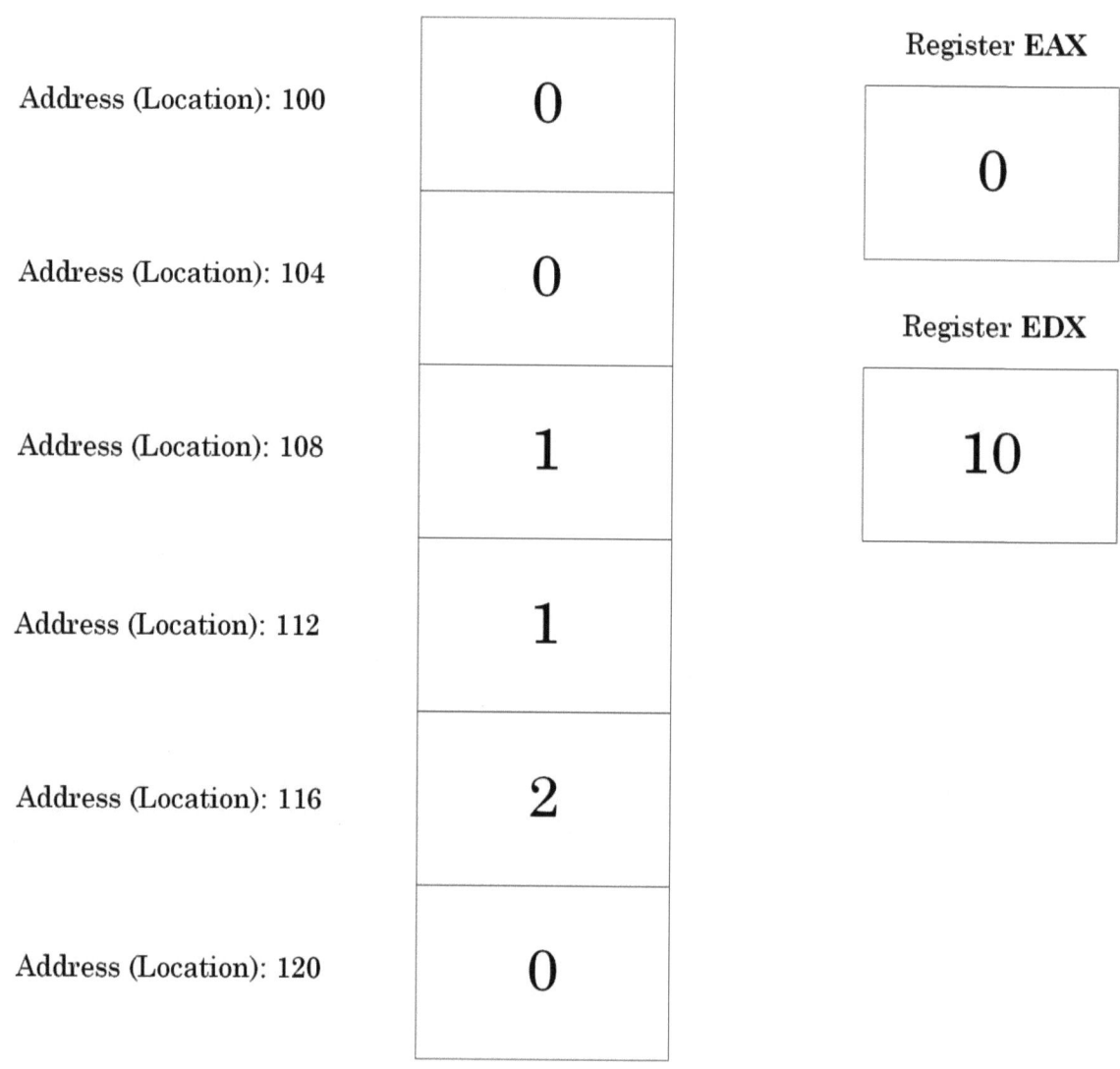

Picture x86.1.2

Because memory cells contain "numbers", we start with a simple arithmetic and ask a PC to compute a sum of two numbers to see how memory and registers change their values. We call our project "Arithmetic".

"Arithmetic" Project: Memory Layout and Registers

For our project, we have two memory addresses (locations) that we call "a" and "b". So we can think about "a" and "b" as names of their respective addresses (locations). Now we introduce a special notation where [a] means contents at the memory address (location) "a". If we use C or C++ language to write our project, then we declare and define memory locations "a" and "b" as:

```
static int a, b;
```

By default, static memory locations are filled with zeroes when we load a program, and we can depict our initial memory layout after loading the program as shown in Picture x86.1.3.

	0	Register **EAX**
		0
Location: **a** (Address 00428500)	0	
		Register **EDX**
Location: **b** (Address 00428504)	0	0
Address (Location): 00428508	0	
	0	
	0	

Picture x86.1.3

"Arithmetic" Project: A Computer Program

We can think of a computer program as a sequence of instructions for the manipulation of contents of memory cells and registers. For example, addition operation: add the contents of memory cell №12 to the contents of memory cell №14. In our pseudo-code, we can write:

`[14] <- [14] + [12]`

Our first program in pseudo-code is shown on the left of the table:

`[a] <- 1`
`[b] <- 1`
`[b] <- [b] + [a]   ; [b] = 2`
`[b] <- [b] * 2     ; [b] = 4`
	Here we put assembly instructions corresponding to pseudo-code.

'<-' means assignment when we replace the contents of a memory location (address) with the new value. ';' is a comment sign, and the rest of the line is a comment. '=' shows the current value at a memory location (address).

To remind, code written in a high-level programming language is translated to a machine language by a compiler. However, the machine language can be readable if its digital codes are represented in some mnemonic system called assembly language. For example, **INC [a]**, to increment by one what is stored at a memory location **a**.

"Arithmetic" Project: Assigning Numbers to Memory Locations

We remind that "a" means location (address) of the memory cell, and it is also the name of the location (address) 00428500 (see Picture x86.1.3). [a] means the contents (number) stored at the address "a".

If we use C or C++ language, "a" is called "variable a", and we write assignment as:

a = 1;

In Intel assembly language, we write:

mov [a], 1

In WinDbg disassembly output, we see the following code where the variable "a" is prefixed by '!' and the name of the executable file (module), which is *ArithmeticProject.exe*:

mov dword ptr [ArithmeticProject!a (00428500)], 1

We show the translation of our pseudo code into assembly language in the right column:

[a] <- 1	mov [a], 1
[b] <- 1	mov [b], 1
[b] <- [b] + [a] ; [b] = 2	
[b] <- [b] * 2 ; [b] = 4	

After executing the first two assembly language instructions, we have the memory layout shown in Picture x86.1.4.

24 "Arithmetic" Project: Assigning Numbers to Memory Locations

Memory		Registers
	0	Register EAX: 0
Location: **a** (Address 00428500)	1	
Location: **b** (Address 00428504)	1	Register EDX: 0
Address (Location): 00428508	0	
	0	
	0	

Picture x86.1.4

Assigning Numbers to Registers

This operation is similar to memory assignments. We can write in pseudo-code:

```
register <- 1 or register <- [a]
```

Note that we do not use brackets when referring to register contents. The latter instruction means assigning (copying) the number at the location (address) "a" to a register.

In assembly language, we write:

```
mov    eax, 1

mov    eax, [a]
```

In WinDbg disassembly output, we would see the following code:

```
mov    eax, [ArithmeticProject!a (00428500)]
```

"Arithmetic" Project: Adding Numbers to Memory Cells

Now let's look at the following pseudo-code statement in more detail:

[b] <- [b] + [a]

To recall, "a" and "b" mean the names of locations (addresses) 00428500 and 00428504, respectively (see Picture x86.1.4). [a] and [b] mean contents at addresses "a" and "b" respectively, simply some numbers stored there.

In C or C++ language we write the following statement:

b = b + a; // or

b += a;

In assembly language, we use the instruction ADD. Due to limitations of Intel x86 architecture, we cannot use both memory addresses in one step (instruction), for example, **add [b], [a]**. We can only use **add [b], register** to add the value stored in the **register** to the contents of memory cell **b**. Recall that a register is like a temporary memory cell itself here:

register <- [a]

[b] <- [b] + register

In assembly language, we write:

mov   eax, [a]

add   [b], eax

In WinDbg disassembly output, we would see the following code:

mov   eax,[ArithmeticProject!a (00428500)]

add   [ArithmeticProject!b (00428504)],eax

Now we can translate our pseudo-code into assembly language:

[a] <- 1		mov	[a], 1
[b] <- 1		mov	[b], 1
	; eax = 1	mov	eax, [a]
[b] <- [b] + [a]	; [b] = 2	add	[b], eax
[b] <- [b] * 2	; [b] = 4		

After the execution of ADD instruction, we have the memory layout illustrated in Picture x86.1.5.

	Register **EAX**
0	
	1
Location: **a** (Address 00428500) → 1	
	Register **EDX**
Location: **b** (Address 00428504) → 2	0
Address (Location): 00428508 → 0	
0	
0	

Picture x86.1.5

Incrementing/Decrementing Numbers in Memory and Registers

In pseudo-code it looks simple and means increment (decrement) a number stored at location (address) "a":

```
[a] <- [a] + 1

[a] <- [a] - 1
```

In C or C++ language, we can write this using three possible ways:

```
a = a + 1; // or

++a; // or

a++;

b = b - 1; // or

--b; // or

b--;
```

In assembly language we use instructions INC and DEC and write:

```
Inc   [a]

inc   eax

dec   [a]

dec   eax
```

In WinDbg disassembly output, we would see the same instruction:

```
inc   eax
```

Now we add this additional increment to our pseudo-code and its assembly language translation (this is needed for subsequent multiplication explained later):

[a] <- 1	mov	[a], 1
[b] <- 1	mov	[b], 1
; eax = 1	mov	eax, [a]
[b] <- [b] + [a] ; [b] = 2	add	[b], eax
eax <- eax + 1 ; eax = 2	**inc**	**eax**
[b] <- [b] * 2 ; [b] = 4		

After the execution of INC instruction, we have the memory layout illustrated in Picture x86.1.6.

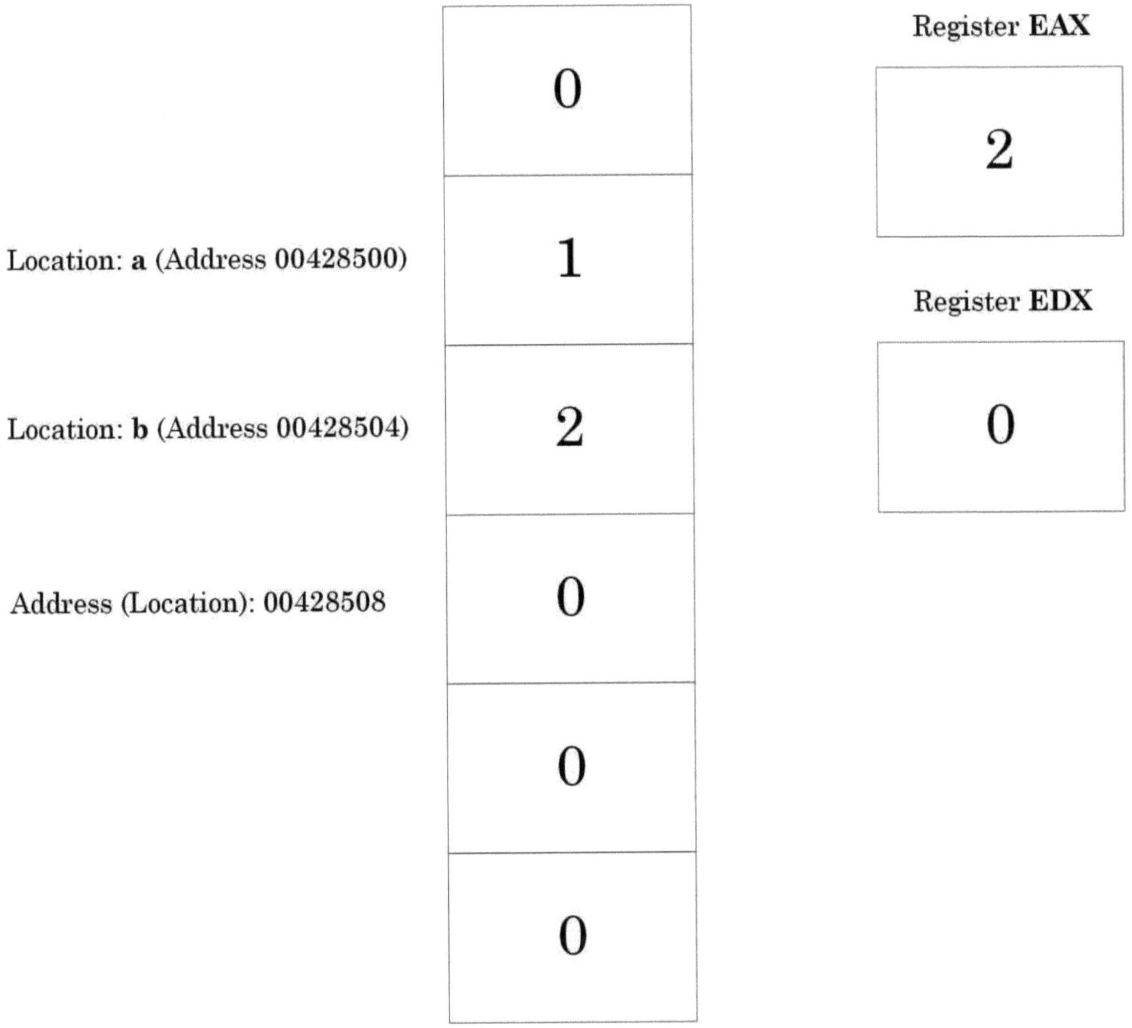
Register EAX
2
Register EDX
0
0
Location: a (Address 00428500)
1
Location: b (Address 00428504)
2
Address (Location): 00428508
0
0
0

Picture x86.1.6

Multiplying Numbers

In pseudo code we write:

```
[b] <- [b] * 2
```

This operation means we multiply the number at the location (address) "b" by 2.

In C or C++ language we can write this using two ways:

```
b = b * 2; // or

b *= 2;
```

In assembly language we use instruction IMUL (Integer MULtiply) and write:

```
imul [b]

mov [b], eax
```

The whole sequence means [b] <- [b] * EAX, so we have to put 2 into EAX (see previous section). Fortunately, we already have 2 in the EAX register. The multiplication result is put into registers EAX and EDX (for reasons why we need the second register, see the next section).

In WinDbg disassembly output, we would see the following code:

```
imul dword ptr [ArithmeticProject!b (00428504)]

mov [ArithmeticProject!b (00428504)],eax
```

Now we add two additional assembly instructions to our pseudo-code assembly language translation:

[a] <- 1		mov [a], 1
[b] <- 1		mov [b], 1
; eax = 1		mov eax, [a]
[b] <- [b] + [a] ; [b] = 2		add [b], eax
eax <- eax + 1 ; eax = 2		inc eax
[b] <- [b] * 2 ; eax = 4		imul [b]
; [b] = 4		mov [b], eax

After executing **imul** and **mov** instructions, we have the memory layout illustrated in Picture x86.1.7.

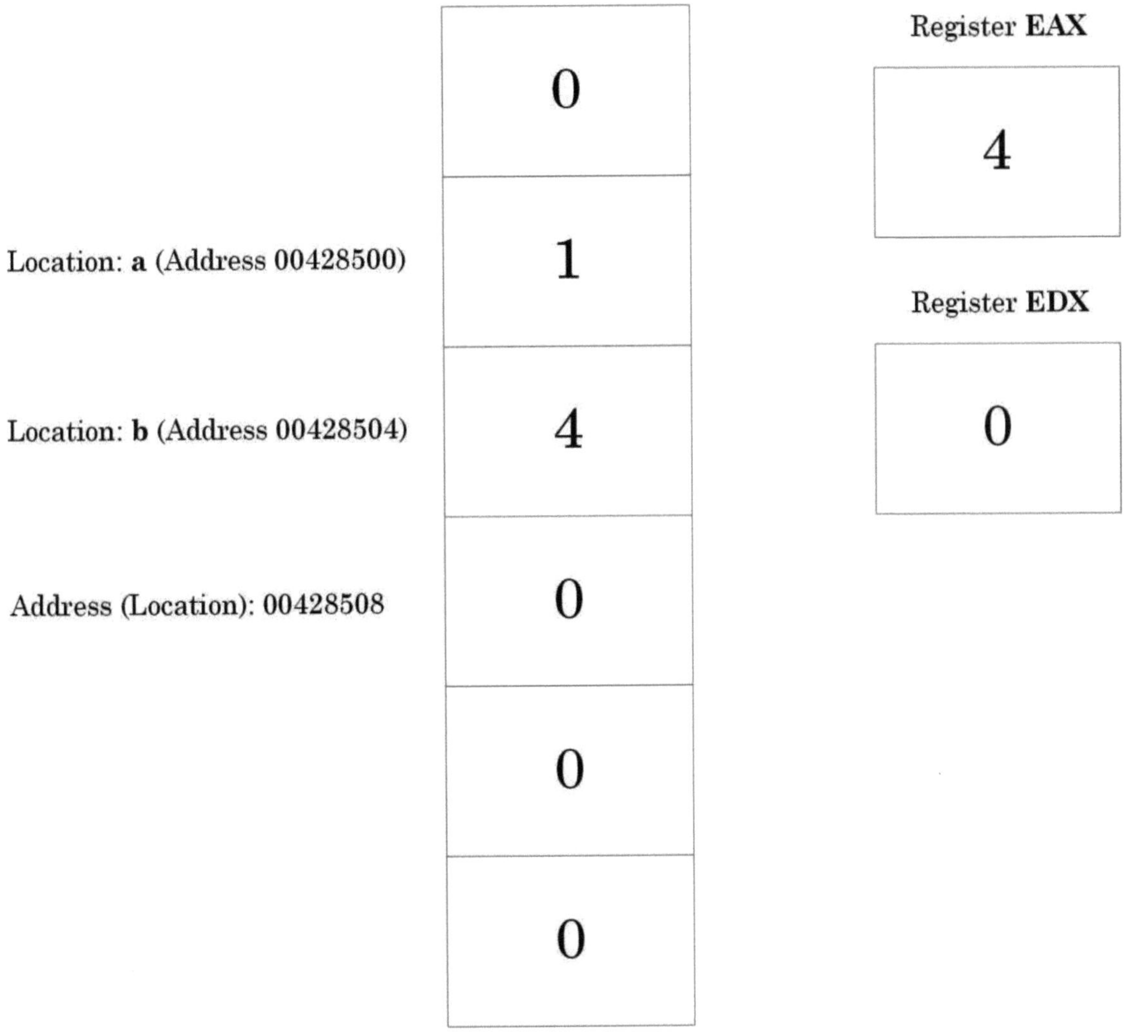
Register **EAX**
4
Register **EDX**
0
0
Location: **a** (Address 00428500)
1
Location: **b** (Address 00428504)
4
Address (Location): 00428508
0
0
0

Picture x86.1.7

Multiplication and Registers

Why do we need two registers to store the result of a multiplication? These two registers are needed because each register or integer memory cell in an x86 computer can contain a number between 2147483648 and 2147483647. If we multiply 2 by 2, the result can be put into one register EAX. However, if we multiply 2147483647 by 2147483647, we get 4611686014132420609. The result is too big to fit into one register or memory cell.

We can think of EDX:EAX pair as two memory cells joined together to hold the large multiplication result.

Chapter x86.2: Debug and Release Binaries

"Arithmetic" Project: C/C++ Program

Let's rewrite our "Arithmetic" program in C/C++. Corresponding assembly language instructions are put in comments:

```
int a, b;
int main(int argc, char* argv[])
{
        a = 1;              // mov   [a], 1
        b = 1;              // mov   [b], 1
        b = b + a;          // mov   eax, [a]
                            // add   [b], eax
        ++a;                // inc   eax
                            // mov   [a], eax
        b = b * a;          // imul  [b]
                            // mov   [b], eax
                            // results: [a] = 2 and [b] = 4

        return 0;
}
```

If we compile and link the program in debug mode, we get the binary executable module which we can load in WinDbg and inspect assembly code.

Downloading and Configuring WinDbg Debugger

WinDbg from Debugging Tools for Windows or WinDbg Preview App can be installed from Microsoft website, or we can use WinDbg.org pointing to Microsoft download links as shown in Picture x86.2.1. In the book, we use WinDbg, but if you choose WinDbg Preview instead, there is no difference in debugger commands output. If you prefer using a Docker environment, please check Appendix x86.

Pattern-Oriented Software Diagnostics

Software Diagnostics Institute

Software Diagnostics Library

Software Diagnostics Technology and Services

Memory Dump Analysis Anthology

Tables of Contents and Indexes of WinDbg Commands from all volumes

WinDbg Quick Links

Download Debugging Tools for Windows

Download WinDbg Preview

Debugging Tools for Windows Help

Debugging Tools for Windows Blog

Symbol Server (Microsoft):

`srv*c:\mss*http://msdl.microsoft.com/download/symbols`

Picture x86.2.1

For x86 chapters, we need to use WinDbg (X86) for debugging 32-bit applications. So, after installing Debugging Tools for Windows, we start WinDbg (X86) as shown in Picture x86.2.2.

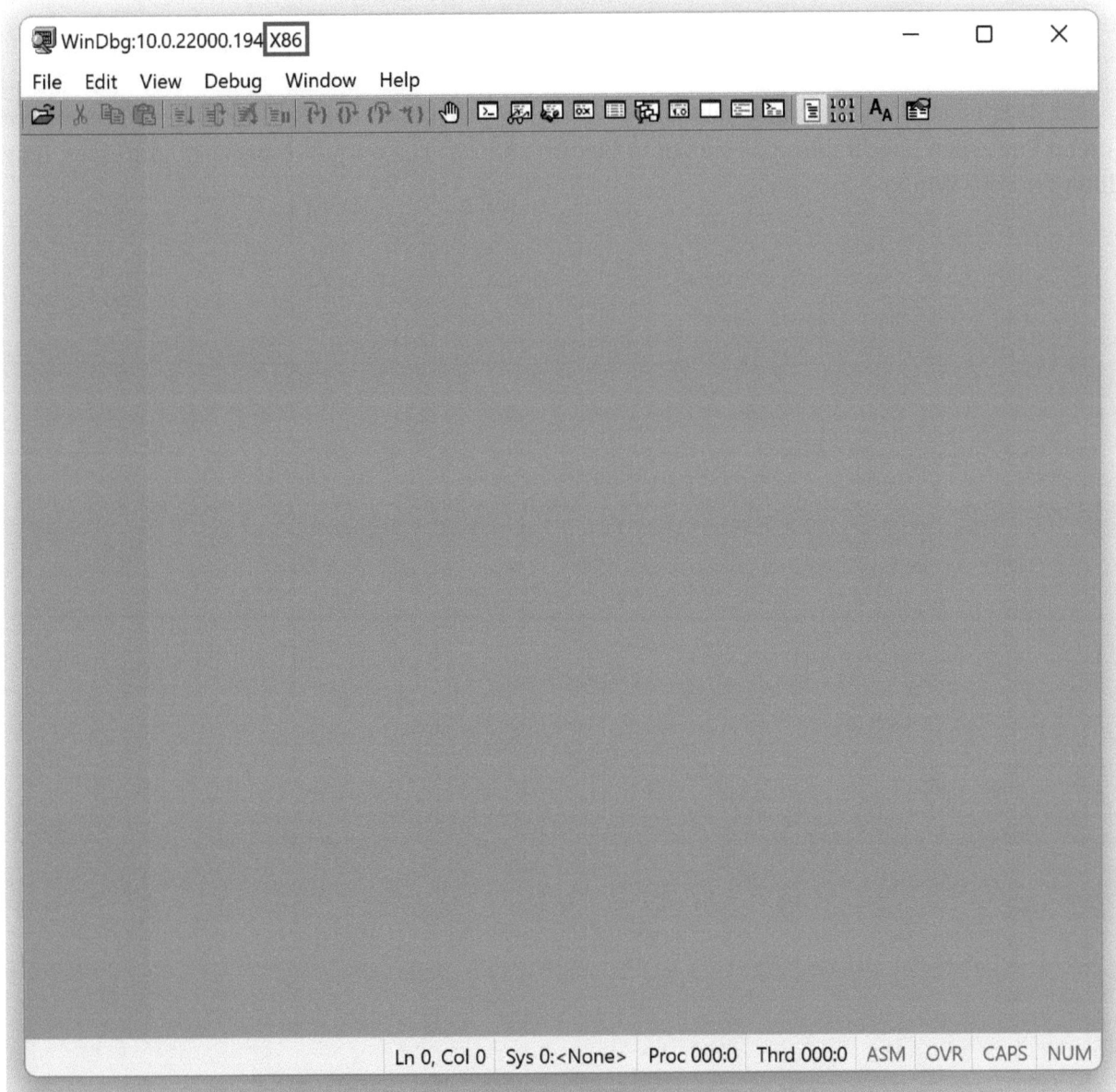

Picture x86.2.2

WinDbg Disassembly Output – Debug Executable

The *Debug* executable can be downloaded from the following location:

https://bitbucket.org/softwarediagnostics/pfwddr2/src/master/x86/Chapter2/

It is located under *Debug* subfolder. We run WinDbg and then load *ArithmeticProjectC.exe* (menu File\Open Executable...) as shown in Picture x86.2.3. The output, especially addresses, may differ for your Windows version.

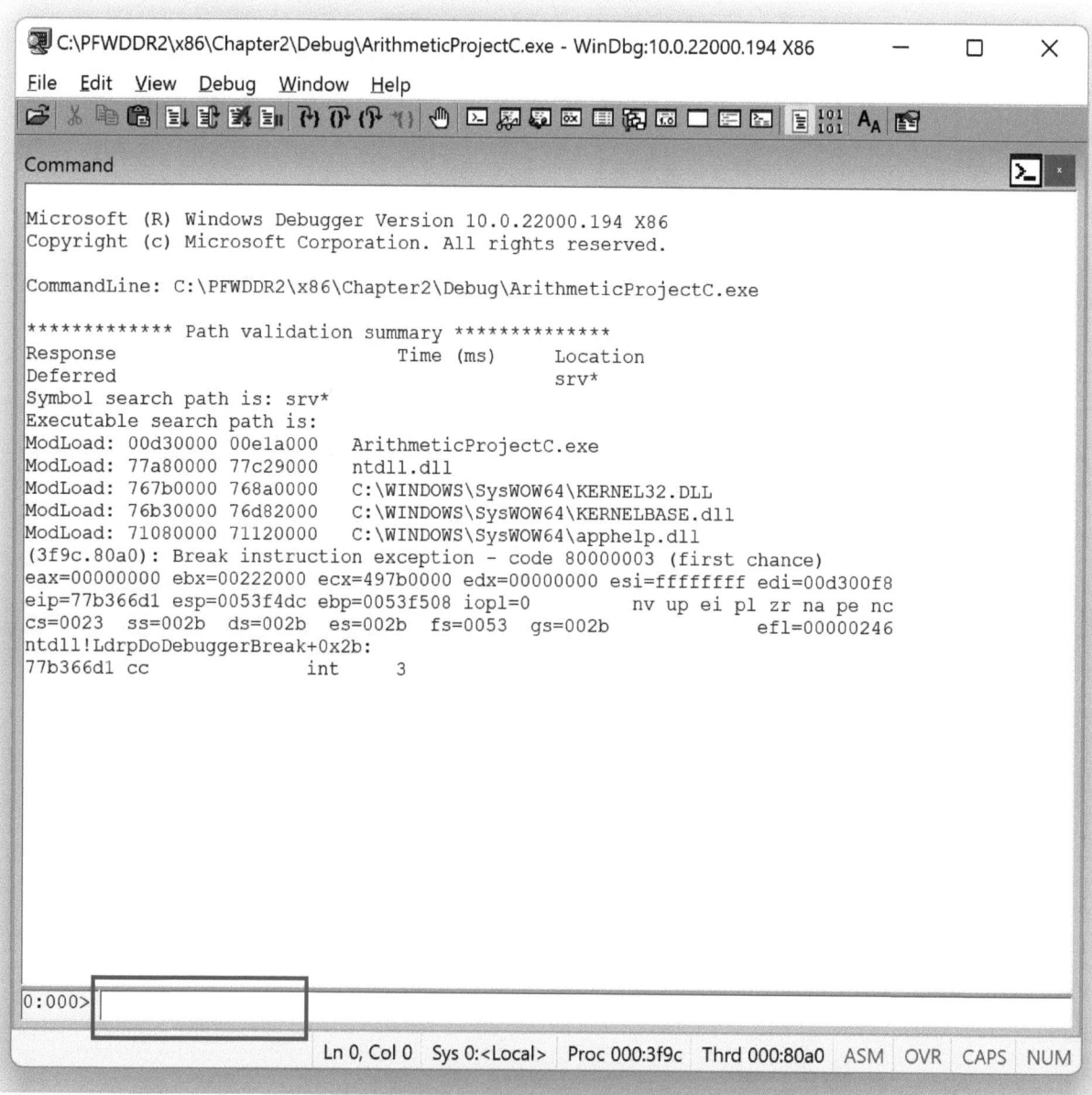

Picture x86.2.3

We see a command line window at the bottom where we can enter WinDbg commands. We also need symbol files for our project to interpret binary data in our own executable file. Fortunately, this symbol file, which has a *.PDB* file extension, is located in the same folder where the *.EXE* file resides, and we don't need a command to specify its path here (**.sympath+** <additional path>).

Next, we put a **b**rea**k**point at our *main* C++ function, as shown in Picture x86.2.4, to allow the program execution to stop at that point and give us a chance to inspect memory and registers. Symbolic names/function names like *main* can be used instead of memory locations of the code when the symbol file is loaded into WinDbg. Showing symbolic names is one useful aspect of a symbol file: we can refer to a function name instead of identifying where the function code resides in memory. Since the *ArithmeticProjectC* executable module is not loaded yet, we specify the fully qualified name in *module!function* format (*ArithmeticProjectC!main*):

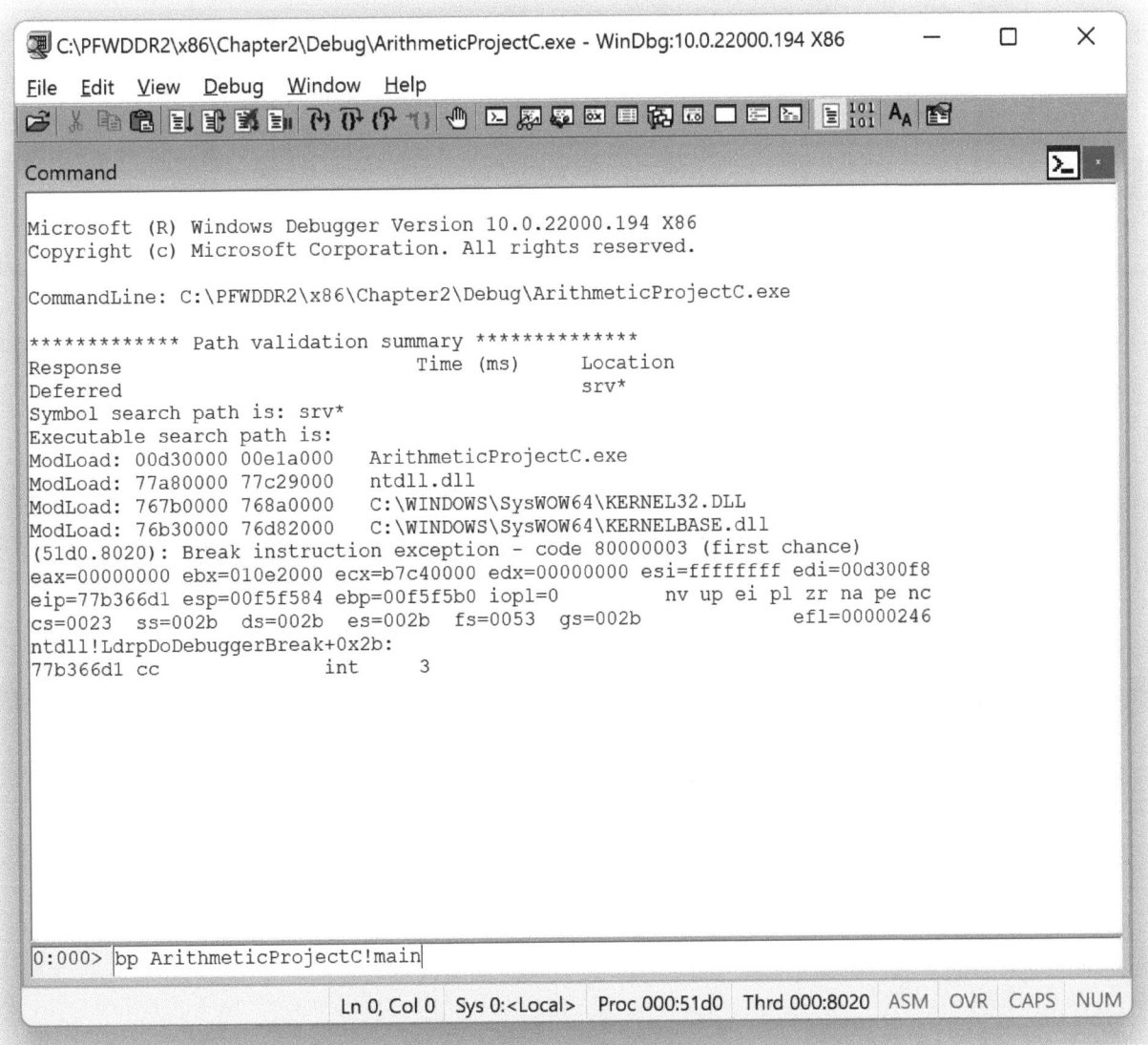

Picture x86.2.4

38   WinDbg Disassembly Output – Debug Executable

Then we start the program's execution (let it **g**o) as shown in Picture x86.2.5.

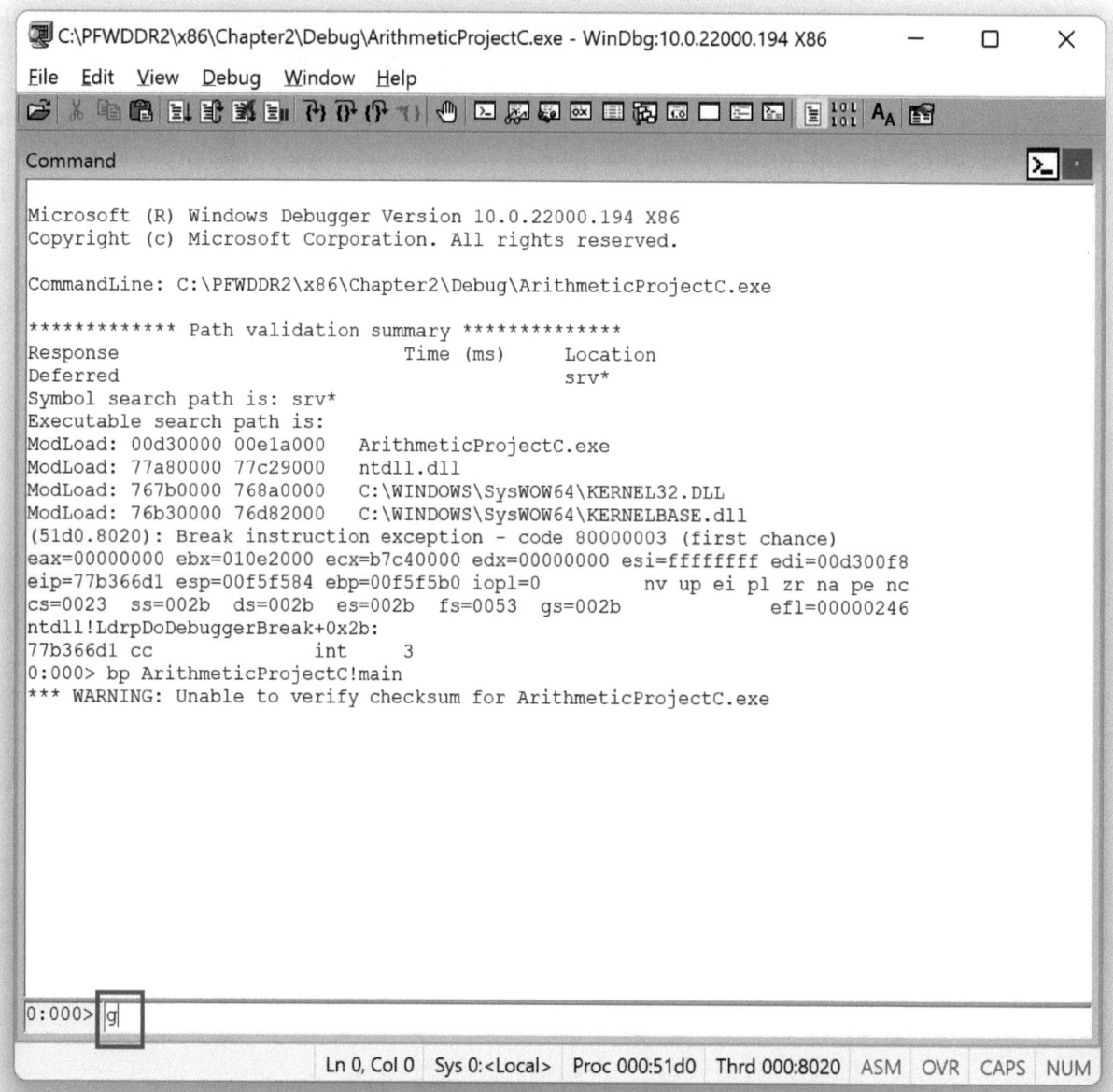

Picture x86.2.5

The program's execution stops at the previously set breakpoint, as shown in Picture x86.2.6.

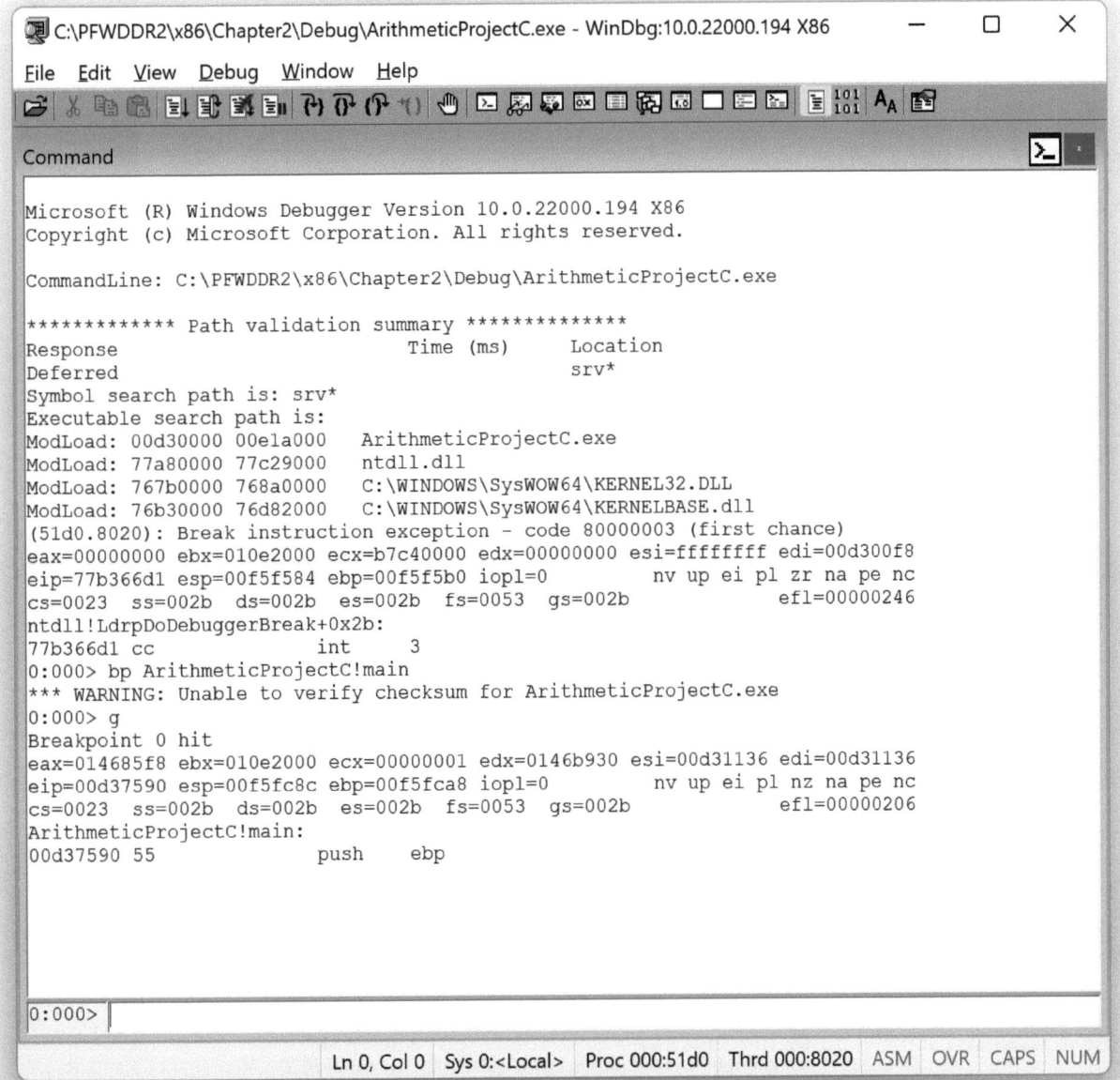

Picture x86.2.6

40 WinDbg Disassembly Output – Debug Executable

Now we **u**nassemble the *main* function as shown in Pictures x86.2.7 and x86.2.8.

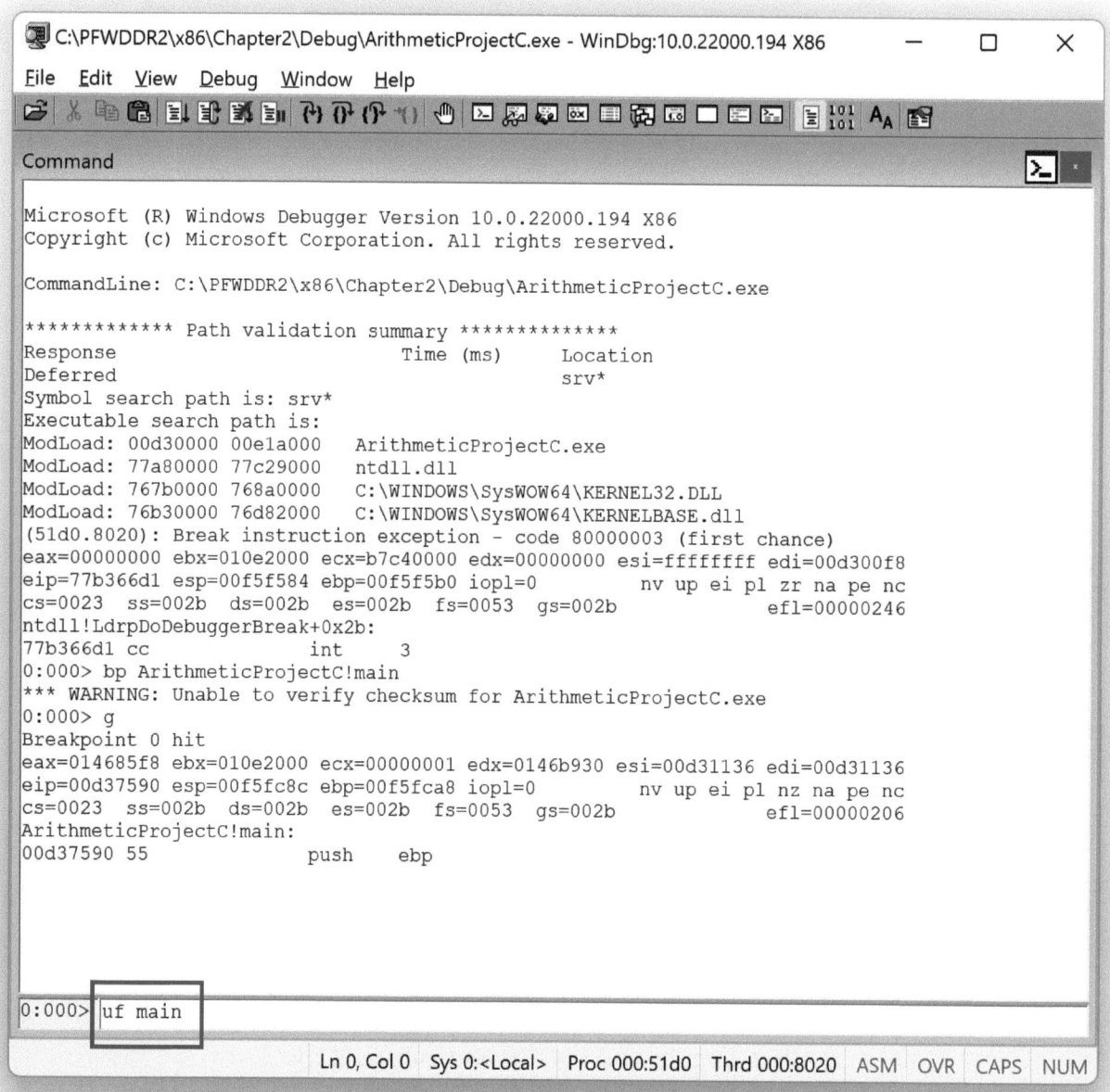

Picture x86.2.7

Chapter x86.2: Debug and Release Binaries

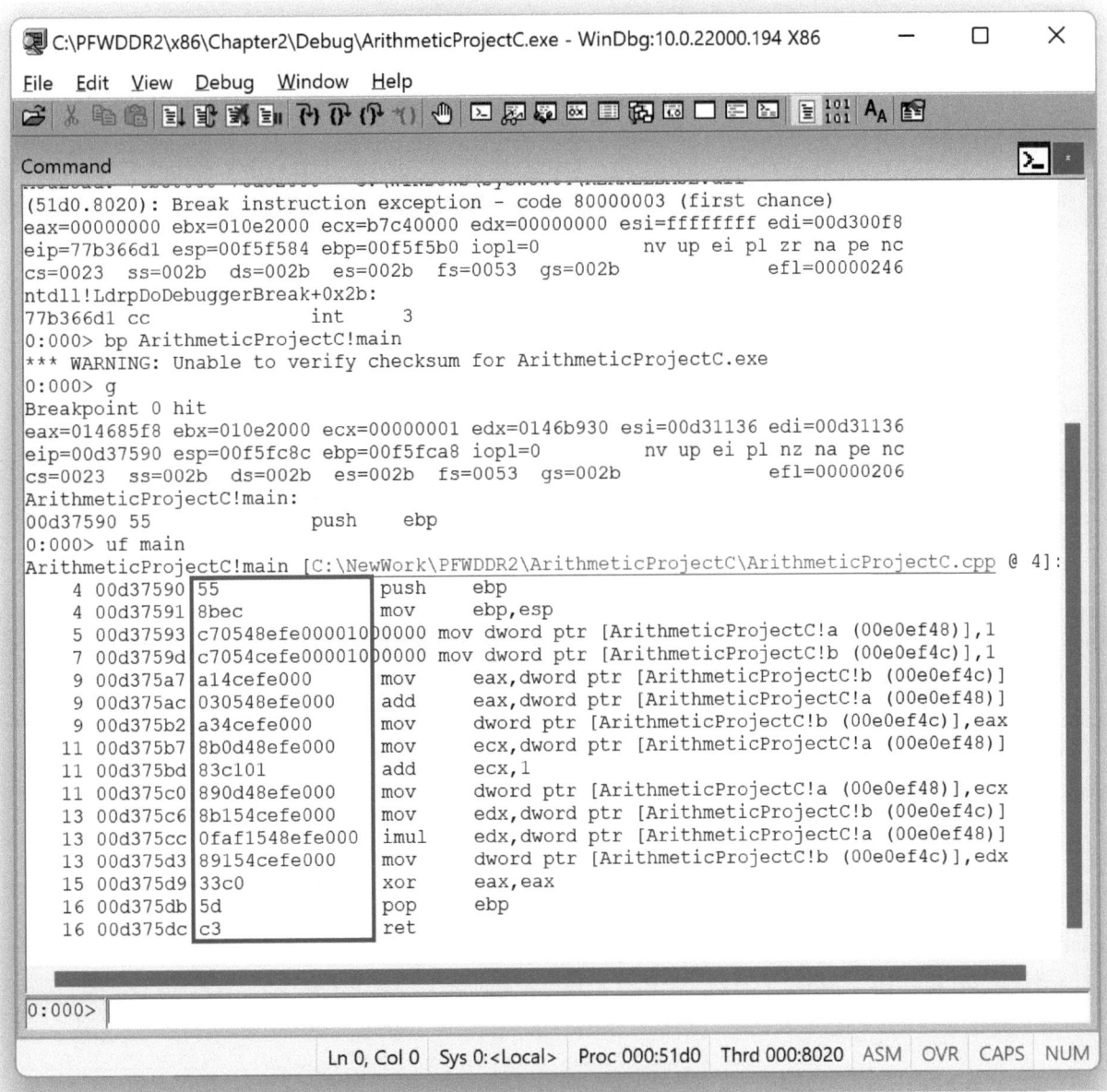

Picture x86.2.8

The middle column shows the binary code we are not interested in, and we opt not to include it in the future, as shown in Picture x86.2.9.

42 WinDbg Disassembly Output – Debug Executable

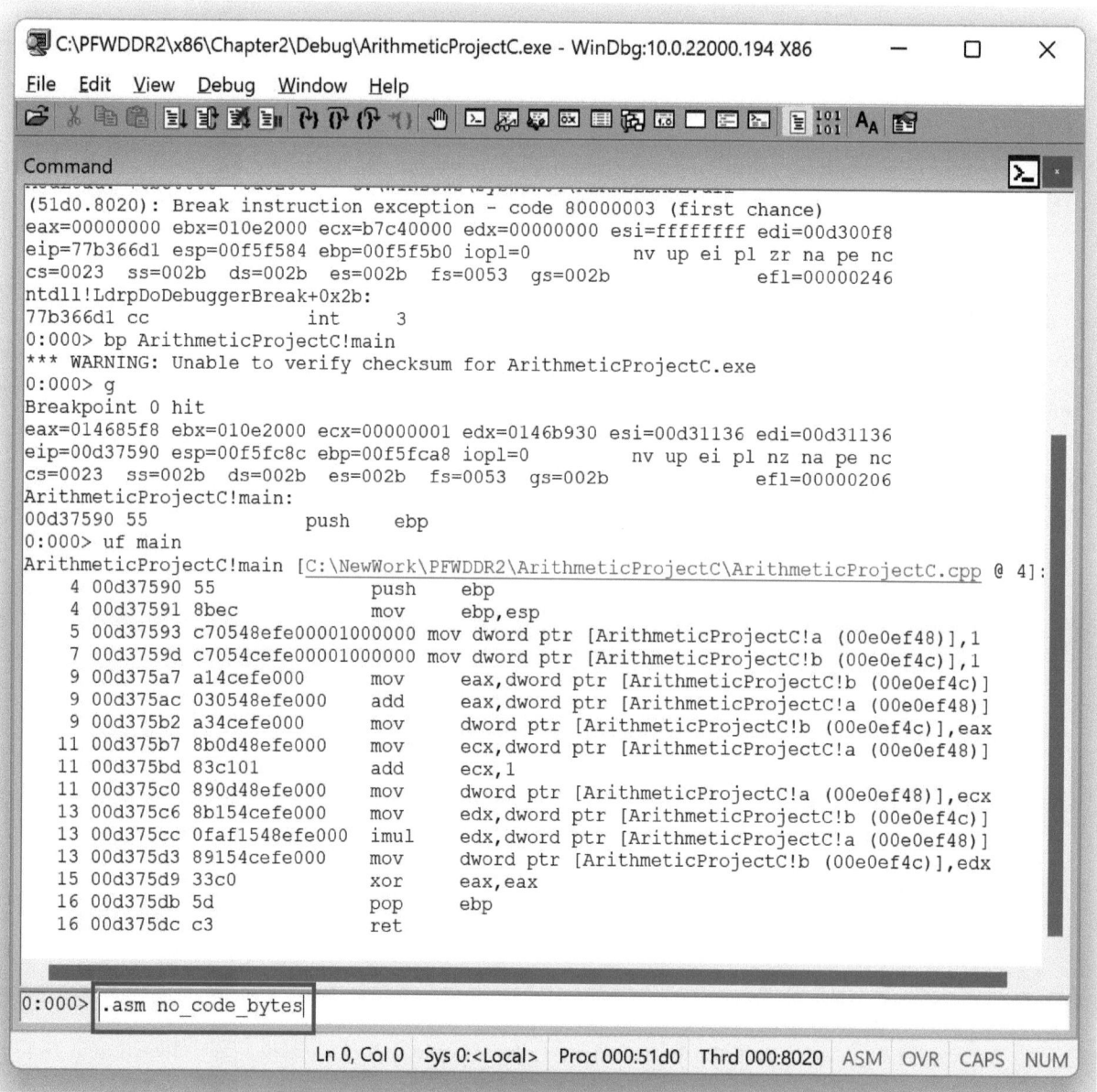

Picture x86.2.9

We repeat our disassembly command, as shown in Picture x86.2.10.

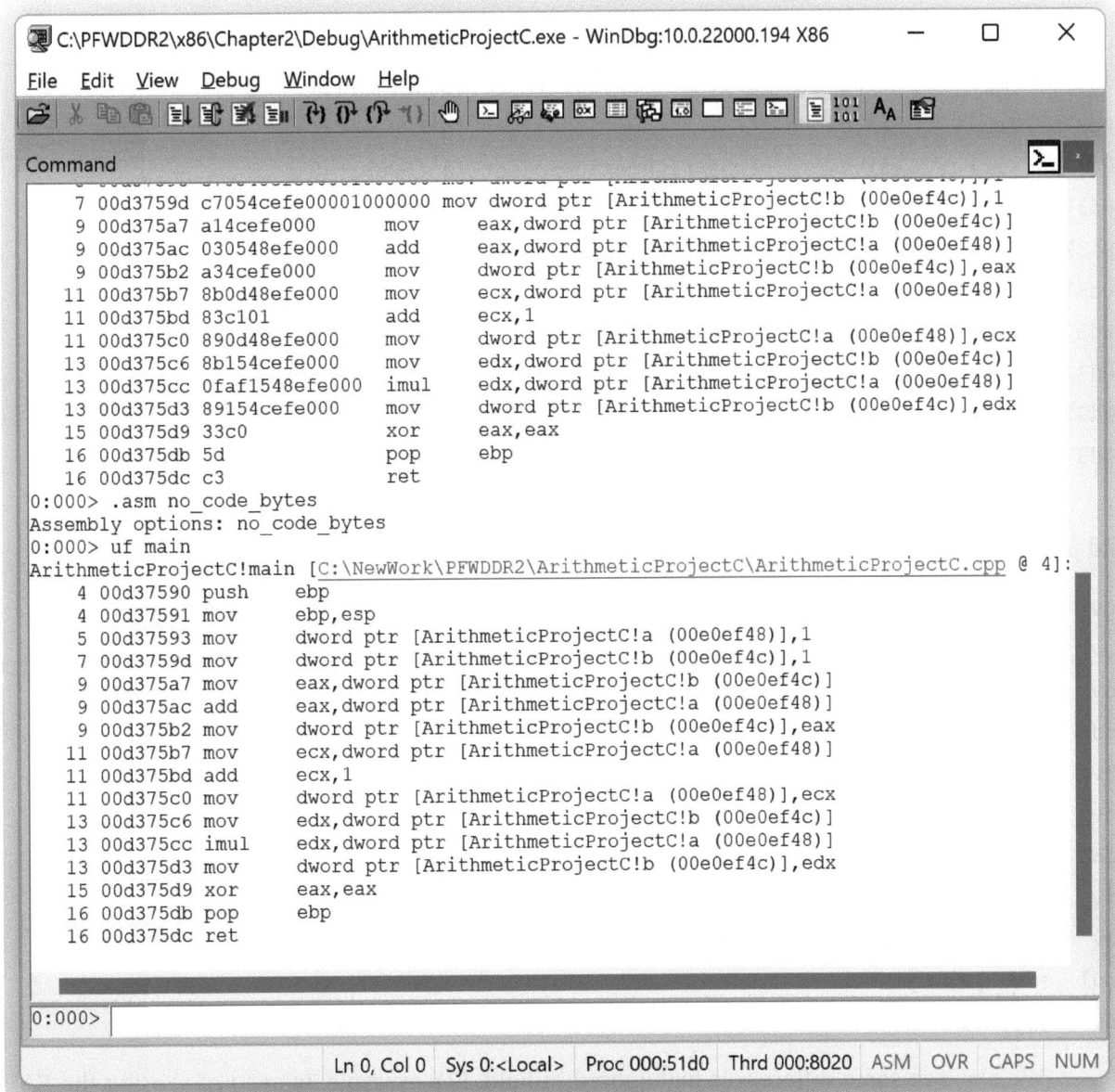

Picture x86.2.10

We repeat the part of the formatted disassembly output here that corresponds to our C++ code where we removed source code line numbers:

```
00d37593 mov     dword ptr [ArithmeticProjectC!a (00e0ef48)],1
00d3759d mov     dword ptr [ArithmeticProjectC!b (00e0ef4c)],1
00d375a7 mov     eax,dword ptr [ArithmeticProjectC!b (00e0ef4c)]
00d375ac add     eax,dword ptr [ArithmeticProjectC!a (00e0ef48)]
00d375b2 mov     dword ptr [ArithmeticProjectC!b (00e0ef4c)],eax
00d375b7 mov     ecx,dword ptr [ArithmeticProjectC!a (00e0ef48)]
00d375bd add     ecx,1
00d375c0 mov     dword ptr [ArithmeticProjectC!a (00e0ef48)],ecx
00d375c6 mov     edx,dword ptr [ArithmeticProjectC!b (00e0ef4c)]
00d375cc imul    edx,dword ptr [ArithmeticProjectC!a (00e0ef48)]
00d375d3 mov     dword ptr [ArithmeticProjectC!b (00e0ef4c)],edx
```

We can directly translate it to similar bare assembly code we used in the previous chapter and put corresponding pseudo-code in comments:

```
mov     [a], 1      ; [a] <- 1
mov     [b], 1      ; [b] <- 1
mov     eax, [b]    ; [b] <- [b] + [a]
add     eax, [a]    ;
mov     [b], eax    ;
mov     ecx, [a]    ; [a] <- [a] + 1
add     ecx, 1      ;
mov     [a], ecx    ;
mov     edx, [b]    ; [b] <- [b] * [a]
imul    edx, [a]    ;
mov     [b], edx    ;
```

We also see some differences highlighted in bold. For example, instead of reusing the EAX register as we did in Chapter 1, ECX and EDX registers were used. The compiler also used a different form of IMUL instruction, the one that multiplies the value of the first operand (a register value) by the value of the second operand (a register value or value at the specified memory address) and puts the result in the first operand (register).

WinDbg Disassembly Output – Release Executable

If we repeat the same procedure for an executable located under *Release* subfolder we get the following output:

```
ArithmeticProjectC!main:
00e41000 mov dword ptr [ArithmeticProjectC!a (00e548d8)],2
00e4100a xor     eax,eax
00e4100c mov dword ptr [ArithmeticProjectC!b (00e548dc)],4
00e41016 ret
```

This corresponds to the following pseudo-code:

```
mov  [a], 2   ; [a] <- 2
mov  [b], 4   ; [b] <- 4
```

What happened to all our previous assembly code in this *Release* executable? If we observe, this code seems to be directly placing the result into [b]. Why is this happening? The answer lies in compiler optimization. When the code is compiled in *Release* mode, the Visual C++ compiler can calculate the final result from the simple C source code itself and generate code only necessary to update corresponding memory locations.

Chapter x86.3: Number Representations

Numbers and Their Representations

Imagine ourselves a herder in ancient times trying to count his sheep. We have a certain number of stones (twelve):

However, we can only count up to three and arrange the total into groups of three:

The last picture is a representation (a kind of notation) of the number of stones. We have one group of three groups of three stones plus a separate group of three stones. If we could count up to ten, we would see a different representation of the same number of stones. We would have one group of ten stones and another group of two stones.

Decimal Representation (Base Ten)

Let's now see how twelve stones are represented in arithmetic notation if we can count up to ten. We have one group of ten numbers plus two:

$12_{dec} = \mathbf{1 * 10 + 2}$ or $\mathbf{1 * 10^1 + 2 * 10^0}$

Here is another exercise with one hundred and twenty-three stones. We have **1** group of ten by ten stones, another group of **2** groups of ten stones and the last group of **3** stones:

$\mathbf{123}_{dec} = \mathbf{1 * 10*10 + 2 * 10 + 3}$ or $\mathbf{1 * 10^2 + 2 * 10^1 + 3 * 10^0}$

We can formalize it in the following summation notation:

$N_{dec} = a_n*10^n + a_{n-1}*10^{n-1} + ... + a_2*10^2 + a_1*10^1 + a_0*10^0 \quad 0 <= a_i <= 9$

Using the summation symbol, we have this formula:

$$N_{dec} = \sum_{i=0}^{n} a_i * 10^i$$

Ternary Representation (Base Three)

Now we come back to our herder's example of twelve stones. We have **1** group of three by three stones, **1** group of three stones, and an empty (**0**) group (which is not empty if we have only one stone or thirteen stones instead of twelve). We can write down the number of groups sequentially: **110**. Therefore **110** is a ternary representation (notation) of twelve stones, and it is equivalent to 12 written in decimal notation:

$12_{dec} = 1*3^2 + 1*3^1 + 0*3^0$

$N_{dec} = a_n*3^n + a_{n-1}*3^{n-1} + ... + a_2*3^2 + a_1*3^1 + a_0*3^0 \qquad a_i = 0 \text{ or } 1 \text{ or } 2$

$$N_{dec} = \sum_{i=0}^{n} a_i*3^i$$

Binary Representation (Base Two)

In the case of counting up to 2, we have more groups for twelve stones: **1100**. Therefore **1100** is a binary representation (notation) for 12 in decimal notation:

$12_{dec} = 1*2^3 + 1*2^2 + 0*2^1 + 0*2^0$

$123_{dec} = 1*2^6 + 1*2^5 + 1*2^4 + 1*2^3 + 0*2^2 + 1*2^1 + 1*2^0$ or 1111011_2

$N_{dec} = a_n*2^n + a_{n-1}*2^{n-1} + ... + a_2*2^2 + a_1*2^1 + a_0*2^0 \qquad a_i = 0 \text{ or } 1$

$$N_{dec} = \sum_{i=0}^{n} a_i*2^i$$

Hexadecimal Representation (Base Sixteen)

If we can count up to sixteen, twelve stones fit in one group, but we need more symbols: **A**, **B**, **C**, **D**, **E**, and **F** for ten, eleven, twelve, thirteen, fourteen, and fifteen respectively:

12_{dec} = C in hexadecimal representation (notation)

$123_{dec} = 7B_{hex}$

$123_{dec} = 7*16^1 + 11*16^0$

$$N_{dec} = \sum_{i=0}^{n} a_i * 16^i$$

Why are Hexadecimals Used?

Consider this number written in binary notation: 110001010011_2. Its equivalent in decimal notation is 3155:

$3155_{dec} = 1*2^{11} + 1*2^{10} + 0*2^9 + 0*2^8 + 0*2^7 + 1*2^6 + 0*2^5 + 1*2^4 + 0*2^3 + 0*2^2 + 1*2^1 + 1*2^0$

Now we divide the binary number digits into groups of four and write them down in decimal and hexadecimal notation:

1100_01010011

12$_{dec}$ **5**$_{dec}$ **3**$_{dec}$

C$_{hex}$ **5**$_{hex}$ **3**$_{hex}$

We see that hexadecimal notation is more compact because every four binary digit group number corresponds to one hexadecimal number. Table x86.3.1 lists hexadecimal equivalents for every four binary digit combination.

In WinDbg and other debuggers, memory addresses are displayed in hexadecimal notation.

Why are Hexadecimals Used?

Binary	Decimal	Hexadecimal
0000	0	0
0001	1	1
0010	2	2
0011	3	3
0100	4	4
0101	5	5
0110	6	6
0111	7	7
1000	8	8
1001	9	9
1010	10	A
1011	11	B
1100	12	C
1101	13	D
1110	14	E
1111	15	F

Table x86.3.1

Chapter x86.4: Pointers

A Definition

The concept of a pointer is one of the most important to understand thoroughly to master Windows debugging. By definition, a pointer is a memory cell or a processor register that contains the address of another memory cell, as shown in Picture x86.4.1. It has its own address as any memory cell. Sometimes, a pointer is called an indirect address (vs. direct address, the address of a memory cell). Iteratively, we can define another level of indirection and introduce a pointer to a pointer as a memory cell or a processor register that contains the address of another memory cell that contains the address of another memory cell, and so on.

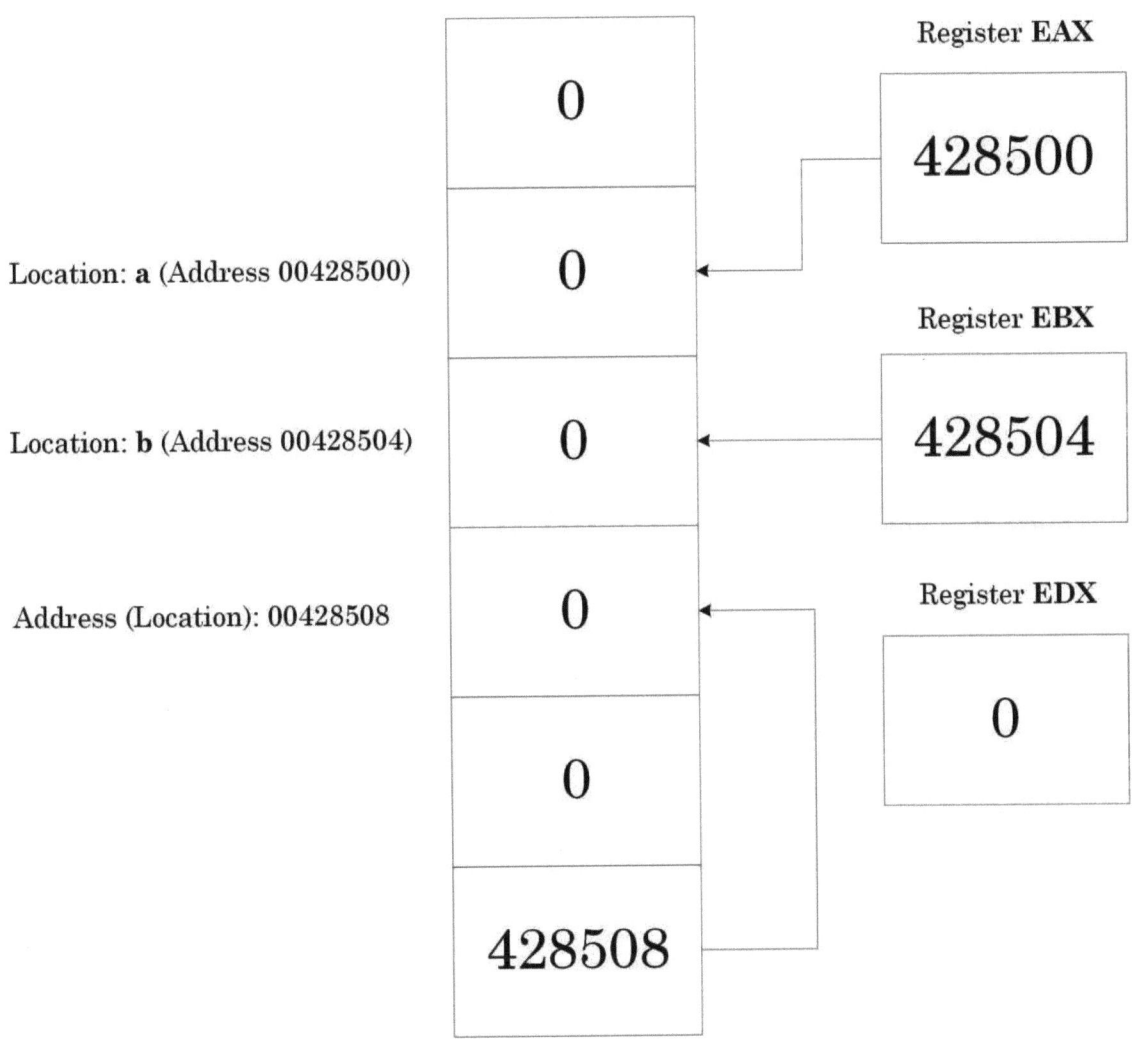

Picture x86.4.1

"Pointers" Project: Memory Layout and Registers

In our debugging project, we have two memory addresses (locations), "a" and "b". We can think about "a" and "b" as names of addresses (locations). We remind that notation [a] means contents at the memory address (location) "a".

We also have registers EAX and EBX as pointers to "a" and "b". These registers contain addresses of "a" and "b", respectively. The notation [EAX] means contents of a memory cell whose address is in register EAX.

In C and C++ languages, we declare and define pointers to "a" and "b" as:

```
int *a, *b;
```

Our project memory layout before program execution is shown in Picture x86.4.2.

Picture x86.4.2

"Pointers" Project: Calculations

To understand pointers better from a low-level assembly language perspective, we perform our old arithmetic calculations from Chapter x86.1 using pointers to memory instead of direct memory addresses:

```
eax <- address a
[eax] <- 1              ; [a] = 1
ebx <- address b
[ebx] <- 1              ; [b] = 1
[ebx] <- [ebx] + [eax]  ; [b] = 2
[ebx] <- [ebx] * 2      ; [b] = 4
```

Using Pointers to Assign Numbers to Memory Cells

First, the following sequence of pseudo-code instructions means that we interpret the contents of the EAX register as the address of a memory cell and then assign a value to that memory cell:

```
eax <- address a
[eax] <- 1
```

In C language, it is called "dereferencing a pointer" and we write:

```
int *a;    // declaration and definition of a pointer
*a = 1;    // get a memory cell (dereference
           // a pointer) and assign a value to it
```

In assembly language, we write:

```
lea   eax, a    ; load the address "a" into eax
mov   [eax], 1  ; use eax as a pointer
```

In WinDbg disassembly output, we would see something like this:

```
00401004 lea       eax,[PointersProject!a (004aba20)]
0040100a mov       byte ptr [eax],1
```

The project for this chapter can be downloaded from:

https://bitbucket.org/softwarediagnostics/pfwddr2/src/master/x86/Chapter4/

The executable is located under *Debug* subfolder. We can load it into WinDbg and disassemble its *main* function as described in Chapter x86.2. From now on, we do not see screenshots of WinDbg windows but the output from the command window instead.

First, we load *PointersProject.exe* using File\Open Executable... menu option in WinDbg and get the following output (the output, especially addresses, may differ for your Windows version):

```
Microsoft (R) Windows Debugger Version 10.0.22000.194 X86
Copyright (c) Microsoft Corporation. All rights reserved.


CommandLine: C:\PFWDDR2\x86\Chapter4\Debug\PointersProject.exe

************* Path validation summary **************
Response                      Time (ms)     Location
Deferred                                    srv*
Symbol search path is: srv*
Executable search path is:
ModLoad: 00400000 004ae000    PointersProject.exe
ModLoad: 77a80000 77c29000    ntdll.dll
ModLoad: 767b0000 768a0000    C:\WINDOWS\SysWOW64\KERNEL32.DLL
ModLoad: 76b30000 76d82000    C:\WINDOWS\SysWOW64\KERNELBASE.dll
ModLoad: 71080000 71120000    C:\WINDOWS\SysWOW64\apphelp.dll
(3170.69cc): Break instruction exception - code 80000003 (first chance)
eax=00000000 ebx=002c2000 ecx=25120000 edx=00000000 esi=ffffffff edi=00400108
eip=77b366d1 esp=0019f7e4 ebp=0019f810 iopl=0         nv up ei pl zr na pe nc
cs=0023  ss=002b  ds=002b  es=002b  fs=0053  gs=002b              efl=00000246
ntdll!LdrpDoDebuggerBreak+0x2b:
77b366d1 cc              int     3
```

Then we put a breakpoint on the *main* function and run the program until WinDbg breaks in:

```
0:000> bp PointersProject!main
*** WARNING: Unable to verify checksum for PointersProject.exe
```

```
0:000> g
Breakpoint 0 hit
eax=006b5cb0 ebx=002c2000 ecx=00000001 edx=006b3008 esi=00401620 edi=00401620
eip=00401000 esp=0019feec ebp=0019ff08 iopl=0         nv up ei pl nz na po nc
cs=0023  ss=002b  ds=002b  es=002b  fs=0053  gs=002b              efl=00000202
PointersProject!main:
00401000 55              push    ebp
```

58 Using Pointers to Assign Numbers to Memory Cells

For visual clarity, we disable the output of binary codes before disassembling *main* function:

```
0:000> .asm no_code_bytes
Assembly options: no_code_bytes
```

```
0:000> uf main
PointersProject!main [C:\NewWork\PFWDDR2\PointersProject\PointersProject.cpp @ 4]:
    4 00401000 push    ebp
    4 00401001 mov     ebp,esp
    4 00401003 push    ebx
    7 00401004 lea     eax,[PointersProject!a (004aba20)]
    8 0040100a mov     byte ptr [eax],1
   10 0040100d lea     ebx,[PointersProject!b (004aba24)]
   11 00401013 mov     byte ptr [ebx],1
   13 00401016 mov     eax,dword ptr [eax]
   14 00401018 add     dword ptr [ebx],eax
   16 0040101a inc     eax
   18 0040101b imul    byte ptr [ebx]
   19 0040101d mov     dword ptr [ebx],eax
   22 0040101f xor     eax,eax
   23 00401021 pop     ebx
   23 00401022 cmp     ebp,esp
   23 00401024 call    PointersProject!_RTC_CheckEsp (004011b0)
   23 00401029 pop     ebp
   23 0040102a ret
```

Because we remember that assigning addresses to registers is most likely done by an LEA (Load Effective Address) instruction, we put a breakpoint on the address of the first such instruction in the code of the *main* function and then resume the program:

```
0:000> bp 00401004
```

```
0:000> g
Breakpoint 1 hit
eax=006b5cb0 ebx=002c2000 ecx=00000001 edx=006b3008 esi=00401620 edi=00401620
eip=00401004 esp=0019fee4 ebp=0019fee8 iopl=0         nv up ei pl nz na po nc
cs=0023  ss=002b  ds=002b  es=002b  fs=0053  gs=002b              efl=00000202
PointersProject!main+0x4:
00401004 lea     eax,[PointersProject!a (004aba20)]
```

Now we examine variables **a** and **b** to verify the memory layout shown previously in Picture x86.4.2 using the **dc** WinDbg command:

```
0:000> dc PointersProject!a L1
004aba20  00000000                                       ....
```

```
0:000> dc PointersProject!b L1
004aba24  00000000
```

We also clear values of EAX, EBX, and EDX registers in accordance with Picture x86.4.2:

```
0:000> r eax = 0
```

```
0:000> r ebx = 0
```

```
0:000> r edx = 0
```

We can verify registers by using the **r** WinDbg command:

```
0:000> r
eax=00000000 ebx=00000000 ecx=00000001 edx=00000000 esi=00401620 edi=00401620
eip=00401004 esp=0019fee4 ebp=0019fee8 iopl=0         nv up ei pl nz na po nc
cs=0023  ss=002b  ds=002b  es=002b  fs=0053  gs=002b              efl=00000202
PointersProject!main+0x4:
00401004 lea     eax,[PointersProject!a (004aba20)]
```

Now we execute the first four instructions that correspond to our pseudo-code using the **t** WinDbg command (the output of the **t** command also shows the instruction to be executed next):

eax <- address a		lea	eax, a
[eax] <- 1	; [a] = 1	mov	[eax], 1
ebx <- address b		lea	ebx, b
[ebx] <- 1	; [b] = 1	mov	[ebx], 1
[ebx] <- [ebx] + [eax]	; [b] = 2		
[ebx] <- [ebx] * 2	; [b] = 4		

60   Using Pointers to Assign Numbers to Memory Cells

```
0:000> t
eax=004aba20 ebx=00000000 ecx=00000001 edx=00000000 esi=00401620 edi=00401620
eip=0040100a esp=0019fee4 ebp=0019fee8 iopl=0         nv up ei pl nz na po nc
cs=0023  ss=002b  ds=002b  es=002b  fs=0053  gs=002b             efl=00000202
PointersProject!main+0xa:
0040100a mov     byte ptr [eax],1                       ds:002b:004aba20=00

0:000> t
eax=004aba20 ebx=00000000 ecx=00000001 edx=00000000 esi=00401620 edi=00401620
eip=0040100d esp=0019fee4 ebp=0019fee8 iopl=0         nv up ei pl nz na po nc
cs=0023  ss=002b  ds=002b  es=002b  fs=0053  gs=002b             efl=00000202
PointersProject!main+0xd:
0040100d lea     ebx,[PointersProject!b (004aba24)]

0:000> t
eax=004aba20 ebx=004aba24 ecx=00000001 edx=00000000 esi=00401620 edi=00401620
eip=00401013 esp=0019fee4 ebp=0019fee8 iopl=0         nv up ei pl nz na po nc
cs=0023  ss=002b  ds=002b  es=002b  fs=0053  gs=002b             efl=00000202
PointersProject!main+0x13:
00401013 mov     byte ptr [ebx],1                       ds:002b:004aba24=00

0:000> t
eax=004aba20 ebx=004aba24 ecx=00000001 edx=00000000 esi=00401620 edi=00401620
eip=00401016 esp=0019fee4 ebp=0019fee8 iopl=0         nv up ei pl nz na po nc
cs=0023  ss=002b  ds=002b  es=002b  fs=0053  gs=002b             efl=00000202
PointersProject!main+0x16:
00401016 mov     eax,dword ptr [eax]                    ds:002b:004aba20=00000001
```

We also see that values of **a** and **b** have changed as expected:

```
0:000> dc PointersProject!a L1
004aba20  00000001                                      ....

0:000> dc PointersProject!b L1
004aba24  00000001                                      ....
```

All this corresponds to a memory layout shown in Picture x86.4.3.

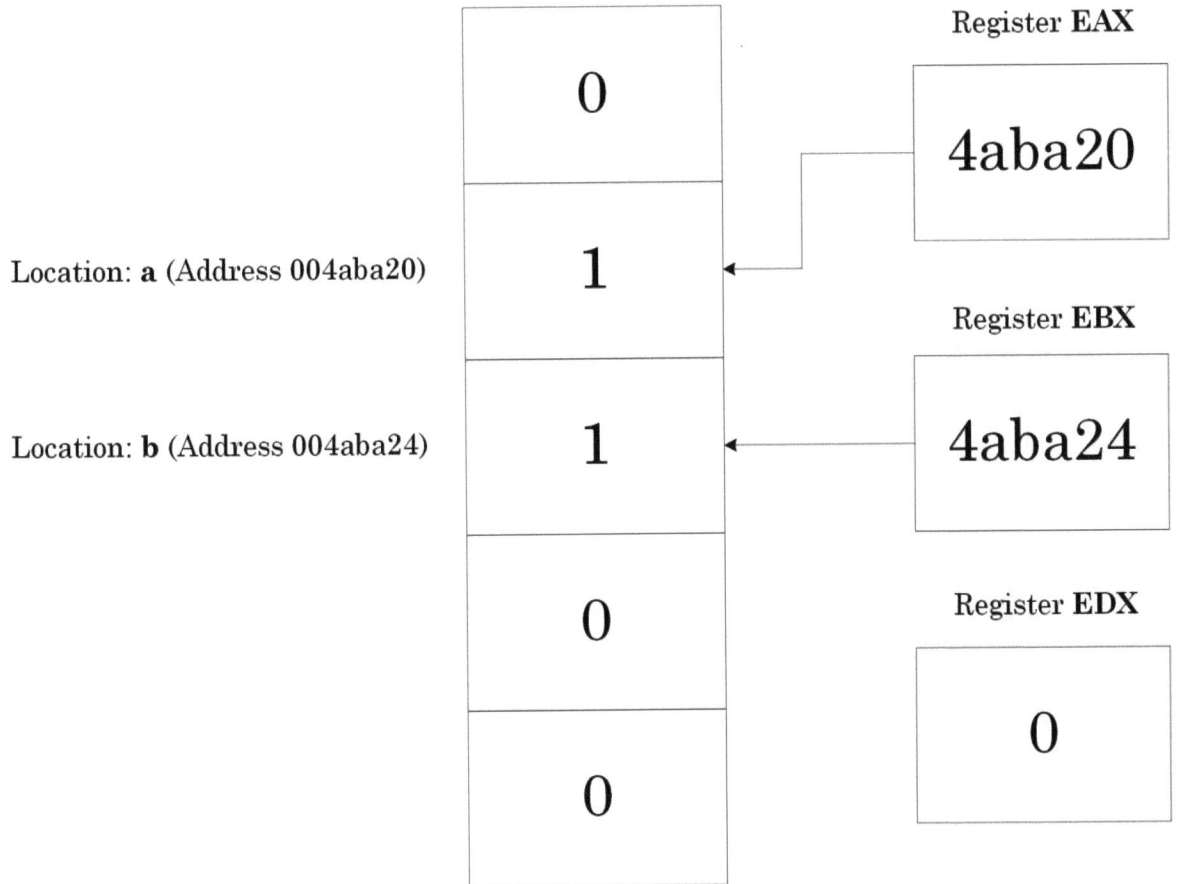

Picture x86.4.3

Adding Numbers Using Pointers

Now we look at the next pseudo-code statement:

```
[ebx] <- [ebx] + [eax]
```

Recall that [eax] and [ebx] mean contents of memory cells whose addresses (locations) are stored in EAX and EBX CPU registers. The statement above is equivalent to the following C or C++ language expression where the '*' operator means to get memory contents pointed to by **pa** or **pb** pointer (also called pointer dereference):

```
*pb = *pb + *pa;
```

In assembly language, we use the instruction ADD for the '+' operator, but we cannot use both memory addresses in one step instruction:

```
add    [ebx], [eax]
```

We can only use one memory reference, and therefore, we need to employ another register as a temporary variable:

```
register <- [eax]
[ebx] <- [ebx] + register
```

In assembly language, we write this sequence of instructions:

```
mov    eax, [eax]
add    [ebx], eax
```

In WinDbg disassembly output, we would see these instructions indeed:

```
00401016 mov        eax,dword ptr [eax]
00401018 add        dword ptr [ebx],eax
```

We add them to our pseudo-code table:

eax <- address a			lea	eax, a
[eax] <- 1	; [a] = 1		mov	[eax], 1
ebx <- address b			lea	ebx, b
[ebx] <- 1	; [b] = 1		mov	[ebx], 1
[ebx] <- [ebx] + [eax]	; [b] = 2		mov	eax, [eax]
			add	[ebx],eax
[ebx] <- [ebx] * 2	; [b] = 4			

Now we execute these two instructions (we remind that the output of the **t** command shows the next instruction to be executed when we use the **t** command again):

```
[From the previous output]
eax=004aba20 ebx=004aba24 ecx=00000001 edx=00000000 esi=00401620 edi=00401620
eip=00401016 esp=0019fee4 ebp=0019fee8 iopl=0         nv up ei pl nz na po nc
cs=0023  ss=002b  ds=002b  es=002b  fs=0053  gs=002b              efl=00000202
PointersProject!main+0x16:
00401016 mov     eax,dword ptr [eax]              ds:002b:004aba20=00000001
```

```
0:000> t
eax=00000001 ebx=004aba24 ecx=00000001 edx=00000000 esi=00401620 edi=00401620
eip=00401018 esp=0019fee4 ebp=0019fee8 iopl=0         nv up ei pl nz na po nc
cs=0023  ss=002b  ds=002b  es=002b  fs=0053  gs=002b              efl=00000202
PointersProject!main+0x18:
00401018 add     dword ptr [ebx],eax              ds:002b:004aba24=00000001
```

```
0:000> t
eax=00000001 ebx=004aba24 ecx=00000001 edx=00000000 esi=00401620 edi=00401620
eip=0040101a esp=0019fee4 ebp=0019fee8 iopl=0         nv up ei pl nz na po nc
cs=0023  ss=002b  ds=002b  es=002b  fs=0053  gs=002b              efl=00000202
PointersProject!main+0x1a:
0040101a inc     eax
```

We also check the memory location of b variable to see that it really changed its value:

```
0:000> dc PointersProject!b L1
004aba24  00000002                                 ....
```

64 Adding Numbers Using Pointers

All this corresponds to a memory layout shown in Picture x86.4.4.

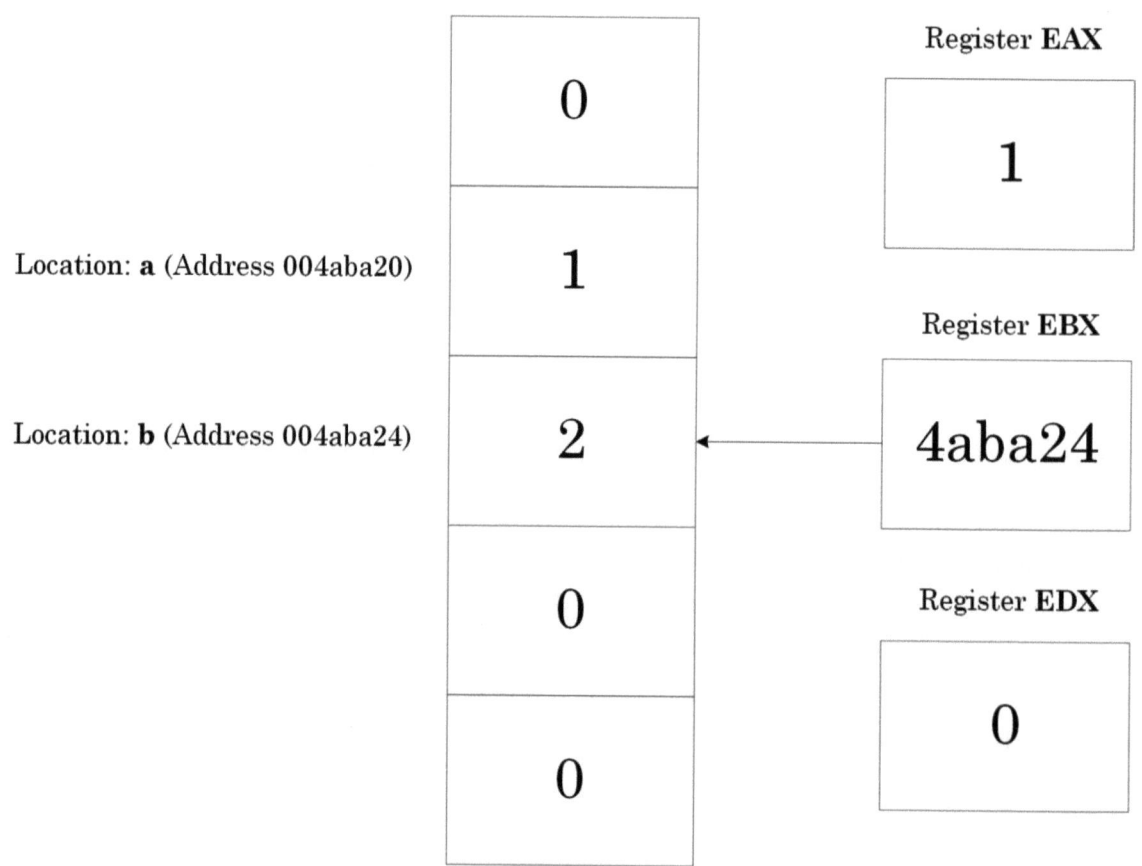

Picture x86.4.4

Multiplying Numbers Using Pointers

Our next pseudo-code statement does multiplication:

```
[ebx] <- [ebx] * 2
```

This statement means that we multiply the contents of the memory whose address is stored in the EBX register by 2. In C or C++ language, we write a similar expression as the addition statement we have seen in the previous section (note that we have two distinct meanings of the '*' operator, pointer dereference and multiplication):

```
*pb = *pb * 2; // or
```

```
*pb *= 2;
```

The latter is a shorthand notation. In assembly language, we use instruction IMUL (Integer MULtiply)

```
imul [ebx]
```

This instruction is equivalent to the following pseudo-code:

```
eax <- [ebx] * eax
```

Therefore, we have to put 2 into the EAX register, but we already have 1 in EAX, so we use INC EAX instruction before IMUL to increment EAX by 1.

In WinDbg disassembly output, we would see this:

```
0040101a inc      eax
0040101b imul     byte ptr [ebx]
0040101d mov      dword ptr [ebx],eax
```

66 Multiplying Numbers Using Pointers

We add instructions to our pseudo-code table:

eax <- address a			lea	eax, a
[eax] <- 1	; [a] = 1		mov	[eax], 1
ebx <- address b			lea	ebx, b
[ebx] <- 1	; [b] = 1		mov	[ebx], 1
[ebx] <- [ebx] + [eax]	; [b] = 2		mov	eax, [eax]
			add	[ebx], eax
[ebx] <- [ebx] * 2	; [b] = 4		inc	eax
			imul	[ebx]
			mov	[ebx], eax

Now we execute these three instructions (we remind that the output of the **t** command shows the next instruction to be executed when we use the **t** command again):

```
[From the previous output]
eax=00000001 ebx=004aba24 ecx=00000001 edx=00000000 esi=00401620 edi=00401620
eip=0040101a esp=0019fee4 ebp=0019fee8 iopl=0         nv up ei pl nz na po nc
cs=0023  ss=002b  ds=002b  es=002b  fs=0053  gs=002b              efl=00000202
PointersProject!main+0x1a:
0040101a inc     eax
```

0:000> t
```
eax=00000002 ebx=004aba24 ecx=00000001 edx=00000000 esi=00401620 edi=00401620
eip=0040101b esp=0019fee4 ebp=0019fee8 iopl=0         nv up ei pl nz na po nc
cs=0023  ss=002b  ds=002b  es=002b  fs=0053  gs=002b              efl=00000202
PointersProject!main+0x1b:
0040101b imul    byte ptr [ebx]                       ds:002b:004aba24=02
```

0:000> t
```
eax=00000004 ebx=004aba24 ecx=00000001 edx=00000000 esi=00401620 edi=00401620
eip=0040101d esp=0019fee4 ebp=0019fee8 iopl=0         nv up ei pl nz na po nc
cs=0023  ss=002b  ds=002b  es=002b  fs=0053  gs=002b              efl=00000202
PointersProject!main+0x1d:
0040101d mov     dword ptr [ebx],eax                  ds:002b:004aba24=00000002
```

```
0:000> t
eax=00000004 ebx=004aba24 ecx=00000001 edx=00000000 esi=00401620 edi=00401620
eip=0040101f esp=0019fee4 ebp=0019fee8 iopl=0         nv up ei pl nz na po nc
cs=0023  ss=002b  ds=002b  es=002b  fs=0053  gs=002b               efl=00000202
PointersProject!main+0x1f:
0040101f xor     eax,eax
```

We check again the memory location of b variable to see that it really changed its value:

```
0:000> dc PointersProject!b L1
004aba24  00000004                                     ....
```

All this corresponds to a memory layout shown in Picture x86.4.5.

Picture x86.4.5

Chapter x86.5: Bytes, Words, and Double Words

Using Hexadecimal Numbers

If we want to use hexadecimal numbers in C language we prefix them with **0x**, for example:

```
a = 12;     // 12_dec

a = 0xC;    // C_hex
```

In WinDbg disassembly, output and when entering commands numbers are interpreted as hexadecimal by default, although we can still prefix them with **0x**. If we want a number to be interpreted as decimal, we prefix it with **0n**, for example:

```
mov    [a], 0n12

mov    [a], C

mov    [a], 0xC
```

or the suffix '**h**' is used to disambiguate between decimal and hexadecimal, for example:

```
mov    [a], 52h
```

Byte Granularity

Picture x86.5.1 shows the difference between bytes, words, and double words in terms of byte granularity. We see that each successive size is double the previous. There are also quad words with the size of 8 bytes.

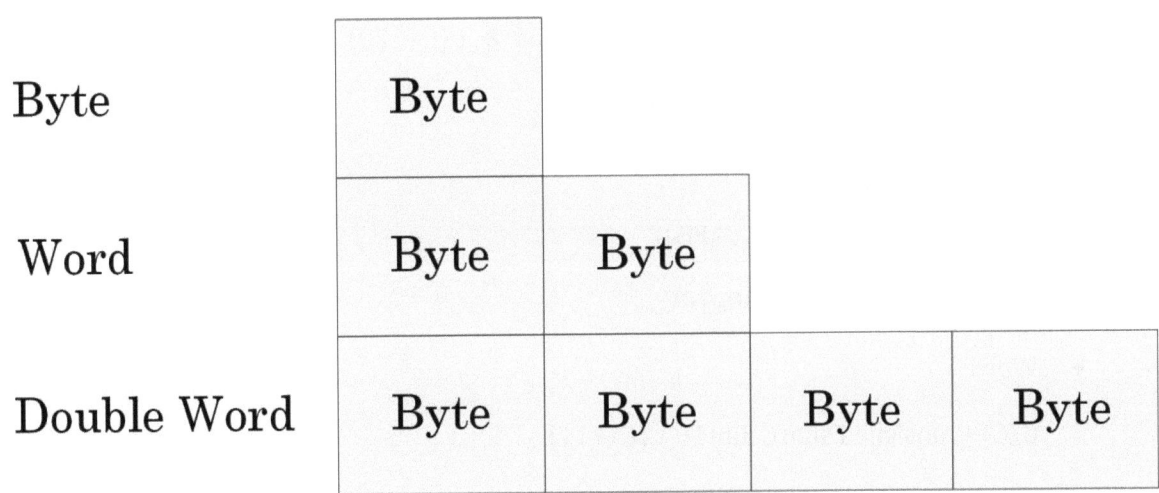

Picture x86.5.1

Bit Granularity

Every byte consists of 8 bits. Every bit has a value of 0 or 1. Here are some examples of bytes, words, and double words shown as bit strings (we can also clearly see the correspondence between the 4-bit sequences and hexadecimal numbers, Table x86.3.1):

- Byte

    C/C++: unsigned char, uint8_t (C++11), char8_t (C++20)

    Windows definitions: BYTE, UCHAR

    8 bits

    Values 0_{dec} - 255_{dec} or 0_{hex} - FF_{hex}

    Example: 12_{dec} 00001100_{bin} $0C_{hex}$

- Word

    C/C++: unsigned short, uint16_t (C++11)

    Windows definitions: USHORT, WORD

    16 bits

    Values 0_{dec} - 65535_{dec} or 0_{hex} - $FFFF_{hex}$

    Example: 0000000000001100_{bin} $000C_{hex}$

- Double word

    C/C++ (ILP32, int, long, and pointer are 32-bit):

    unsigned int, unsigned, unsigned long, uint32_t (C++11)

    Windows definitions (Win32 API): DWORD, UINT, ULONG

    32 bits

    Values 0_{dec} - 4294967295_{dec} or 0_{hex} - $FFFFFFFF_{hex}$

    Example: $00000000000000000000000000001100_{bin}$

    $0000000C_{hex}$

Memory Layout

The minimum addressable element of memory is a byte. The maximum addressable element is a **double word** or **dword** on 32-bit machines and a **quad word** or **qword** on 64-bit machines. All general registers are 32-bit on 32-bit processors or presented as such when the 32-bit mode is emulated on 64-bit processors and can contain a double word value. Picture x86.5.2 shows a typical memory layout, and Picture x86.5.3 shows the byte layout of some general CPU registers.

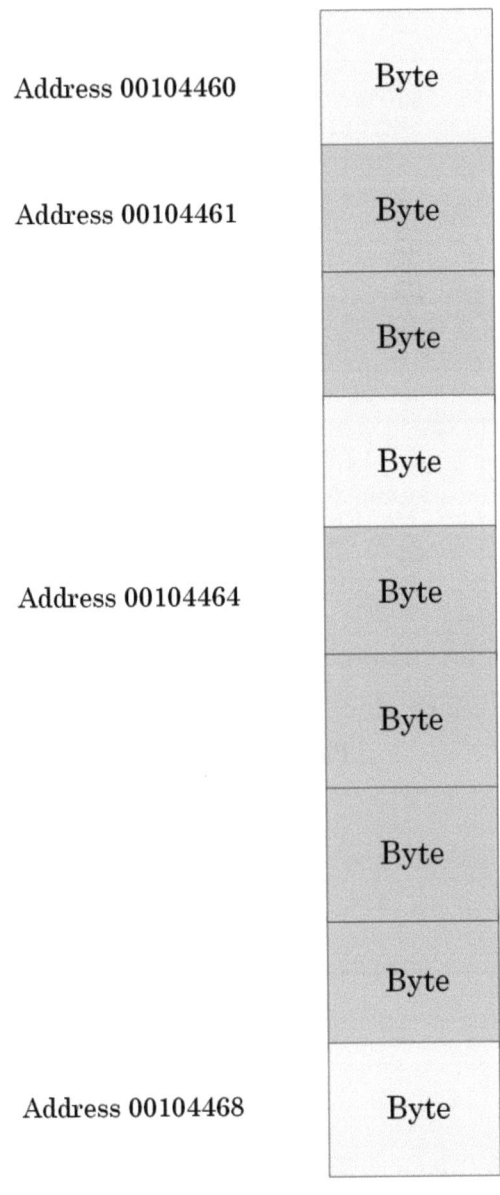

Picture x86.5.2

72 Memory Layout

EAX	Byte	Byte	Byte	Byte
EBX	Byte	Byte	Byte	Byte
ECX	Byte	Byte	Byte	Byte
EDX	Byte	Byte	Byte	Byte

Picture x86.5.3

Chapter x86.6: Pointers to Memory

Pointers Revisited

The pointer is a memory cell or a register that contains the address of another memory cell. Memory pointers have their own addresses because they are memory cells too. On 32-bit Windows, pointers are always 32-bit. On 64-bit Windows, pointers are 64-bit except in emulation mode when executing 32-bit applications and services.

Addressing Types

As seen in Chapter x86.5, memory cells can be of one byte, word, or double-word sizes. Therefore, we can have a pointer to a byte (**byte ptr**), a pointer to a word (**word ptr**), and a pointer to a double word (**dword ptr**). WinDbg disassembly output in Chapter x86.4 has **byte ptr** and **dword ptr** prefixes in instructions involving pointers to memory.

Here are some illustrated examples:

```
mov   byte ptr [eax], 0xFF
```

The layout of memory before instruction execution is shown in Picture x86.6.1, and the layout of memory after execution is shown in Picture x86.6.2.

```
mov   word ptr [eax], 0xFF
```

```
mov   dword ptr [eax], 0xFF
```

The layout of memory before instruction execution is shown in Picture x86.6.3, and the layout of memory after execution is shown in Picture x86.6.4. We can see that although we specify just one byte 0xFF as a source operand to MOV instruction, it replaces all other 3 bytes of a double word in memory because we specify the destination as a pointer to 4 bytes, and 0xFF is really 0x000000FF as a double word. So we need to specify **dword ptr** prefix to disambiguate moving a double word value from moving a byte value. In the following equivalent instruction, we don't need to specify **dword ptr** prefix:

```
mov   [eax], 0x000000FF
```

Picture x86.6.5 shows a summary of various addressing modes.

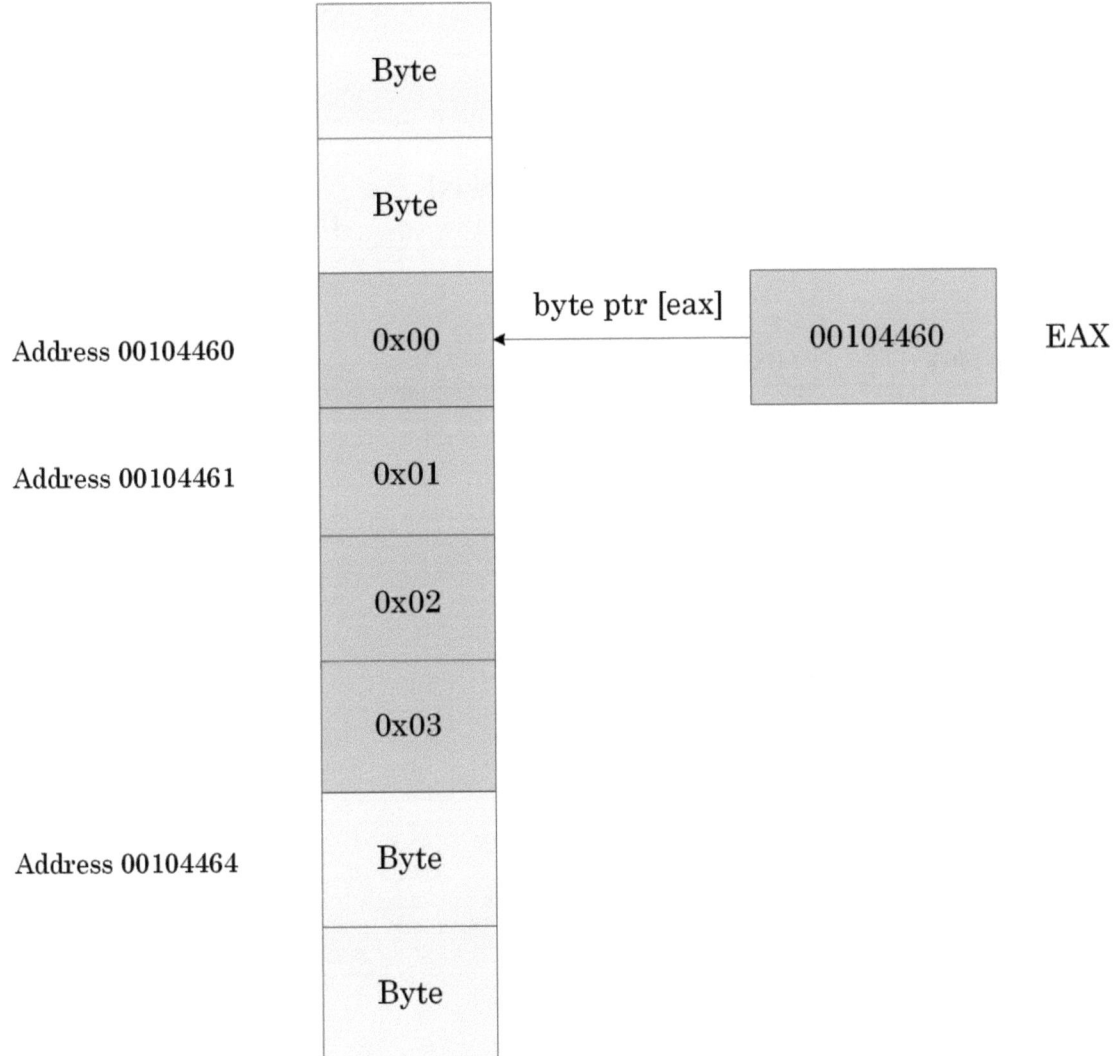

Picture x86.6.1

Addressing Types

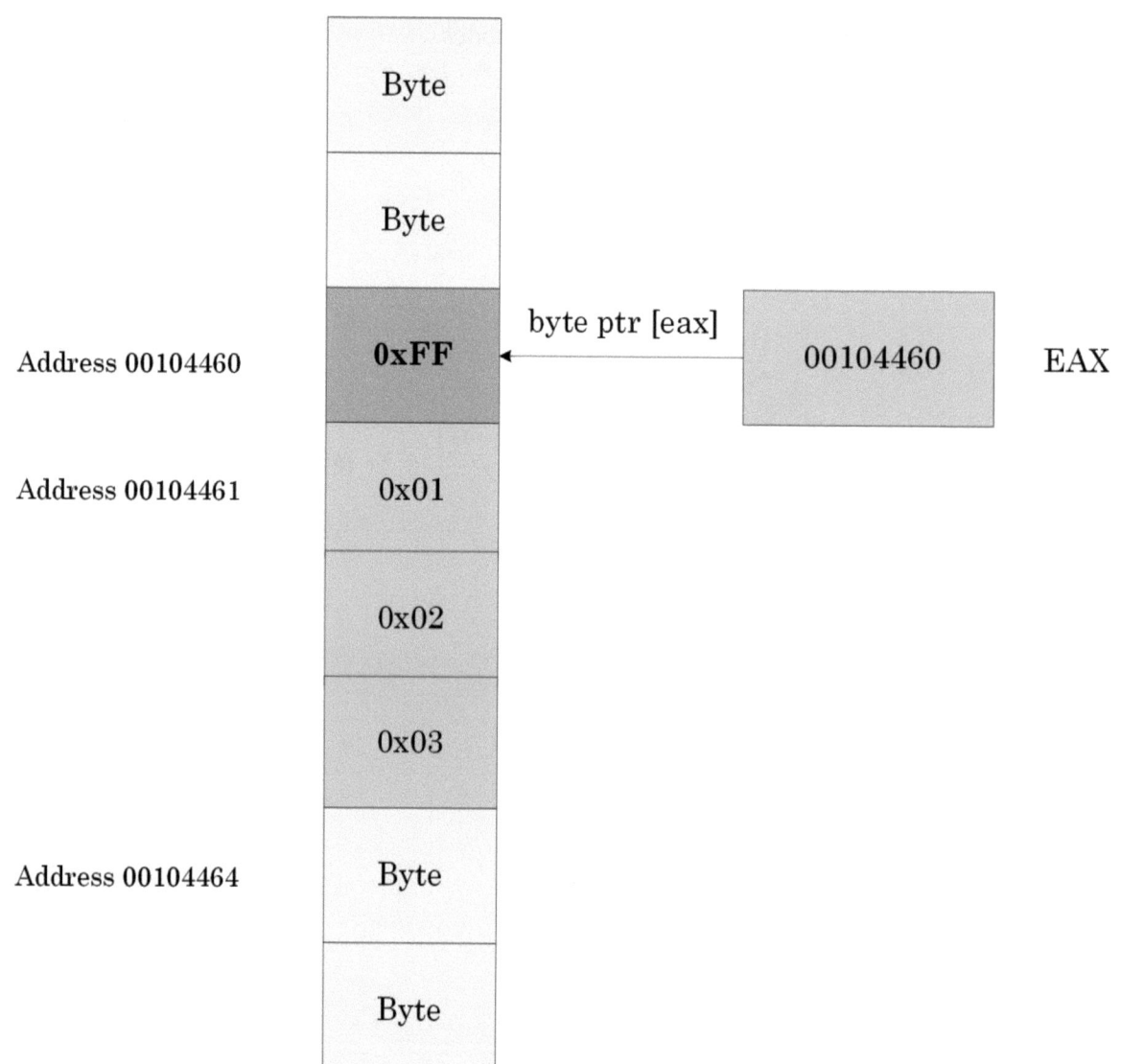

Picture x86.6.2

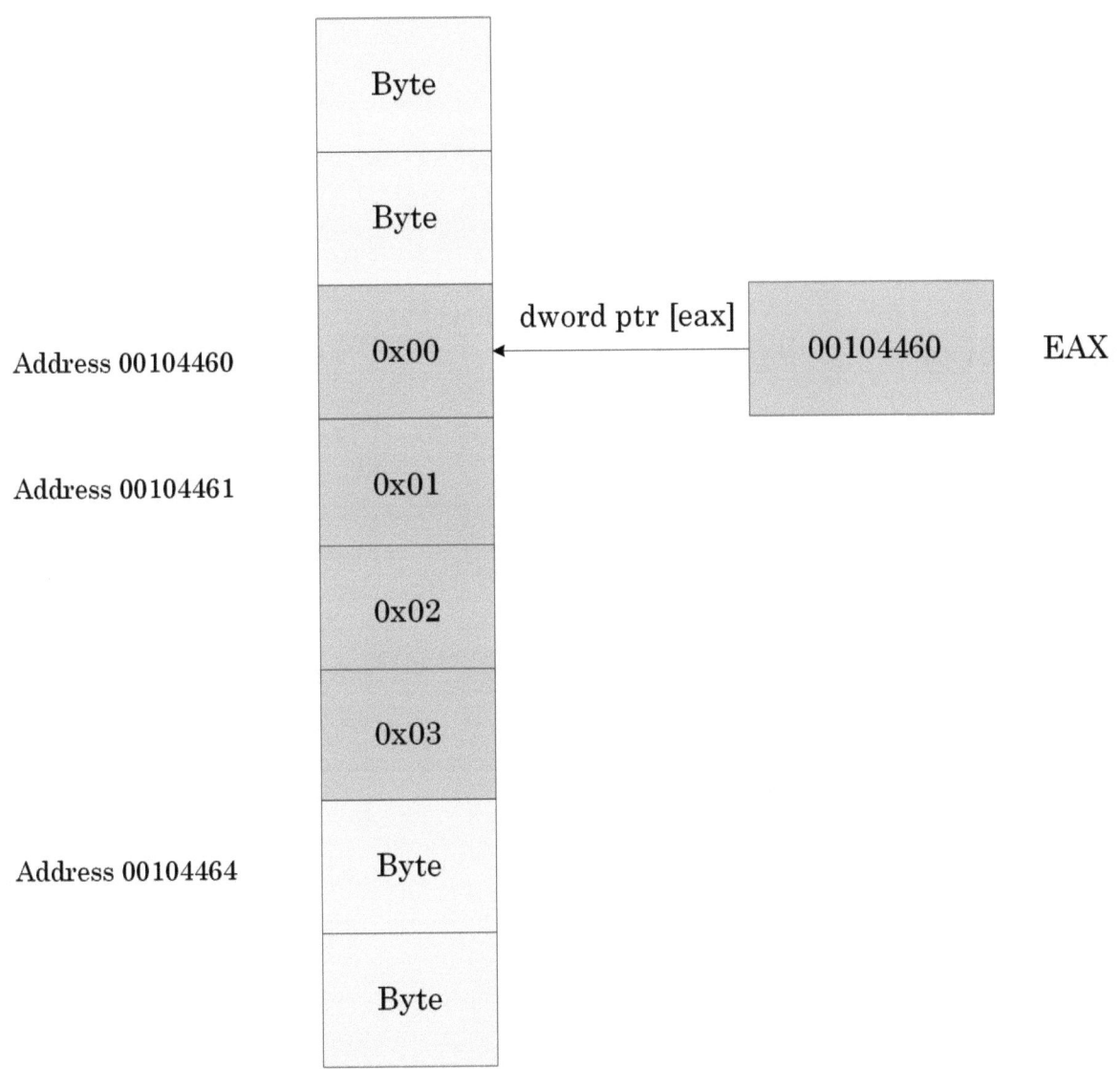

Picture x86.6.3

Addressing Types

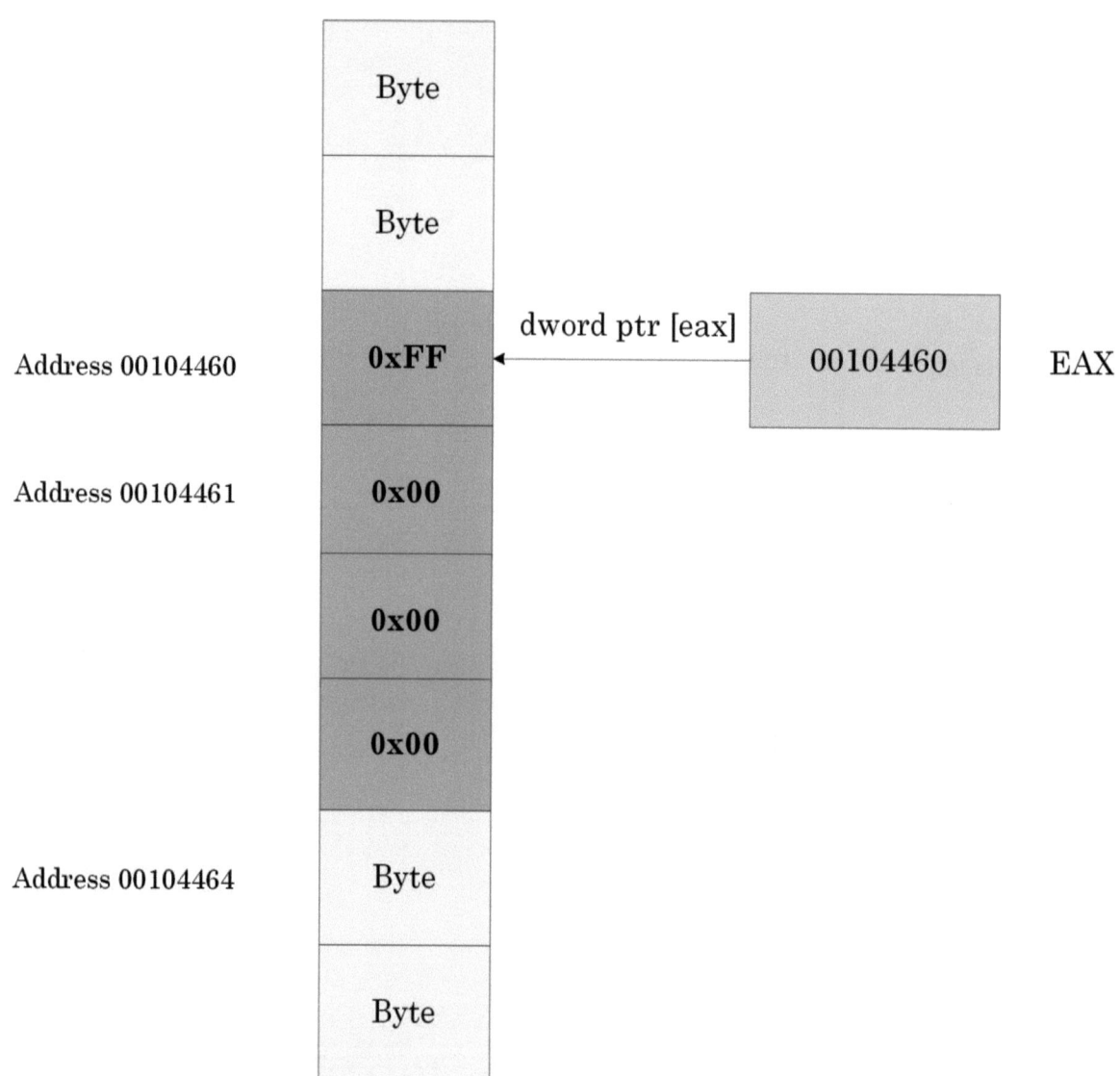

Picture x86.6.4

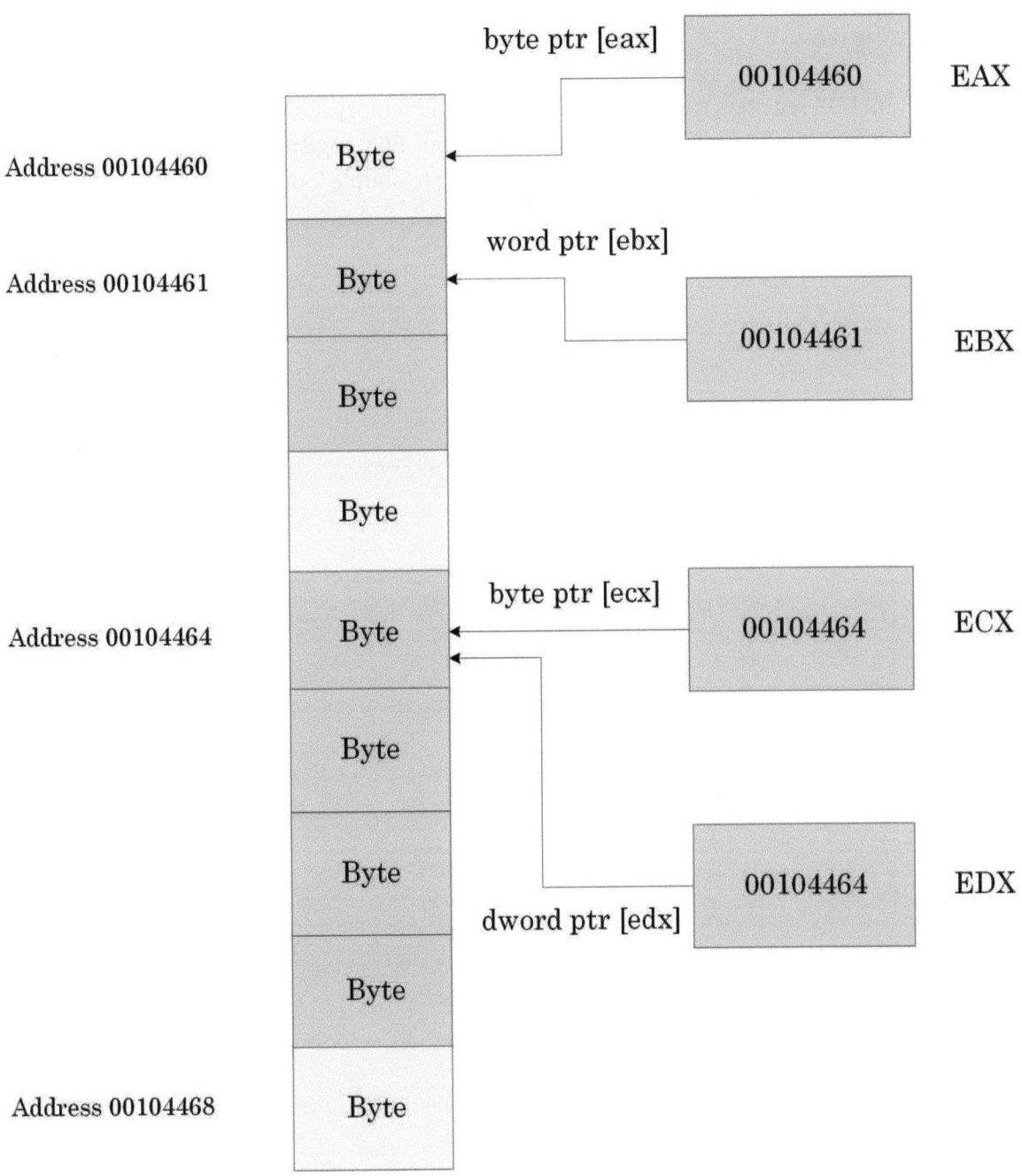

Picture x86.6.5

Registers Revisited

EAX, EBX, ECX, and EDX registers can be used as pointers to memory. EAX and EDX registers contain the multiplication result after executing IMUL instruction. ECX register is often used as a loop counter, E(Counter)X, in assembly language corresponding to simple loops in C and C++ code:

```
for (int i = 0; i < N; ++i)
```

NULL Pointers

Addresses 0x00000000 – 0x0000FFFF are specifically made inaccessible in Windows. The following code will force an application crash or BSOD if executed inside a driver:

```
mov    eax, 0xF
mov    [eax], 1   ; Access violation
```

Invalid Pointers

There are different kinds of invalid pointers that cause an access violation when we try to dereference them:

- NULL pointers
- Pointers to inaccessible memory
- Pointers to read-only memory when writing

Other pointers may or may not cause an access violation, and some of them are discussed in the subsequent chapters:

- Pointers pointing to "random" memory
- Uninitialized pointers having random values inherited from past code execution
- Dangling pointers

The last pointers are similar to pointers pointing to "random" memory locations and arise when we forget to set pointer variables to zero (NULL) after disposing (deallocating) of the memory they point to. By nullifying pointers, we indicate that they no longer point to memory.

Variables as Pointers

Suppose we have two memory addresses (locations) "a" and "b" declared and defined in C and C++ as:

```
int a, b;
```

These are normal variables "a" and "b". In addition, we can have another two memory addresses (locations), "pa" and "pb" declared and defined in C and C++ as:

```
int *pa, *pb;
```

Here **pa** is a pointer to an *int* or, in other words, the memory cell **pa** contains the address of another memory cell that contains an integer value.

Pointer Initialization

In order to have pointers to point to memory we need to initialize them with corresponding memory addresses. Here is typical C or C++ code that does what we need:

```
int a;              // uninitialized variable

int *pa;            // uninitialized pointer

pa = &a;            // [pa] now contains the address a

int b = 12;         // initialized variable

int *pb = &b;       // initialized pointer
```

We can see that pointers are also variables and can change their values, effectively pointing to different memory locations during program execution.

Note: Initialized and Uninitialized Data

A bit of additional information about initialized and uninitialized variables that is useful to know: an executable program on Windows is divided into different sections. One of them is called **.data**, where all global and static variables (including pointers) are put.

Consider this C or C++ data definition:

```
int array[1000000]; // size 4,000,000 bytes or 3.815Mb
```

We would expect the size of the *.EXE* file to be about 4Mb. However, the program size on a disk is only 32Kb. It is because the uninitialized array contains only information about its size. When we launch the program, this array is recreated from its size information and filled with zeroes. The size of the program in memory becomes about 4Mb.

In the case of the initialized array the program size on disk 3.84Mb:

```
int array[1000000] = { 12 };
```

This is because the array was put into a .data section and contains the following sequence of integers { 12, 0, 0, 0, 0 ... }.

More Pseudo Notation

We remind that **[a]** means contents of memory at the address **a**, and **[eax]** means contents of memory at the address stored in the EAX register (here, EAX is a pointer).

We also introduce an additional notation to employ in this and subsequent chapters: ***[pa]** means contents at the address stored at the address **pa** and is called dereferencing a pointer whose address is **pa**. The corresponding C code is similar:

```
int *pa = &a;
int b = *pa;
```

"MemoryPointers" Project: Memory Layout

This project is very similar to the "Pointers" project from Chapter x86.4. We have this data declaration and definition in C or C++ language:

```
int a, b;

int *pa, *pb = &b;
```

The project code corresponds to the following pseudo-code and assembly language:

`[pa] <- address a`		`lea`	`eax, a`
		`mov`	`[pa], eax`
`*[pa] <- 1`	`; [a] = 1`	`mov`	`eax, [pa]`
		`mov`	`[eax], 1`
`*[pb] <- 1`	`; [b] = 1`	`mov`	`ebx, [pb]`
		`mov`	`[ebx], 1`
`*[pb] <- *[pb] + *[pa]`	`; [b] = 2`	`mov`	`ecx, [eax]`
		`add`	`ecx, [ebx]`
		`mov`	`[ebx], ecx`

The project for this chapter can be downloaded from:

https://bitbucket.org/softwarediagnostics/pfwddr2/src/master/x86/Chapter6/

    The executable is located in *Debug* subfolder. We can load it into WinDbg and disassemble its *main* function as described in Chapter x86.2 or Chapter x86.4.

    First, we load *MemoryPointers.exe* using File\Open Executable… menu option in WinDbg and get the following output (the output, especially addresses, may differ for your Windows version):

```
Microsoft (R) Windows Debugger Version 10.0.22000.194 X86
Copyright (c) Microsoft Corporation. All rights reserved.


CommandLine: C:\PFWDDR2\x86\Chapter6\Debug\MemoryPointers.exe


************* Path validation summary **************
Response                         Time (ms)     Location
Deferred                                       srv*
```

```
Symbol search path is: srv*
Executable search path is:
ModLoad: 00400000 004e4000   MemoryPointers.exe
ModLoad: 77a80000 77c29000   ntdll.dll
ModLoad: 767b0000 768a0000   C:\WINDOWS\SysWOW64\KERNEL32.DLL
ModLoad: 76b30000 76d82000   C:\WINDOWS\SysWOW64\KERNELBASE.dll
ModLoad: 71080000 71120000   C:\WINDOWS\SysWOW64\apphelp.dll
(5c9c.682c): Break instruction exception - code 80000003 (first chance)
eax=00000000 ebx=0022a000 ecx=0edd0000 edx=00000000 esi=ffffffff edi=00400108
eip=77b366d1 esp=0019f7e4 ebp=0019f810 iopl=0         nv up ei pl zr na pe nc
cs=0023  ss=002b  ds=002b  es=002b  fs=0053  gs=002b           efl=00000246
ntdll!LdrpDoDebuggerBreak+0x2b:
77b366d1 cc              int     3
```

Then we put a breakpoint at the *main* function and run the program until WinDbg breaks in:

```
0:000> bp MemoryPointers!main
*** WARNING: Unable to verify checksum for MemoryPointers.exe
```

```
0:000> g
Breakpoint 0 hit
eax=006154b8 ebx=0022a000 ecx=00000001 edx=006188e8 esi=00401136 edi=00401136
eip=004075b0 esp=0019feec ebp=0019ff08 iopl=0         nv up ei pl nz na pe nc
cs=0023  ss=002b  ds=002b  es=002b  fs=0053  gs=002b           efl=00000206
MemoryPointers!main:
004075b0 55              push    eb
```

For visual clarity we disable the output of binary codes before disassembling *main* function:

```
0:000> .asm no_code_bytes
Assembly options: no_code_bytes
```

```
0:000> uf main
MemoryPointers!main [C:\NewWork\PFWDDR2\MemoryPointers\MemoryPointers.cpp @ 5]:
    5 004075b0 push    ebp
    5 004075b1 mov     ebp,esp
    5 004075b3 push    ebx
    8 004075b4 lea     eax,[MemoryPointers!a (004def60)]
    9 004075ba mov     dword ptr [MemoryPointers!pa (004def68)],eax
   11 004075bf mov     eax,dword ptr [MemoryPointers!pa (004def68)]
   12 004075c4 mov     byte ptr [eax],1
```

```
14 004075c7 mov     ebx,dword ptr [MemoryPointers!pb (004de000)]
15 004075cd mov     byte ptr [ebx],1
17 004075d0 mov     ecx,dword ptr [eax]
18 004075d2 add     ecx,dword ptr [ebx]
20 004075d4 mov     dword ptr [ebx],ecx
23 004075d6 xor     eax,eax
24 004075d8 pop     ebx
24 004075d9 cmp     ebp,esp
24 004075db call    MemoryPointers!ILT+7805(__RTC_CheckEsp) (00402e82)
24 004075e0 pop     ebp
24 004075e1 ret
```

Because our real project code starts with LEA instruction, we find its code address in the listing above, set a breakpoint on it, and resume our program execution:

```
0:000> bp 004075b4
```

```
0:000> g
Breakpoint 1 hit
eax=006154b8 ebx=0022a000 ecx=00000001 edx=006188e8 esi=00401136 edi=00401136
eip=004075b4 esp=0019fee4 ebp=0019fee8 iopl=0         nv up ei pl nz na pe nc
cs=0023  ss=002b  ds=002b  es=002b  fs=0053  gs=002b              efl=00000206
MemoryPointers!main+0x4:
004075b4 lea     eax,[MemoryPointers!a (004def60)]
```

Then we clear EAX, EBX and ECX registers to set up memory layout that is easy to follow:

```
0:000> r eax = 0
```

```
0:000> r ebx = 0
```

```
0:000> r ecx = 0
```

```
0:000> r
eax=00000000 ebx=00000000 ecx=00000000 edx=006188e8 esi=00401136 edi=00401136
eip=004075b4 esp=0019fee4 ebp=0019fee8 iopl=0         nv up ei pl nz na pe nc
cs=0023  ss=002b  ds=002b  es=002b  fs=0053  gs=002b              efl=00000206
MemoryPointers!main+0x4:
004075b4 lea     eax,[MemoryPointers!a (004def60)]
```

We check the values and addresses of **a**, **b**, **pa**, and **pb** variables:

```
0:000> dc MemoryPointers!a L1
004def60  00000000                              ....

0:000> dc MemoryPointers!b L1
004def64  00000000                              ....

0:000> dc MemoryPointers!pa L1
004def68  00000000                              ....

0:000> dc MemoryPointers!pb L1
004de000  004def64                              d.M.
```

These values correspond to the memory layout before executing the first LEA instruction, and it is shown in Picture x86.6.6.

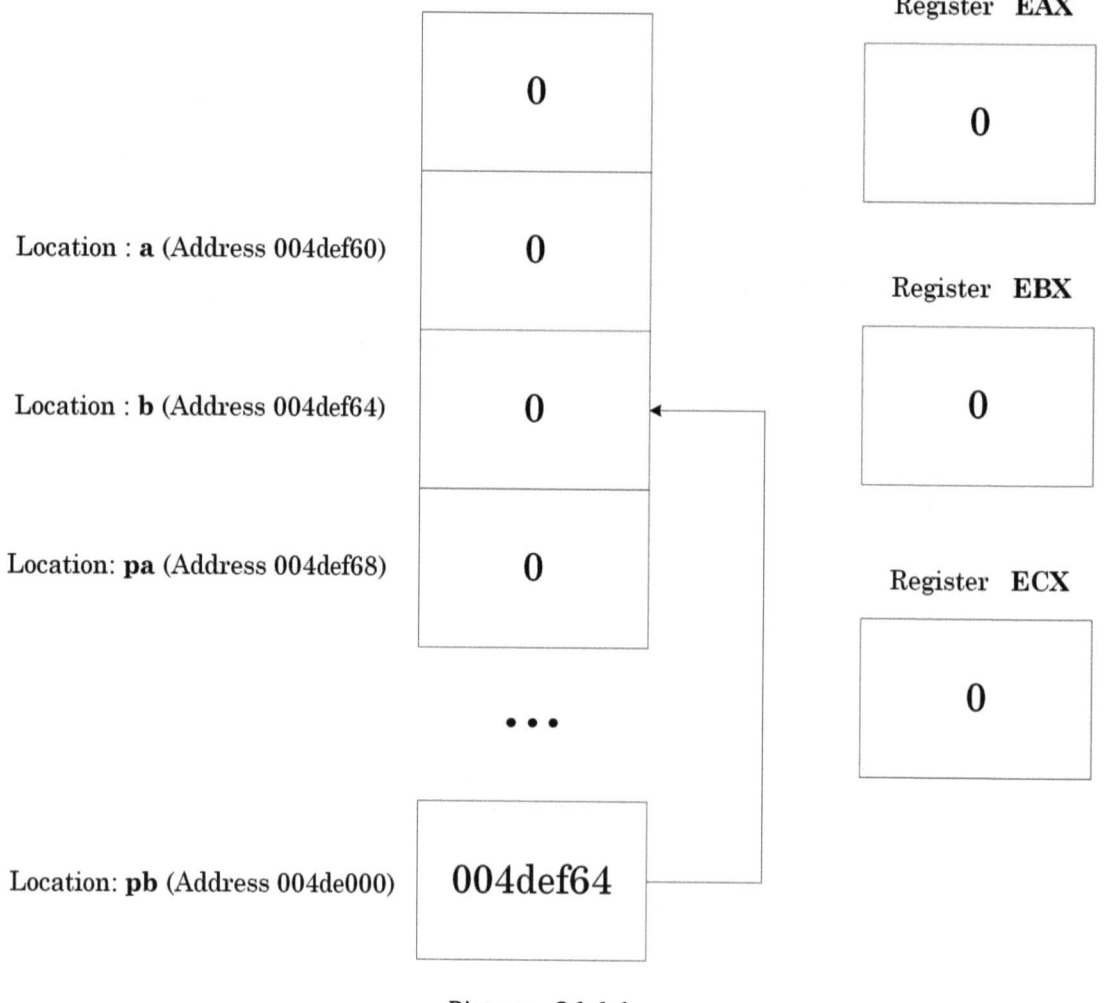

Picture x86.6.6

We then execute our code step by step. Changes in registers and memory are highlighted in bold.

```
[From the previous output]
eax=00000000 ebx=00000000 ecx=00000000 edx=006188e8 esi=00401136 edi=00401136
eip=004075b4 esp=0019fee4 ebp=0019fee8 iopl=0         nv up ei pl nz na pe nc
cs=0023  ss=002b  ds=002b  es=002b  fs=0053  gs=002b              efl=00000206
MemoryPointers!main+0x4:
004075b4 lea     eax,[MemoryPointers!a (004def60)]
```

```
0:000> t
eax=004def60 ebx=00000000 ecx=00000000 edx=006188e8 esi=00401136 edi=00401136
eip=004075ba esp=0019fee4 ebp=0019fee8 iopl=0         nv up ei pl nz na pe nc
cs=0023  ss=002b  ds=002b  es=002b  fs=0053  gs=002b              efl=00000206
MemoryPointers!main+0xa:
004075ba mov     dword ptr [MemoryPointers!pa (004def68)],eax
ds:002b:004def68=00000000
```

```
0:000> t
eax=004def60 ebx=00000000 ecx=00000000 edx=006188e8 esi=00401136 edi=00401136
eip=004075bf esp=0019fee4 ebp=0019fee8 iopl=0         nv up ei pl nz na pe nc
cs=0023  ss=002b  ds=002b  es=002b  fs=0053  gs=002b              efl=00000206
MemoryPointers!main+0xf:
004075bf mov     eax,dword ptr [MemoryPointers!pa (004def68)]
ds:002b:004def68={MemoryPointers!a (004def60)}
```

```
0:000> dc MemoryPointers!pa L1
004def68  004def60                                     `.M.
```

```
0:000> t
eax=004def60 ebx=00000000 ecx=00000000 edx=006188e8 esi=00401136 edi=00401136
eip=004075c4 esp=0019fee4 ebp=0019fee8 iopl=0         nv up ei pl nz na pe nc
cs=0023  ss=002b  ds=002b  es=002b  fs=0053  gs=002b              efl=00000206
MemoryPointers!main+0x14:
004075c4 mov     byte ptr [eax],1                          ds:002b:004def60=00
```

"MemoryPointers" Project: Memory Layout

```
0:000> t
eax=004def60 ebx=00000000 ecx=00000000 edx=006188e8 esi=00401136 edi=00401136
eip=004075c7 esp=0019fee4 ebp=0019fee8 iopl=0         nv up ei pl nz na pe nc
cs=0023  ss=002b  ds=002b  es=002b  fs=0053  gs=002b             efl=00000206
MemoryPointers!main+0x17:
004075c7 mov     ebx,dword ptr [MemoryPointers!pb (004de000)]
ds:002b:004de000={MemoryPointers!b (004def64)}

0:000> dc @eax L1
004def60  00000001                                     ....

0:000> dc MemoryPointers!a L1
004def60  00000001                                     ....

0:000> t
eax=004def60 ebx=004def64 ecx=00000000 edx=006188e8 esi=00401136 edi=00401136
eip=004075cd esp=0019fee4 ebp=0019fee8 iopl=0         nv up ei pl nz na pe nc
cs=0023  ss=002b  ds=002b  es=002b  fs=0053  gs=002b             efl=00000206
MemoryPointers!main+0x1d:
004075cd mov     byte ptr [ebx],1                     ds:002b:004def64=00

0:000> t
eax=004def60 ebx=004def64 ecx=00000000 edx=006188e8 esi=00401136 edi=00401136
eip=004075d0 esp=0019fee4 ebp=0019fee8 iopl=0         nv up ei pl nz na pe nc
cs=0023  ss=002b  ds=002b  es=002b  fs=0053  gs=002b             efl=00000206
MemoryPointers!main+0x20:
004075d0 mov     ecx,dword ptr [eax]                  ds:002b:004def60=00000001

0:000> dc MemoryPointers!b L1
004def64  00000001                                     ....

0:000> dc @ebx L1
004def64  00000001                                     ....
```

```
0:000> t
eax=004def60 ebx=004def64 ecx=00000001 edx=006188e8 esi=00401136 edi=00401136
eip=004075d2 esp=0019fee4 ebp=0019fee8 iopl=0         nv up ei pl nz na pe nc
cs=0023  ss=002b  ds=002b  es=002b  fs=0053  gs=002b              efl=00000206
MemoryPointers!main+0x22:
004075d2 add     ecx,dword ptr [ebx]            ds:002b:004def64=00000001

0:000> t
eax=004def60 ebx=004def64 ecx=00000002 edx=006188e8 esi=00401136 edi=00401136
eip=004075d4 esp=0019fee4 ebp=0019fee8 iopl=0         nv up ei pl nz na po nc
cs=0023  ss=002b  ds=002b  es=002b  fs=0053  gs=002b              efl=00000202
MemoryPointers!main+0x24:
004075d4 mov     dword ptr [ebx],ecx            ds:002b:004def64=00000001

0:000> t
eax=004def60 ebx=004def64 ecx=00000002 edx=006188e8 esi=00401136 edi=00401136
eip=004075d6 esp=0019fee4 ebp=0019fee8 iopl=0         nv up ei pl nz na po nc
cs=0023  ss=002b  ds=002b  es=002b  fs=0053  gs=002b              efl=00000202
MemoryPointers!main+0x26:
004075d6 xor     eax,eax

0:000> dc MemoryPointers!b L1
004def64  00000002                                     ....

0:000> dc @ebx L1
004def64  00000002                                     ....
```

94 "MemoryPointers" Project: Memory Layout

Final memory layout and registers are shown in Picture x86.6.7.

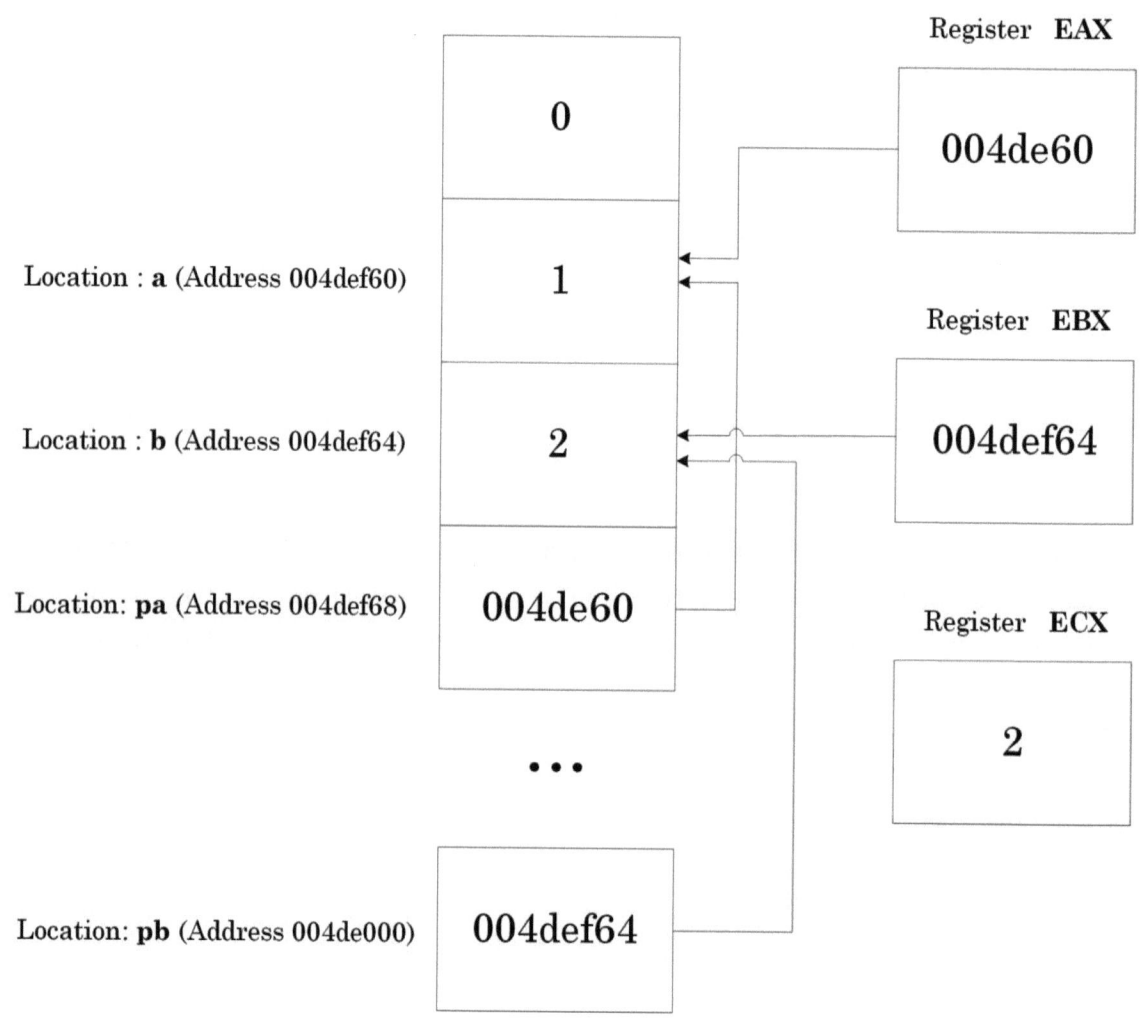

Picture x86.6.7

Chapter x86.7: Logical Instructions and EIP

Instruction Format

We have seen that assembly language instructions have uniform format:

Opcode *operand*

Opcode *destination_operand, source_operand*

Operands can be registers (reg), memory reference (mem) or some number, called immediate value (imm). Typical notational examples:

```
inc   mem/reg
dec   mem/reg
add   mem/reg, reg/imm
add   reg, mem/imm
```

And some concrete assembly language examples:

```
inc   dword ptr [eax]
dec   byte ptr [a]
add   byte ptr [eax], 10
add   eax, dword ptr [a]
```

Logical Shift Instructions

In addition to arithmetic instructions, there are so-called logical shift instructions that just shift a bit string to the left or the right.

Shift to the left:

```
11111111   ->   11111110    ; shift by 1
11111110   ->   11110000    ; shift by 3
shl   mem/reg, imm/reg
shl   eax, 1
shl   byte ptr [eax], 2
```

Shift to the right:

```
11111111   ->   01111111    ; shift by 1
01111111   ->   00001111    ; shift by 3
shr   mem/reg, imm/reg
shr   eax, 1
shr   byte ptr [eax], 2
```

Logical Operations

Here we recall logical operations and corresponding truth tables you probably learned earlier. Here we abbreviate True as T and False as F.

AND

```
1 and 1 = 1    T and T = T
1 and 0 = 0    T and F = F
0 and 1 = 0    F and T = F
0 and 0 = 0    F and F = F
```

OR

```
1 or 1 = 1     T or T = T
1 or 0 = 1     T or F = T
0 or 1 = 1     F or T = T
0 or 0 = 0     F or F = F
```

Zeroing Memory or Registers

There are several ways to put a zero value into a register or a memory location:

1. Move a value:

```
mov    dword ptr [a], 0
```

```
mov    eax, 0
```

2. Use XOR (Exclusive OR) logical operation:

```
xor    eax, eax
```

XOR

1 xor 1 = 0   T xor T = F

1 xor 0 = 1   T xor F = T

0 xor 1 = 1   F xor T = T

0 xor 0 = 0   F xor F = F

This operation clears its destination operand because the source operand is the same, and the same bits are cleared.

Instruction Pointer

Consider these two execution steps from the previous chapter project:

```
0:000> t
eax=004def60 ebx=004def64 ecx=00000002 edx=006188e8 esi=00401136 edi=00401136
eip=004075d4 esp=0019fee4 ebp=0019fee8 iopl=0         nv up ei pl nz na po nc
cs=0023  ss=002b  ds=002b  es=002b  fs=0053  gs=002b             efl=00000202
MemoryPointers!main+0x24:
004075d4 mov     dword ptr [ebx],ecx              ds:002b:004def64=00000001
```

```
0:000> t
eax=004def60 ebx=004def64 ecx=00000002 edx=006188e8 esi=00401136 edi=00401136
eip=004075d6 esp=0019fee4 ebp=0019fee8 iopl=0         nv up ei pl nz na po nc
cs=0023  ss=002b  ds=002b  es=002b  fs=0053  gs=002b             efl=00000202
MemoryPointers!main+0x26:
004075d6 xor     eax,eax
```

When MOV instruction at 004075d4 address is being executed, another CPU register EIP points to the next instruction at 004075d6 address to be executed. It is shown in Picture x86.7.1.

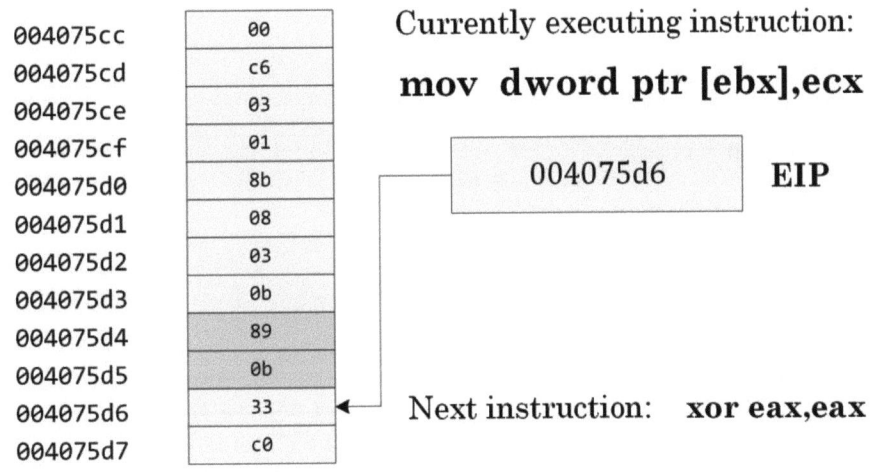

Picture x86.7.1

Note: Code Section

Recall that in Chapter x86.6, we discussed **.data** section where the program data is put. The program code is put into the **.text** section.

The **!dh** WinDbg command lists various program sections and their information:

```
0:000> !dh MemoryPointers


File Type: EXECUTABLE IMAGE
FILE HEADER VALUES
     14C machine (i386)
       6 number of sections
6240D927 time date stamp Sun Mar 27 22:37:43 2022

       0 file pointer to symbol table
       0 number of symbols
      E0 size of optional header
     103 characteristics
            Relocations stripped
            Executable
            32 bit word machine

OPTIONAL HEADER VALUES
     10B magic #
   14.31 linker version
   B5E00 size of code
   2A400 size of initialized data
       0 size of uninitialized data
    1136 address of entry point
    1000 base of code
         ----- new -----
00400000 image base
    1000 section alignment
     200 file alignment
       3 subsystem (Windows CUI)
    6.00 operating system version
    0.00 image version
    6.00 subsystem version
   E4000 size of image
```

```
     400 size of headers
       0 checksum
00100000 size of stack reserve
00001000 size of stack commit
00100000 size of heap reserve
00001000 size of heap commit
[Skipped]

SECTION HEADER #1
   .text name
   B5D85 virtual size
    1000 virtual address
   B5E00 size of raw data
     400 file pointer to raw data
       0 file pointer to relocation table
       0 file pointer to line numbers
       0 number of relocations
       0 number of line numbers
60000020 flags
         Code
         (no align specified)
         Execute Read
[Skipped]

SECTION HEADER #3
   .data name
    26B4 virtual size
   DE000 virtual address
    1000 size of raw data
   DCA00 file pointer to raw data
       0 file pointer to relocation table
       0 file pointer to line numbers
       0 number of relocations
       0 number of line numbers
C0000040 flags
         Initialized Data
         (no align specified)
         Read Write
[Skipped]
```

Chapter x86.8: Reconstructing a Program with Pointers

Example of Disassembly Output: No Optimization

The ability to reconstruct approximate C or C++ code from code disassembly is very important in memory dump analysis and debugging.

The project for this chapter can be downloaded from:

https://bitbucket.org/softwarediagnostics/pfwddr2/src/master/x86/Chapter8

The executable is located under *Debug* subfolder. We load it into WinDbg and disassemble its *main* function.

First, we load *PointersAsVariables.exe* using File\Open Executable... menu option in WinDbg and get the following output (the output, especially addresses, may differ for your Windows version):

```
Microsoft (R) Windows Debugger Version 10.0.22000.194 X86
Copyright (c) Microsoft Corporation. All rights reserved.


CommandLine: C:\PFWDDR2\x86\Chapter8\Debug\PointersAsVariables.exe

************* Path validation summary **************
Response                         Time (ms)     Location
Deferred                                       srv*
Symbol search path is: srv*
Executable search path is:
ModLoad: 00400000 004e4000   PointersAsVariables.exe
ModLoad: 77a80000 77c29000   ntdll.dll
ModLoad: 767b0000 768a0000   C:\WINDOWS\SysWOW64\KERNEL32.DLL
ModLoad: 76b30000 76d82000   C:\WINDOWS\SysWOW64\KERNELBASE.dll
ModLoad: 71080000 71120000   C:\WINDOWS\SysWOW64\apphelp.dll
(22a0.8358): Break instruction exception - code 80000003 (first chance)
eax=00000000 ebx=0035e000 ecx=42160000 edx=00000000 esi=ffffffff edi=004000f8
eip=77b366d1 esp=0019f7e4 ebp=0019f810 iopl=0         nv up ei pl zr na pe nc
cs=0023  ss=002b  ds=002b  es=002b  fs=0053  gs=002b             efl=00000246
ntdll!LdrpDoDebuggerBreak+0x2b:
77b366d1 cc              int     3
```

Then we put a breakpoint at the *main* function and run the program until WinDbg breaks in:

```
0:000> bp PointersAsVariables!main
*** WARNING: Unable to verify checksum for PointersAsVariables.exe
```

```
0:000> g
Breakpoint 0 hit
eax=008a5500 ebx=0035e000 ecx=00000001 edx=008a8938 esi=00401136 edi=00401136
eip=00407590 esp=0019feec ebp=0019ff08 iopl=0         nv up ei pl nz na po nc
cs=0023  ss=002b  ds=002b  es=002b  fs=0053  gs=002b          efl=00000202
PointersAsVariables!main:
00407590 55              push    ebp
```

Next we disassemble our *main* function:

```
0:000> .asm no_code_bytes
Assembly options: no_code_bytes
```

```
0:000> uf main
PointersAsVariables!main
[C:\NewWork\PFWDDR2\PointersAsVariables\PointersAsVariables.cpp @ 5]:
    5 00407590 push    ebp
    5 00407591 mov     ebp,esp
    6 00407593 mov     dword ptr [PointersAsVariables!pa (004def50)],offset PointersAsVariables!a (004def48)
    7 0040759d mov     dword ptr [PointersAsVariables!pb (004def54)],offset PointersAsVariables!b (004def4c)
    9 004075a7 mov     eax,dword ptr [PointersAsVariables!pa (004def50)]
    9 004075ac mov     dword ptr [eax],1
   10 004075b2 mov     ecx,dword ptr [PointersAsVariables!pb (004def54)]
   10 004075b8 mov     dword ptr [ecx],1
   12 004075be mov     edx,dword ptr [PointersAsVariables!pb (004def54)]
   12 004075c4 mov     eax,dword ptr [edx]
   12 004075c6 mov     ecx,dword ptr [PointersAsVariables!pa (004def50)]
   12 004075cc add     eax,dword ptr [ecx]
   12 004075ce mov     edx,dword ptr [PointersAsVariables!pb (004def54)]
   12 004075d4 mov     dword ptr [edx],eax
   14 004075d6 mov     eax,dword ptr [PointersAsVariables!pb (004def54)]
   14 004075db mov     ecx,dword ptr [eax]
   14 004075dd shl     ecx,1
   14 004075df mov     edx,dword ptr [PointersAsVariables!pb (004def54)]
   14 004075e5 mov     dword ptr [edx],ecx
   16 004075e7 xor     eax,eax
   17 004075e9 pop     ebp
   17 004075ea ret
```

Reconstructing C/C++ Code: Part 1

Now we go from instruction to instruction and try to reconstruct pseudo-code which is shown as comments to assembly language code.

```
mov     dword ptr [PointersAsVariables!pa (004def50)],offset PointersAsVariables!a (004def48)
; [pa]   <- address of a
mov     dword ptr [PointersAsVariables!pb (004def54)],offset PointersAsVariables!b (004def4c)
; [pb]   <- address of b
mov     eax,dword ptr [PointersAsVariables!pa (004def50)]
; eax    <- [pa]
mov     dword ptr [eax],1
; [eax]  <- 1
mov     ecx,dword ptr [PointersAsVariables!pb (004def54)]
; ecx    <- [pb]
mov     dword ptr [ecx],1
; [ecx]  <- 1
mov     edx,dword ptr [PointersAsVariables!pb (004def54)]
; edx    <- [pb]
mov     eax,dword ptr [edx]
; eax    <- [edx]
mov     ecx,dword ptr [PointersAsVariables!pa (004def50)]
; ecx    <- [pa]
add     eax,dword ptr [ecx]
; eax    <- eax + [ecx]
mov     edx,dword ptr [PointersAsVariables!pb (004def54)]
; edx    <- [pb]
mov     dword ptr [edx],eax
; [edx]  <- eax
mov     eax,dword ptr [PointersAsVariables!pb (004def54)]
; eax    <- [pb]
mov     ecx,dword ptr [eax]
; ecx    <- [eax]
shl     ecx,1
; ecx    <- ecx * 2
mov     edx,dword ptr [PointersAsVariables!pb (004def54)]
; edx    <- [pb]
mov     dword ptr [edx],ecx
; [edx]  <- ecx
```

Reconstructing C/C++ Code: Part 2

Now we group pseudo-code together with possible mixed C/C++ and assembly language equivalents:

```
[pa]   <- address of a      ;  int a; int *pa; pa = &a;


[pb]   <- address of b      ;  int b; int *pb; pb = &b;


eax    <- [pa]              ;  *pa = 1;
[eax]  <- 1


ecx    <- [pb]              ;  *pb = 1;
[ecx]  <- 1


edx    <- [pb]              ;  eax = *pb;
eax    <- [edx]


ecx    <- [pa]              ;  eax = eax + *pa;
eax    <- eax + [ecx]


edx    <- [pb]              ;  *pb = eax;
[edx]  <- eax


eax    <- [pb]              ;  ecx = *pb;
ecx    <- [eax]


ecx    <- ecx * 2           ;  ecx = ecx * 2;


edx    <- [pb]              ;  *pb = ecx;
[edx]  <- ecx
```

Reconstructing C/C++ Code: Part 3

Next we combine more mixed statements into C/C++ language code:

```
int a, b;
int *pa, *pb;

pa = &a;
pb = &b;

*pa = 1;
*pb = 1;

eax = *pb;
eax = eax + *pa;
*pb = eax;          ; *pb = *pb + *pa;

ecx = *pb;
ecx = ecx * 2;
*pb = ecx;          ; *pb = *pb * 2;
```

Reconstructing C/C++ Code: C/C++ program

Finally, we have something that looks like complete C/C++ code:

```
int a, b;
int *pa, *pb;

pa = &a;
pb = &b;

*pa = 1;
*pb = 1;

*pb = *pb + *pa;
*pb = *pb * 2;
```

If we look at the project source code *PointersAsVariables.cpp*, we see exactly the same code that was compiled into our executable file that we were disassembling.

Example of Disassembly Output: Optimized Program

A fully optimized program from the *Release* project folder contains fewer CPU instructions:

```
0:000> uf main
PointersAsVariables!main
[C:\NewWork\PFWDDR2\PointersAsVariables\PointersAsVariables.cpp @ 5]:
    5 00401000 mov     dword ptr [PointersAsVariables!pa (004148e0)],offset
PointersAsVariables!a (004148d8)
   16 0040100a xor     eax,eax
   16 0040100c mov     dword ptr [PointersAsVariables!pb (004148e4)],offset
PointersAsVariables!b (004148dc)
   16 00401016 mov     dword ptr [PointersAsVariables!a (004148d8)],1
   16 00401020 mov     dword ptr [PointersAsVariables!b (004148dc)],4
   17 0040102a ret
```

We see that the Visual C++ compiler was able to figure out the result of computation: a = 1; b = 4; However, one question remains, why did the compiler not optimize away the first two instructions initializing pa and pb variables? The answer lies in the nature of separate compilation model in C and C++. We can compile several compilation units (*.c* or *.cpp*) files separately and independently. Therefore there is no guarantee that another compilation unit would not reference our globally declared and defined pa and pb variables.

Chapter x86.9: Memory and Stacks

Stack: A Definition

A stack is a simple computational device with two operations, push and pop, that allows us to pile up data to remember it in LIFO (Last In First Out) manner and help in easy retrieval of the last piled data item, as shown in Picture x86.9.1.

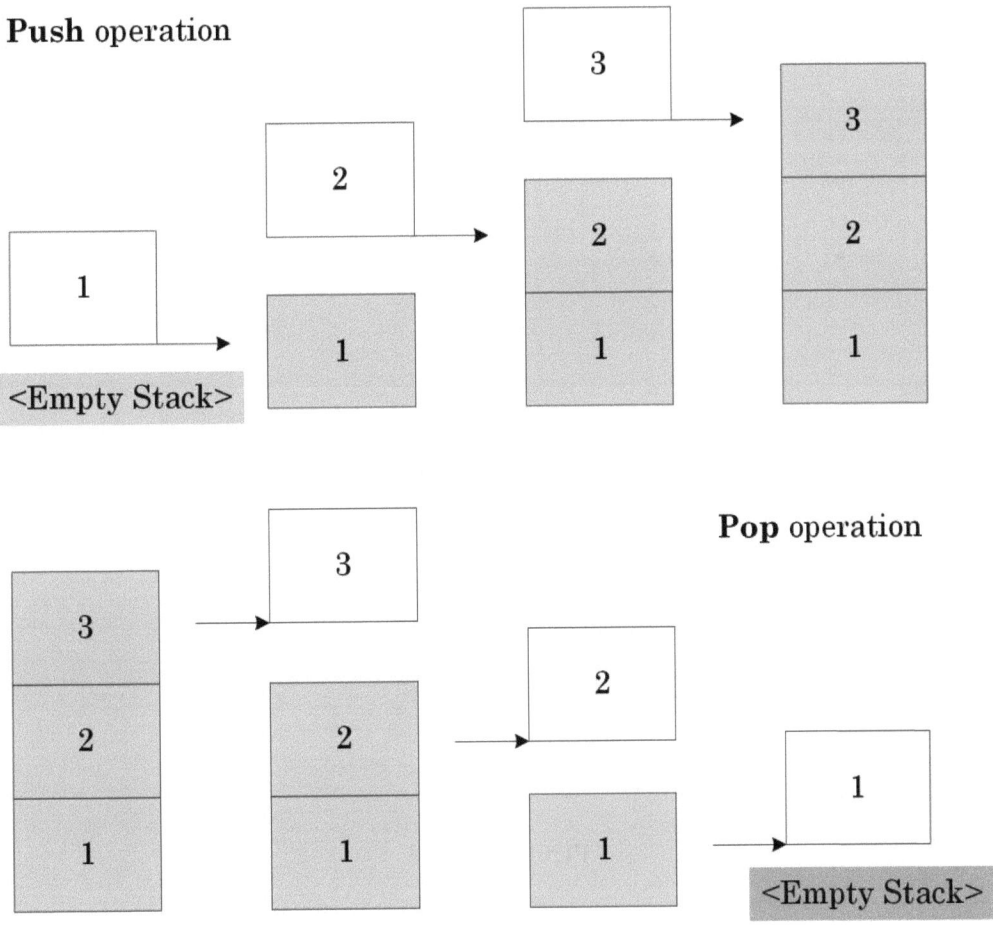

Picture x86.9.1

Stack Implementation in Memory

CPU ESP register (Stack Pointer) points to the top of a stack. As shown in Picture x86.9.2, a stack grows towards lower memory addresses with every push instruction, and this is implemented as the ESP register decrement by 4. We can read the top stack value using the following instruction:

```
mov    eax, [esp]
```

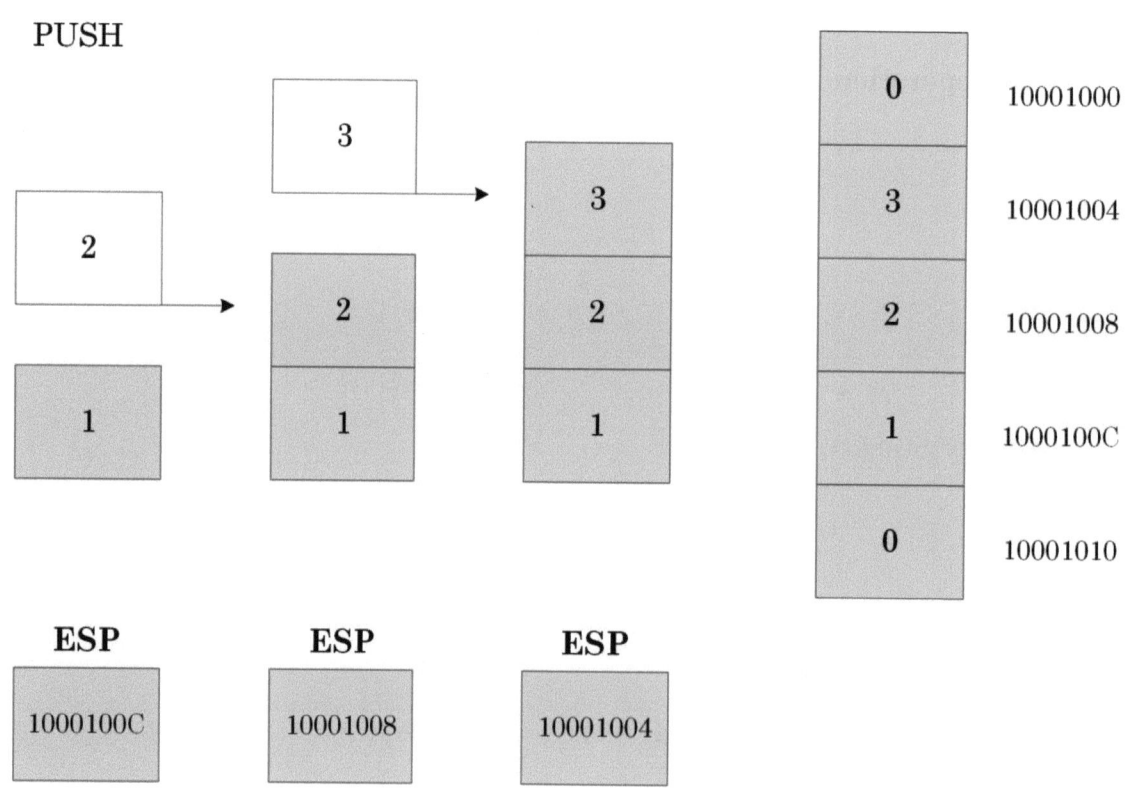

Picture x86.9.2

The opposite POP instruction increments the value of the ESP register, as shown in Picture x86.9.3.

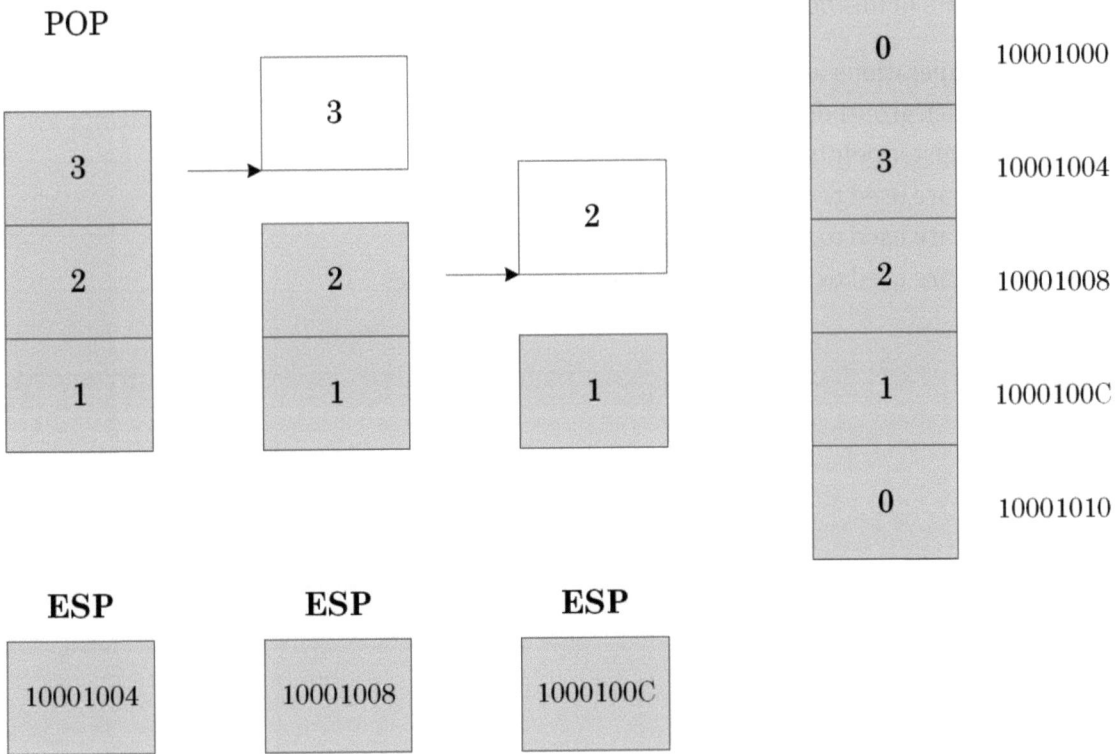

Picture x86.9.3

Things to Remember

Here is the summary of what we have learned about stacks with the last 3 points covered in the subsequent chapters of this book:

- Stack operations are LIFO – Last In First Out
- The stack grows down in memory
- ESP register points to the top of a stack
- Stacks are used to store return addresses for CALL instructions
- Stacks are used to pass parameters to functions
- Stacks are used to store local and temporary variables

PUSH Instruction

We can push a value stored in a register, a value stored at a memory address, or a constant (an immediate operand):

PUSH r/mem/imm

Here is PUSH simplified pseudo-code adopted from Intel manual:

```
IF OperandSize = 32
     THEN
          ESP <- ESP - 4
          [ESP] <- OperandValue   ; double word
     ELSE
          ESP <- ESP - 2
          [ESP] <- OperandValue   ; word
FI
```

Examples:

```
push eax
```

```
push dword ptr [ebx]
```

```
push byte ptr [ecx]
```

```
push 0
```

POP instruction

We can pop a value stored on the top of a stack to a register or a memory address:

POP   r/mem

Here is POP simplified pseudo-code adopted from Intel manual:

```
IF OperandSize = 32
      THEN
              OperandValue <- [ESP] ; double word
              ESP <- ESP + 4
      ELSE
              OperandValue <- [ESP] ; word
              ESP <- ESP + 2
FI
```

Examples:

```
pop   eax

pop   dword ptr [ebx]

pop   byte ptr [ecx]
```

Register Review

So far, we have seen and used general-purpose CPU registers:

- EAX (among its specific uses are to contain function return values and the lower part of a multiplication result)
- EBX
- ECX (among its specific uses is a loop counter)
- EDX (among its specific uses is to contain the higher part of a multiplication result if it exceeds the maximum 32-bit value)

We also have special registers:

- EIP (Instruction Pointer)
- ESP (Stack Pointer)

Application Memory Simplified

When an executable file is loaded into memory, its header and sections are mapped to memory pages. Some data and code are copied unmodified, but some data is initialized and expanded. The first stack is also created at this stage. EIP register is set to point to the first program instruction, and ESP points to the top of the stack. This simplified process is shown in Picture x86.9.4.

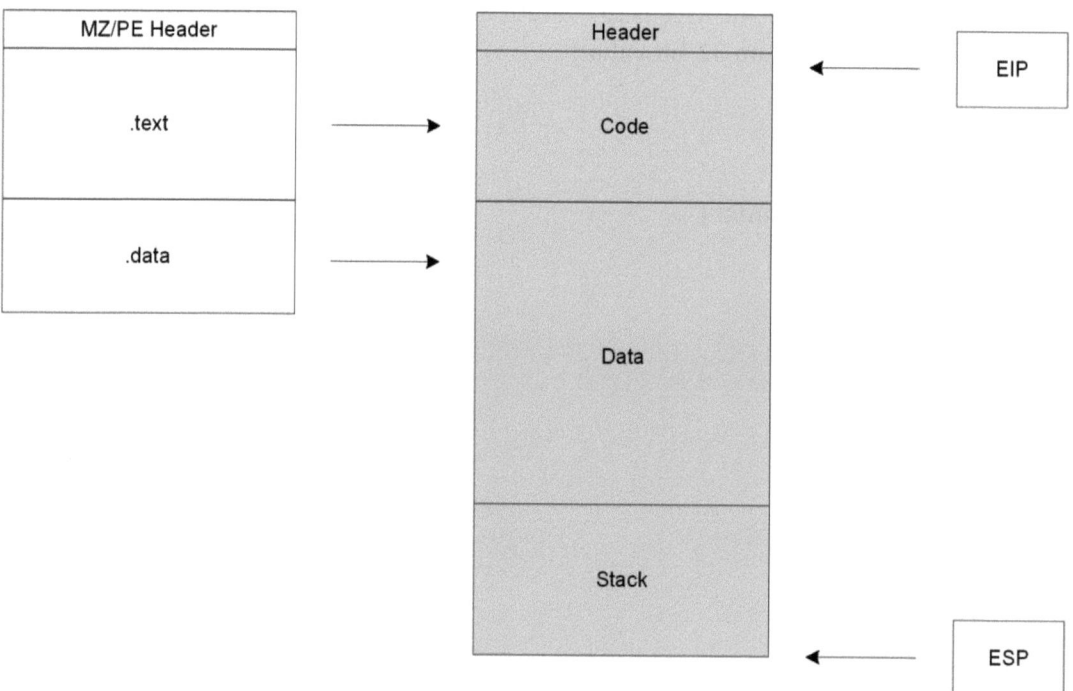

Picture x86.9.4

Stack Overflow

By default, the stack size is 1Mb (compiler dependent). However, this limit can be changed by the linker /STACK option or done via the Visual C++ project Linker\System option, as shown in Picture x86.9.5.

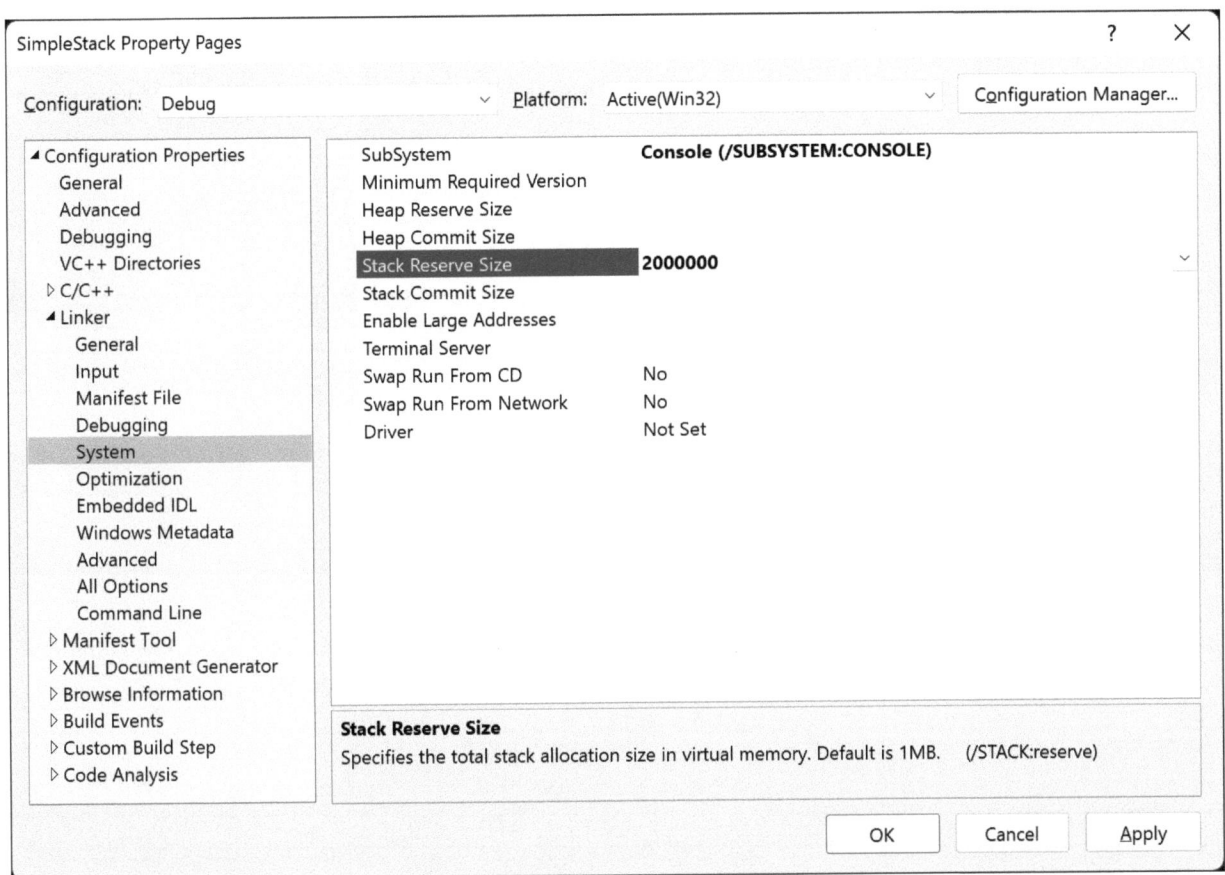

Picture x86.9.5

If a stack grows beyond the reserve limit, then a stack overflow exception occurs (exception code C00000FD). This exception might be caused by an unlimited recursion or very deep recursion:

```
int func()
{
    func();
    return 0;
}
```

Or by very large local variables:

```
int func()
{
      int array[1000000] = { 1 };
      printf("%d", array[1000000-1]);
      // use array to prevent the compiler to optimize it away
}
```

Jumps

Another instruction we need to know and understand before we look deeper into C and C++ functions is called JMP (Jump). Picture x86.9.6 shows instructions in memory and corresponding values of the EIP register.

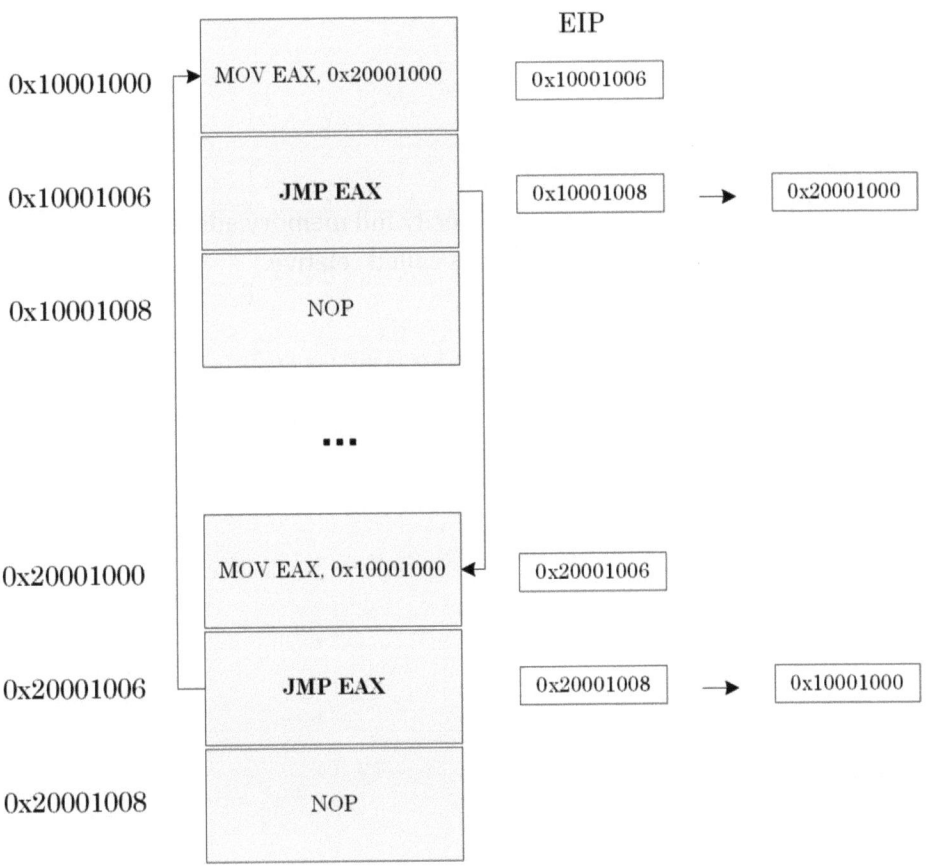

Picture x86.9.6

We see that JMP instruction changes EIP to point to another memory address, and the program execution continues from that location. The code shown in Picture x86.9.6 loops indefinitely: this can be considered a hang and CPU spike.

Here is a pseudo-code for absolute JMP instructions adopted from Intel manuals and some examples:

```
; Format and arguments:

  JMP   r/mem32

; Pseudo-code:

  EIP <- DEST ; new destination address for execution

; Examples:

  JMP   EAX

  JMP   [EAX]
```

The jump is called absolute because we specify full memory addresses and not a relative +/- number to the current EIP value. The latter jump is called relative.

Calls

Now we discuss two very important instructions that make the implementation of C and C++ function calls much easier. They are called CALL and RET. Picture x86.9.7 shows instructions in memory and corresponding values of EIP and ESP registers.

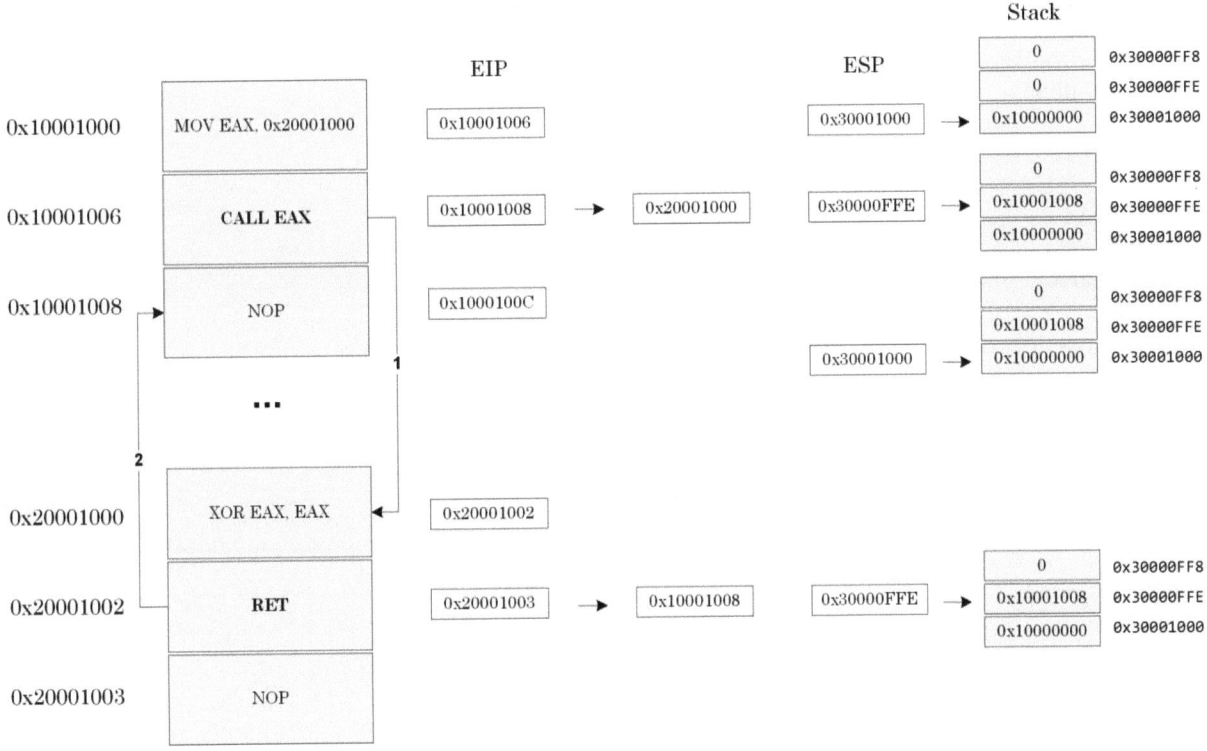

Picture x86.9.7

We see that CALL instruction pushes the current value of EIP to the stack and changes EIP to point to another memory address. Then the program execution continues from the new location. RET instruction pops the saved EIP value from the stack to the EIP register. Then the program execution resumes at the memory location after the CALL instruction.

Here is a pseudo-code for CALL instructions and some examples adopted from Intel manuals:

```
; Format and arguments:
  CALL r/mem32
; Pseudo-code:
  PUSH (EIP)
  EIP <- DEST
; Examples:
  CALL EAX
  CALL [EAX]
```

Here is a pseudo-code for RET instruction adopted from Intel manuals:

```
; Format:
  RET
; Pseudo-code:
  EIP <- POP()
```

Call Stack

If one function (the caller) calls another function (the callee) in C and C++, the resulting code is implemented using CALL instruction, and during its execution, the return address is saved on the stack. If the callee calls another function, the return address is also saved on the stack, and so on. Therefore, we have the so-called call stack of return addresses. Let's see this with a simple but trimmed down example.

Suppose we have 3 functions with their code occupying the following addresses:

```
func   0x10001000 - 0x10001100
func2  0x10001101 - 0x10001200
func3  0x10001201 - 0x10001300
```

We also have the following code where *func* calls *func2*, and *func2* calls *func3*:

```
void func()
{
   func2();
}
void func2()
{
   func3();
}
```

When *func* calls *func2*, the caller return address is pushed to the stack, and ESP points to some value in the 0x10001000 – 0x10001100 range, say 0x10001020. When *func2* calls *func3*, the caller return address is also pushed to the stack, and ESP points to some value in the 0x10001101 – 0x10001200 range, say 0x10001180. If we interrupt *func3* with a debugger and inspect EIP, we would find its value in the 0x10001201 – 0x10001300 range, say 0x10001250. Therefore, we have the following memory and register layout shown in Picture x86.9.8 (the usual function prolog is not shown: we learn about it in the next chapter).

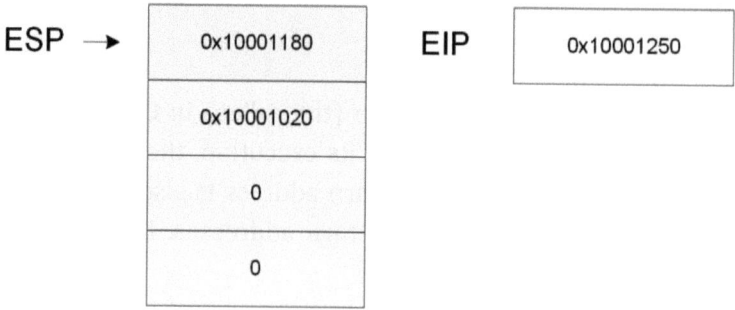

Picture x86.9.8

The debugger examines the value of EIP and the values on top of the stack and reconstructs this call stack:

func3
func2
func

The debugger gets address ranges corresponding to *func*, *func2*, and *func3* functions from the so-called symbol files, which have the *.PDB* file extension. Downloaded projects also contain *.PDB* files corresponding to *.EXE* files to allow WinDbg debugger to understand the memory location of the *main* function, for example.

Exploring Stack in WinDbg

To see call stack in real action we have a project called "SimpleStack", and it can be downloaded from:

https://bitbucket.org/softwarediagnostics/pfwddr2/src/master/x86/Chapter9

The executable is located in *Release* subfolder. We load *SimpleStack.exe* using File\Open Executable... menu option in WinDbg and get the following output (the output, especially addresses, may differ for your Windows version):

```
Microsoft (R) Windows Debugger Version 10.0.22000.194 X86
Copyright (c) Microsoft Corporation. All rights reserved.


CommandLine: C:\PFWDDR2\x86\Chapter9\Release\SimpleStack.exe

************* Path validation summary **************
Response                         Time (ms)     Location
Deferred                                       srv*
Symbol search path is: srv*
Executable search path is:
ModLoad: 00400000 00417000   SimpleStack.exe
ModLoad: 77a80000 77c29000   ntdll.dll
ModLoad: 767b0000 768a0000   C:\WINDOWS\SysWOW64\KERNEL32.DLL
ModLoad: 76b30000 76d82000   C:\WINDOWS\SysWOW64\KERNELBASE.dll
ModLoad: 71080000 71120000   C:\WINDOWS\SysWOW64\apphelp.dll
(92e0.9760): Break instruction exception - code 80000003 (first chance)
eax=00000000 ebx=003aa000 ecx=19950000 edx=00000000 esi=ffffffff edi=004000f8
eip=77b366d1 esp=0019f7e4 ebp=0019f810 iopl=0         nv up ei pl zr na pe nc
cs=0023  ss=002b  ds=002b  es=002b  fs=0053  gs=002b             efl=00000246
ntdll!LdrpDoDebuggerBreak+0x2b:
77b366d1 cc              int     3
```

Then we put a breakpoint to the *main* function and run the program until WinDbg breaks in:

```
0:000> bp SimpleStack!main
*** WARNING: Unable to verify checksum for SimpleStack.exe


0:000> g
Breakpoint 0 hit
eax=00414e20 ebx=003aa000 ecx=00000000 edx=35dd281f esi=00743410 edi=007487a8
eip=00401030 esp=0019ff30 ebp=0019ff74 iopl=0         nv up ei pl nz na po nc
cs=0023  ss=002b  ds=002b  es=002b  fs=0053  gs=002b             efl=00000202
```

Exploring Stack in WinDbg

```
SimpleStack!main:
00401030 55                   push    ebp
```

The function *func3* has a breakpoint instruction inside that allows a debugger to break in and stop the program execution to inspect its state. We resume our program execution from our breakpoint in *main* function to allow *main* function to call *func*, *func* to call *func2*, *func2* to call *func3*, and inside *func3* to execute the explicit breakpoint:

```
0:000> g
(92e0.9760): Break instruction exception - code 80000003 (first chance)
eax=00414e20 ebx=003aa000 ecx=00000000 edx=35dd281f esi=00743410 edi=007487a8
eip=00401023 esp=0019ff14 ebp=0019ff14 iopl=0         nv up ei pl nz na po nc
cs=0023  ss=002b  ds=002b  es=002b  fs=0053  gs=002b              efl=00000202
SimpleStack!func3+0x3:
00401023 cc                   int     3
```

Now we can inspect the top of the stack:

```
0:000> dd esp
0019ff14  0019ff1c 00401018 0019ff24 00401008
0019ff24  0019ff2c 00401038 0019ff74 004011fb
0019ff34  00000001 00743410 007487a8 afd2f3d1
0019ff44  00401283 00401283 003aa000 00000000
0019ff54  00000000 00000000 0019ff40 00000000
0019ff64  0019ffcc 00401bc0 af8a3e6d 00000000
0019ff74  0019ff84 767c6739 003aa000 767c6720
0019ff84  0019ffdc 77ae8e7f 003aa000 2250223a
```

The data is meaningless for us, and we use another command called **dds** to dump memory with corresponding symbols from PDB files (we can also use **dps** command instead):

```
0:000> dds esp
0019ff14  0019ff1c
0019ff18  00401018 SimpleStack!func2+0x8 [C:\NewWork\PFWDDR2\SimpleStack\func2.c @ 6]
0019ff1c  0019ff24
0019ff20  00401008 SimpleStack!func+0x8 [C:\NewWork\PFWDDR2\SimpleStack\func.c @ 6]
0019ff24  0019ff2c
0019ff28  00401038 SimpleStack!main+0x8 [C:\NewWork\PFWDDR2\SimpleStack\SimpleStack.c @ 6]
0019ff2c  0019ff74
0019ff30  004011fb SimpleStack!__scrt_common_main_seh+0xfa [d:\a01\_work\38\s\src\vctools\crt\vcstartup\src\startup\exe_common.inl @ 288]
0019ff34  00000001
```

```
0019ff38  00743410
0019ff3c  007487a8
0019ff40  afd2f3d1
0019ff44  00401283 SimpleStack!mainCRTStartup
[d:\a01\_work\38\s\src\vctools\crt\vcstartup\src\startup\exe_main.cpp @ 15]
0019ff48  00401283 SimpleStack!mainCRTStartup
[d:\a01\_work\38\s\src\vctools\crt\vcstartup\src\startup\exe_main.cpp @ 15]
0019ff4c  003aa000
0019ff50  00000000
0019ff54  00000000
0019ff58  00000000
0019ff5c  0019ff40
0019ff60  00000000
0019ff64  0019ffcc
0019ff68  00401bc0 SimpleStack!_except_handler4
[d:\a01\_work\38\s\src\vctools\crt\vcruntime\src\eh\i386\chandler4.c @ 316]
0019ff6c  af8a3e6d
0019ff70  00000000
0019ff74  0019ff84
0019ff78  767c6739 KERNEL32!BaseThreadInitThunk+0x19
0019ff7c  003aa000
0019ff80  767c6720 KERNEL32!BaseThreadInitThunk
0019ff84  0019ffdc
0019ff88  77ae8e7f ntdll!__RtlUserThreadStart+0x2b
0019ff8c  003aa000
```

The current value of EIP points to *func3* and return addresses on the stack are shown in bold. WinDbg is able to reconstruct the following call stack or stack trace:

```
0:000> k
 # ChildEBP RetAddr
00 0019ff14 00401018     SimpleStack!func3+0x3 [C:\NewWork\PFWDDR2\SimpleStack\func3.c @ 3]
01 0019ff1c 00401008     SimpleStack!func2+0x8 [C:\NewWork\PFWDDR2\SimpleStack\func2.c @ 6]
02 0019ff24 00401038     SimpleStack!func+0x8 [C:\NewWork\PFWDDR2\SimpleStack\func.c @ 6]
03 0019ff2c 004011fb     SimpleStack!main+0x8 [C:\NewWork\PFWDDR2\SimpleStack\SimpleStack.c @ 6]
04 (Inline) --------     SimpleStack!invoke_main+0x1c
[d:\a01\_work\38\s\src\vctools\crt\vcstartup\src\startup\exe_common.inl @ 78]
05 0019ff74 767c6739     SimpleStack!__scrt_common_main_seh+0xfa
[d:\a01\_work\38\s\src\vctools\crt\vcstartup\src\startup\exe_common.inl @ 288]
06 0019ff84 77ae8e7f     KERNEL32!BaseThreadInitThunk+0x19
07 0019ffdc 77ae8e4d     ntdll!__RtlUserThreadStart+0x2b
08 0019ffec 00000000     ntdll!_RtlUserThreadStart+0x1b
```

Chapter x86.10: Frame Pointer and Local Variables

Stack Usage

In addition to storage for return addresses of CALL instructions, the stack is used to pass parameters to functions and store local variables. The stack is also used to save and restore values held in registers when we want to preserve them during some computation or across function calls. For example, suppose we want to do multiplication, but at the same time, we have other valuable data in register EAX and EDX. The multiplication result overwrites EAX and EDX values, and we temporarily put their values on the stack to avoid that:

```
mov     eax, 10
mov     edx, 20
...
...
...                     ; now we want to preserve EAX and EDX
push    eax
push    edx
imul    edx
mov     dword ptr [result], eax
pop     edx             ; pop in reverse order
pop     eax             ; stack is LIFO
```

Register Review

So far, we have encountered these general-purpose registers:

- EAX (among its specific uses are to contain function return values and the lower part of a multiplication result)
- EBX
- ECX (among its specific uses is a loop counter)
- EDX (among its specific uses is to contain the higher part of a multiplication result if it exceeds the maximum 32-bit value)
- EIP (Instruction Pointer, points to the next instruction to be executed)
- ESP (Stack Pointer, points to the top of the stack)

Now we come to the next important register on 32-bit platforms called **Base Pointer** register or sometimes as Stack Frame Pointer register:

EBP

Addressing Array Elements

We can also consider stack memory as an array of memory cells, and often EBP register is used to address stack memory elements in the way shown in Picture x86.10.1, where it slides into the frame of stack memory called a stack frame.

	Address	Address of the element	Value of the element
0	0x10001000	EBP-10	[EBP-10]
0	0x10001004	EBP-C	[EBP-C]
0	0x10001008	EBP-8	[EBP-8]
0	0x1000100C	EBP-4	[EBP-4]
0	0x10001010	EBP	[EBP]
0	0x10001014	EBP+4	[EBP+4]
0	0x10001018	EBP+8	[EBP+8]
0	0x1000101C	EBP+C	[EBP+C]

EBP → points to 0x10001010

Picture x86.10.1

Stack Structure (No Function Parameters)

Suppose the following function is called:

```
void func()
{
    int var1, var2;
    // Body Code
    // ...
}
```

Before the function body code is executed, the following pointers are set up:

- [EBP] contains previous EBP
- [EBP-4] contains local variable var1 (DWORD)
- [EBP-8] contains local variable var2 (DWORD)

This memory layout is illustrated in Picture x86.10.2.

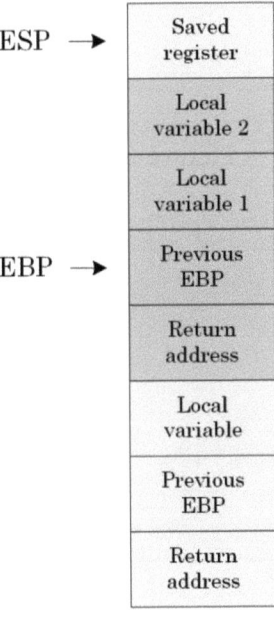

Picture x86.10.2

Function Prolog

The sequence of instructions resulting in the initialization of EBP register and making room for local variables is called function prolog. One example is in Picture x86.10.3, where *func* calls *func2*, which has one local variable *var*. Sometimes saving necessary registers is also considered part of a function prolog.

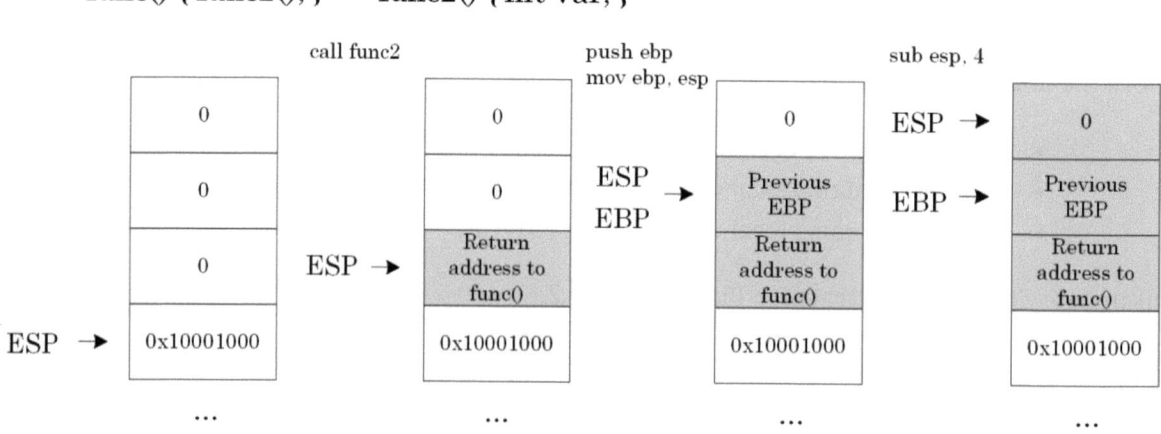

Picture x86.10.3

Raw Stack (No Local Variables and Function Parameters)

Now we can understand additional data (the previous RBP that was equal to the previous RSP before the function call) that appear on the raw stack together with function return addresses that we saw in Chapter x86.9 project "SimpleStack":

```
0:000> r
eax=00414e20 ebx=003aa000 ecx=00000000 edx=35dd281f esi=00743410 edi=007487a8
eip=00401023 esp=0019ff14 ebp=0019ff14 iopl=0         nv up ei pl nz na po nc
cs=0023  ss=002b  ds=002b  es=002b  fs=0053  gs=002b              efl=00000202
SimpleStack!func3+0x3:
00401023 cc              int     3
```

```
0:000> dds esp
0019ff14  0019ff1c
0019ff18  00401018 SimpleStack!func2+0x8 [C:\NewWork\PFWDDR2\SimpleStack\func2.c @ 6]
0019ff1c  0019ff24
0019ff20  00401008 SimpleStack!func+0x8 [C:\NewWork\PFWDDR2\SimpleStack\func.c @ 6]
0019ff24  0019ff2c
0019ff28  00401038 SimpleStack!main+0x8 [C:\NewWork\PFWDDR2\SimpleStack\SimpleStack.c @ 6]
0019ff2c  0019ff74
0019ff30  004011fb SimpleStack!__scrt_common_main_seh+0xfa
[d:\a01\_work\38\s\src\vctools\crt\vcstartup\src\startup\exe_common.inl @ 288]
0019ff34  00000001
0019ff38  00743410
0019ff3c  007487a8
0019ff40  afd2f3d1
0019ff44  00401283 SimpleStack!mainCRTStartup
[d:\a01\_work\38\s\src\vctools\crt\vcstartup\src\startup\exe_main.cpp @ 15]
0019ff48  00401283 SimpleStack!mainCRTStartup
[d:\a01\_work\38\s\src\vctools\crt\vcstartup\src\startup\exe_main.cpp @ 15]
0019ff4c  003aa000
0019ff50  00000000
0019ff54  00000000
0019ff58  00000000
0019ff5c  0019ff40
0019ff60  00000000
0019ff64  0019ffcc
0019ff68  00401bc0 SimpleStack!_except_handler4
[d:\a01\_work\38\s\src\vctools\crt\vcruntime\src\eh\i386\chandler4.c @ 316]
```

Raw Stack (No Local Variables and Function Parameters)

```
0019ff6c  af8a3e6d
0019ff70  00000000
0019ff74  0019ff84
0019ff78  767c6739 KERNEL32!BaseThreadInitThunk+0x19
0019ff7c  003aa000
0019ff80  767c6720 KERNEL32!BaseThreadInitThunk
0019ff84  0019ffdc
0019ff88  77ae8e7f ntdll!__RtlUserThreadStart+0x2b
0019ff8c  003aa000
0019ff90  2250223a
```

We can also use the **dps** command instead since pointers and double words have the same size on the x86 platform.

Function Epilog

Before the function code makes a return to the caller, it must restore the previous value of ESP and EBP registers to allow the caller to resume its execution from the correct address previously saved on the stack and to continue addressing its own stack frame properly. This sequence of instructions is called the function epilog, and it is shown in Picture x86.10.4.

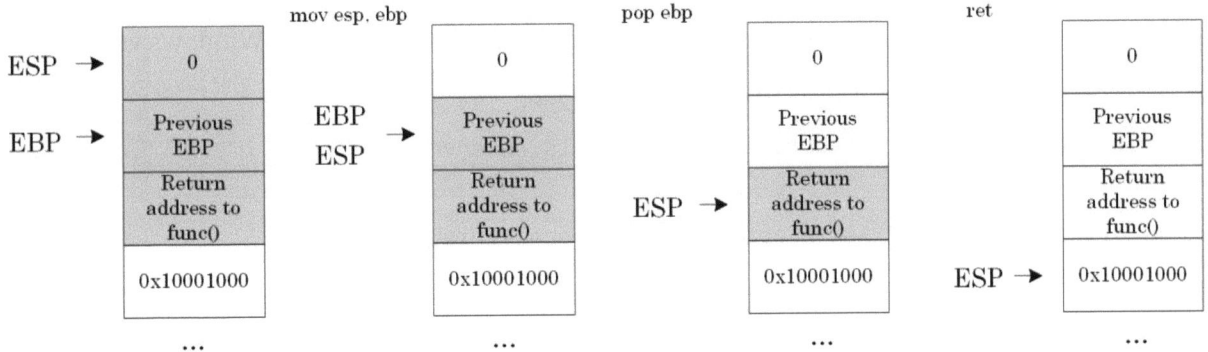

Picture x86.10.4

"Local Variables" Project

The project for this chapter can be downloaded from:

https://bitbucket.org/softwarediagnostics/pfwddr2/src/master/x86/Chapter10

The executable is located in *Debug* subfolder. We load it into WinDbg and disassemble its *main* function.

First, we load *LocalVariables.exe* using File\Open Executable… menu option in WinDbg and get the following output (the output, especially addresses, may differ for your Windows version):

```
Microsoft (R) Windows Debugger Version 10.0.22000.194 X86
Copyright (c) Microsoft Corporation. All rights reserved.


CommandLine: C:\PFWDDR2\x86\Chapter10\Debug\LocalVariables.exe

************* Path validation summary **************
Response                         Time (ms)     Location
Deferred                                       srv*
Symbol search path is: srv*
Executable search path is:
ModLoad: 00400000 004e4000   LocalVariables.exe
ModLoad: 77a80000 77c29000   ntdll.dll
ModLoad: 767b0000 768a0000   C:\WINDOWS\SysWOW64\KERNEL32.DLL
ModLoad: 76b30000 76d82000   C:\WINDOWS\SysWOW64\KERNELBASE.dll
ModLoad: 71080000 71120000   C:\WINDOWS\SysWOW64\apphelp.dll
(3554.89cc): Break instruction exception - code 80000003 (first chance)
eax=00000000 ebx=002ec000 ecx=47000000 edx=00000000 esi=ffffffff edi=004000f8
eip=77b366d1 esp=0019f7e4 ebp=0019f810 iopl=0         nv up ei pl zr na pe nc
cs=0023  ss=002b  ds=002b  es=002b  fs=0053  gs=002b             efl=00000246
ntdll!LdrpDoDebuggerBreak+0x2b:
77b366d1 cc              int     3
```

Then, we put a breakpoint to the *main* function and run the program until WinDbg breaks in:

```
0:000> bp LocalVariables!main
*** WARNING: Unable to verify checksum for LocalVariables.exe
```

```
0:000> g
Breakpoint 0 hit
eax=006d54c0 ebx=002ec000 ecx=00000001 edx=006d88f0 esi=00401136 edi=00401136
eip=00407590 esp=0019feec ebp=0019ff08 iopl=0         nv up ei pl nz na pe nc
cs=0023  ss=002b  ds=002b  es=002b  fs=0053  gs=002b           efl=00000206
LocalVariables!main:
00407590 55              push    ebp
```

Next, we disassemble our *main* function:

```
0:000> .asm no_code_bytes
Assembly options: no_code_bytes
```

```
0:000> uf main
LocalVariables!main [C:\NewWork\PFWDDR2\LocalVariables\LocalVariables.cpp @ 2]:
    2 00407590 push    ebp
    2 00407591 mov     ebp,esp
    2 00407593 sub     esp,8
    5 00407596 mov     dword ptr [ebp-4],1
    6 0040759d mov     dword ptr [ebp-8],1
    8 004075a4 mov     eax,dword ptr [ebp-8]
    8 004075a7 add     eax,dword ptr [ebp-4]
    8 004075aa mov     dword ptr [ebp-8],eax
    9 004075ad mov     ecx,dword ptr [ebp-4]
    9 004075b0 add     ecx,1
    9 004075b3 mov     dword ptr [ebp-4],ecx
   10 004075b6 mov     edx,dword ptr [ebp-4]
   10 004075b9 imul    edx,dword ptr [ebp-8]
   10 004075bd mov     dword ptr [ebp-8],edx
   12 004075c0 xor     eax,eax
   13 004075c2 mov     esp,ebp
   13 004075c4 pop     ebp
   13 004075c5 ret
```

Its source code is the following:

```
int main(int argc, char* argv[])
{
    int a, b;
    a = 1;
    b = 1;
    b = b + a;
    ++a;
    b = a * b;
    return 0;
}
```

Below is the same assembly language code but with comments showing operations in pseudo-code and highlighting function prolog and epilog:

```
LocalVariables!main:
push    ebp                             ; establishing stack frame
mov     ebp,esp                         ;
sub     esp,8                           ; creating stack frame for locals
mov     dword ptr [ebp-4],1             ; [a] = 1      ([ebp-0x4])
mov     dword ptr [ebp-8],1             ; [b] = 1      ([ebp-0x8])
mov     eax,dword ptr [ebp-8]           ; eax <- [b]
add     eax,dword ptr [ebp-4]           ; eax <- eax + [a]
mov     dword ptr [ebp-8],eax           ; [b] <- eax   (b = b + a)
mov     ecx,dword ptr [ebp-4]           ; ecx <- [a]
add     ecx,1                           ; ecx <- ecx + 1
mov     dword ptr [ebp-4],ecx           ; [a] <- ecx   (++a)
mov     edx,dword ptr [ebp-4]           ; edx <- [a]
imul    edx,dword ptr [ebp-8]           ; edx <- edx * [b]
mov     dword ptr [ebp-8],edx           ; [b] <- edx   (b = a * b)
xor     eax,eax                         ; eax <- 0     (return value)
mov     esp,ebp                         ; restoring previous stack pointer
pop     ebp                             ; restoring previous stack frame
ret                                     ; return 0
```

Disassembly of Optimized Executable (Release Configuration)

If we load *LocalVariables.exe* from the *Release* project folder, we would see very simple code that just returns 0:

```
0:000> uf main
LocalVariables!main [C:\NewWork\PFWDDR2\LocalVariables\LocalVariables.cpp @ 2]:
    2 00401000 33c0              xor     eax,eax
   13 00401002 c3                ret
```

Where is all the code we have seen in *Debug* version? It was optimized away by the Visual C++ compiler because the results of our calculation are never used. Variables **a** and **b** are local to the *main* function, and their values are not accessible outside when we return from the function.

Advanced Topic: FPO

FPO stands for Frame Pointer Omission, a kind of 32-bit code optimization where only the ESP register is used to address local variables and parameters, but EBP is used as a general-purpose register like EAX.

Here is the same project assembly language code when compiled with FPO optimization enabled with comments showing operations in pseudo-code:

```
LocalVariables!main:
sub     esp,0x8                 ; allocating stack space for locals
mov     eax,0x1                 ; eax <- 1
mov     [esp],eax               ; [a] <- eax   ([esp])
mov     [esp+0x4],eax           ; [b] <- eax   ([esp+0x4])
mov     eax,[esp+0x4]           ; eax <- [b]
add     eax,[esp]               ; eax <- eax + [a]
mov     [esp+0x4],eax           ; [b] <- eax   (b = b + a)
mov     ecx,[esp]               ; ecx <- [a]
inc     ecx                     ; ecx <- ecx + 1
mov     [esp],ecx               ; [a] <- ecx   (++a)
mov     edx,[esp+0x4]           ; edx <- [b]
mov     eax,[esp]               ; eax <- [a]
imul    edx,eax                 ; edx <- edx * eax
mov     [esp+0x4],edx           ; [b] <- edx   (b = b * a)
xor     eax,eax                 ; eax <- 0
add     esp,0x8                 ; clearing stack space
ret                             ; return 0
```

Chapter x86.11: Function Parameters

"FunctionParameters" Project

In this chapter, we learn how a caller function passes its parameters via stack memory and how a callee (the called function) accesses them. We use the following project that can be downloaded from this link:

https://bitbucket.org/softwarediagnostics/pfwddr2/src/master/x86/Chapter11

Here is the project source code:

```
// FunctionParameters.cpp
int arithmetic (int a, int b);
int main(int argc, char* argv[])
{
      int result = arithmetic (1, 1);
      return 0;
}


// Arithmetic.cpp
int arithmetic (int a, int b)
{
      b = b + a;
      ++a;
      b = a * b;
      return b;
}
```

Stack Structure

Recall from the previous chapter that the EBP register is used to address stack memory locations. This usage was illustrated by Picture x86.10.1. Here we provide an example of the stack memory layout for the following function:

```
void func(int Param1, int Param2)
{
    int var1, var2;
    // stack memory layout at this point
    // ...
    // [EBP-8]   = var2 (DWORD)
    // [EBP-4]   = var1 (DWORD)
    // [EBP]     = previous EBP (DWORD)
    // [EBP+4]   = return address (DWORD)
    // [EBP+8]   = Param1 (DWORD)
    // [EBP+C]   = Param2 (DWORD)
    // ...
}
```

The stack frame memory layout for the function with 2 arguments and 2 local variables is illustrated by Picture x86.11.1.

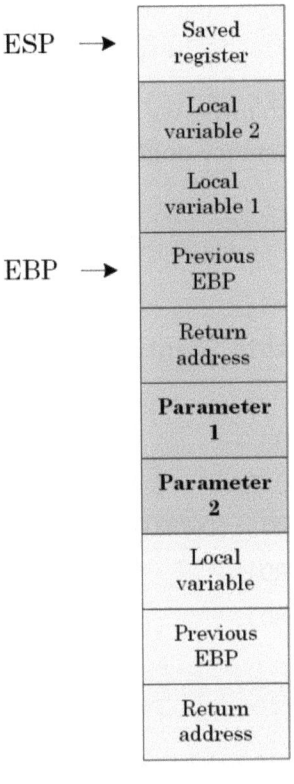

Picture x86.11.1

Stack Structure with FPO

With FPO introduced in the previous chapter, we have the same stack memory layout, but now the ESP register is used to address stack memory double words:

```
void func(int Param1, int Param2)
{
    int var1, var2;
    // stack memory layout at this point
    // ...
    // [ESP]     = var2 (DWORD)
    // [ESP+4]   = var1 (DWORD)
    // [ESP+8]   = return address (DWORD)
    // [ESP+C]   = Param1 (DWORD)
    // [ESP+10]  = Param2 (DWORD)
    // ...
}
```

The stack frame memory layout for the function with 2 arguments and 2 local variables with FPO optimization enabled is illustrated in Picture x86.11.2.

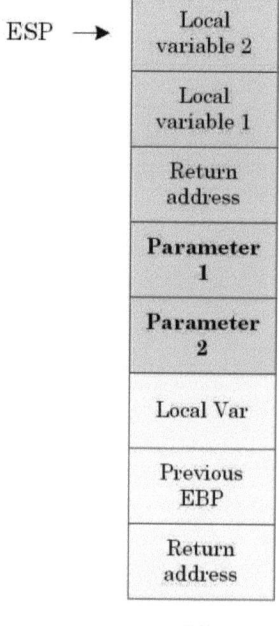

Picture x86.11.2

Function Prolog and Epilog

Now, before we try to make sense of the *FunctionParameters* project disassembly, we look at the very simple case with one function parameter and one local variable to illustrate the standard function prolog and epilog sequence of instructions and corresponding stack memory changes.

Function prolog is illustrated in Picture x86.11.3, and function epilog is illustrated in Picture x86.11.4.

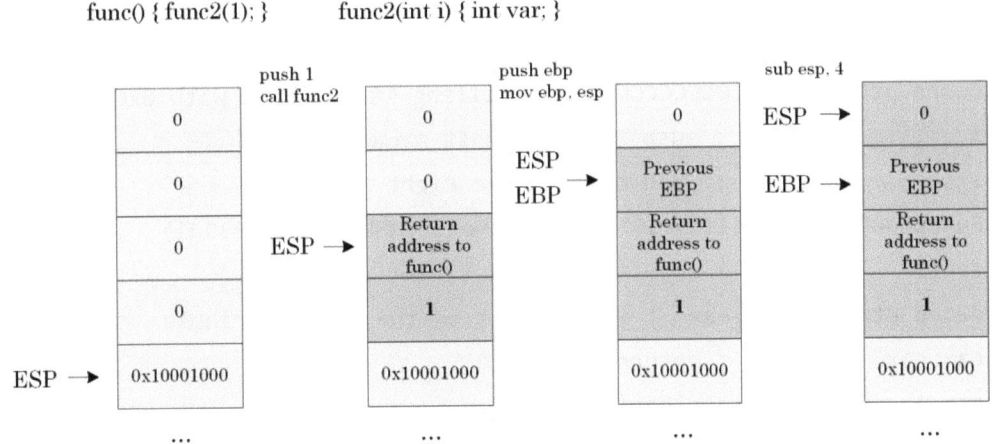

Picture x86.11.3

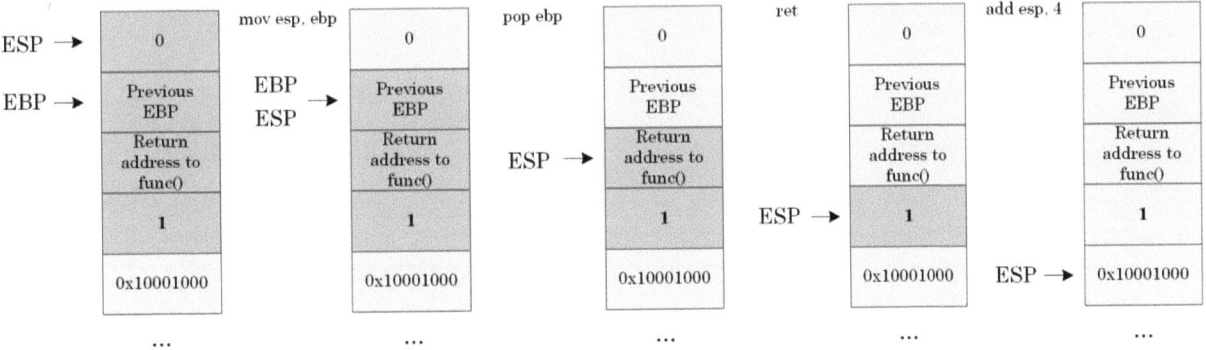

Picture x86.11.4

Project Disassembled Code with Comments

Here is commented code disassembly of *main* and *arithmetic* functions from *Debug* version of *FunctionParameters.exe* done by the **uf** WinDbg command with memory addresses and codes removed for visual clarity.

```
FunctionParameters!main:
push    ebp                             ; establishing stack frame
mov     ebp,esp                         ;
push    ecx                             ; creating stack frame for local variable
                                        ; the same as sub esp, 4
mov     dword ptr [ebp-4],0CCCCCCCCh    ; filling stack frame with 0xCC
push    1                               ; push the rightmost parameter
push    1                               ; push next to the right parameter
call    FunctionParameters!ILT+10700(?arithmeticYAHHHZ) (004039d1)
add     esp,8                           ; adjusting stack (2 int parameters)
mov     dword ptr [ebp-4],eax           ; save result to the local variable
xor     eax,eax                         ; return value (0)
add     esp,4                           ; clearing stack
cmp     ebp,esp                         ; ESP == EBP ?
call    FunctionParameters!ILT+7800(__RTC_CheckEsp) (00402e7d)
mov     esp,ebp                         ; restoring previous stack pointer
pop     ebp                             ; restoring previous stack frame
ret                                     ; return 0
```

```
FunctionParameters!arithmetic:
push    ebp                          ; establishing stack frame
mov     ebp,esp                      ;
mov     eax,dword ptr [ebp+0Ch]      ; eax <- [b]
add     eax,dword ptr [ebp+8]        ; eax <- eax + [a]
mov     dword ptr [ebp+0Ch],eax      ; [b] <- eax (b = b + a)
mov     ecx,dword ptr [ebp+8]        ; ecx <- [a]
add     ecx,1                        ; ecx <- ecx + 1
mov     dword ptr [ebp+8],ecx        ; [a] <- ecx (++a)
mov     edx,dword ptr [ebp+8]        ; edx <- [a]
imul    edx,dword ptr [ebp+0Ch]      ; edx <- edx * [b]
mov     dword ptr [ebp+0Ch],edx      ; [b] <- edx (b = a * b)
mov     eax,dword ptr [ebp+0Ch]      ; eax <- [b] (return value, b)
                                     ; no need to restore previous stack pointer
                                     ;     because there was no space allocated for
                                     ;     local variables in this function
pop     ebp                          ; restoring previous stack frame
ret                                  ; return (return value, b)
```

We can put a breakpoint on the first arithmetic calculations address and examine raw stack data pointed to by the ESP register:

```
0:000> .asm no_code_bytes
Assembly options: no_code_bytes
```

```
0:000> uf FunctionParameters!arithmetic
FunctionParameters!arithmetic [C:\NewWork\PFWDDR2\FunctionParameters\Arithmetic.cpp @ 3]:
    3 004075c0 push      ebp
    3 004075c1 mov       ebp,esp
    4 004075c3 mov       eax,dword ptr [ebp+0Ch]
    4 004075c6 add       eax,dword ptr [ebp+8]
    4 004075c9 mov       dword ptr [ebp+0Ch],eax
    5 004075cc mov       ecx,dword ptr [ebp+8]
    5 004075cf add       ecx,1
    5 004075d2 mov       dword ptr [ebp+8],ecx
    6 004075d5 mov       edx,dword ptr [ebp+8]
    6 004075d8 imul      edx,dword ptr [ebp+0Ch]
    6 004075dc mov       dword ptr [ebp+0Ch],edx
    8 004075df mov       eax,dword ptr [ebp+0Ch]
```

```
         9 004075e2 pop     ebp
         9 004075e3 ret
```

`0:000> bp 004075c3`

`0:000> g`
```
Breakpoint 1 hit
eax=006e5528 ebx=0024e000 ecx=00000001 edx=006e8968 esi=00401136 edi=00401136
eip=004075c3 esp=0019fed4 ebp=0019fed4 iopl=0         nv up ei pl nz na po nc
cs=0023  ss=002b  ds=002b  es=002b  fs=0053  gs=002b              efl=00000202
FunctionParameters!arithmetic+0x3:
004075c3 mov     eax,dword ptr [ebp+0Ch]          ss:002b:0019fee0=00000001
```

`0:000> dds esp L8`
```
0019fed4  0019fee8 ; previous EBP
0019fed8  00407604 FunctionParameters!main+0x14
[C:\NewWork\PFWDDR2\FunctionParameters\FunctionParameters.cpp @ 5] ; return address
0019fedc  00000001 ; parameter 1
0019fee0  00000001 ; parameter 2
0019fee4  cccccccc
0019fee8  0019ff08
0019feec  00407cd3 FunctionParameters!invoke_main+0x33
[d:\a01\_work\38\s\src\vctools\crt\vcstartup\src\startup\exe_common.inl @ 78]
0019fef0  00000001
```

Release Build with FPO Enabled

The *Release* version of *FunctionParameters.exe* was compiled with FPO enabled (Picture x86.11.5), and here is the corresponding code disassembly with comments:

FunctionParameters!main:
```
push    1                               ; parameter 2
push    1                               ; parameter 1
call    FunctionParameters!arithmetic (00401000)
add     esp,8                           ; adjusting stack
xor     eax,eax                         ; return result 0
ret
```

FunctionParameters!arithmetic:
```
mov     ecx,dword ptr [esp+4]           ; ecx <- [a]
mov     eax,dword ptr [esp+8]           ; eax <- [b]
add     eax,ecx                         ; eax <- eax + ecx (b = b + a)
inc     ecx                             ; ecx <- ecx + 1   (++a)
imul    eax,ecx                         ; eax <- eax * ecx (b = b * a)
ret                                     ; return result in eax (b)
```

150 Release Build with FPO Enabled

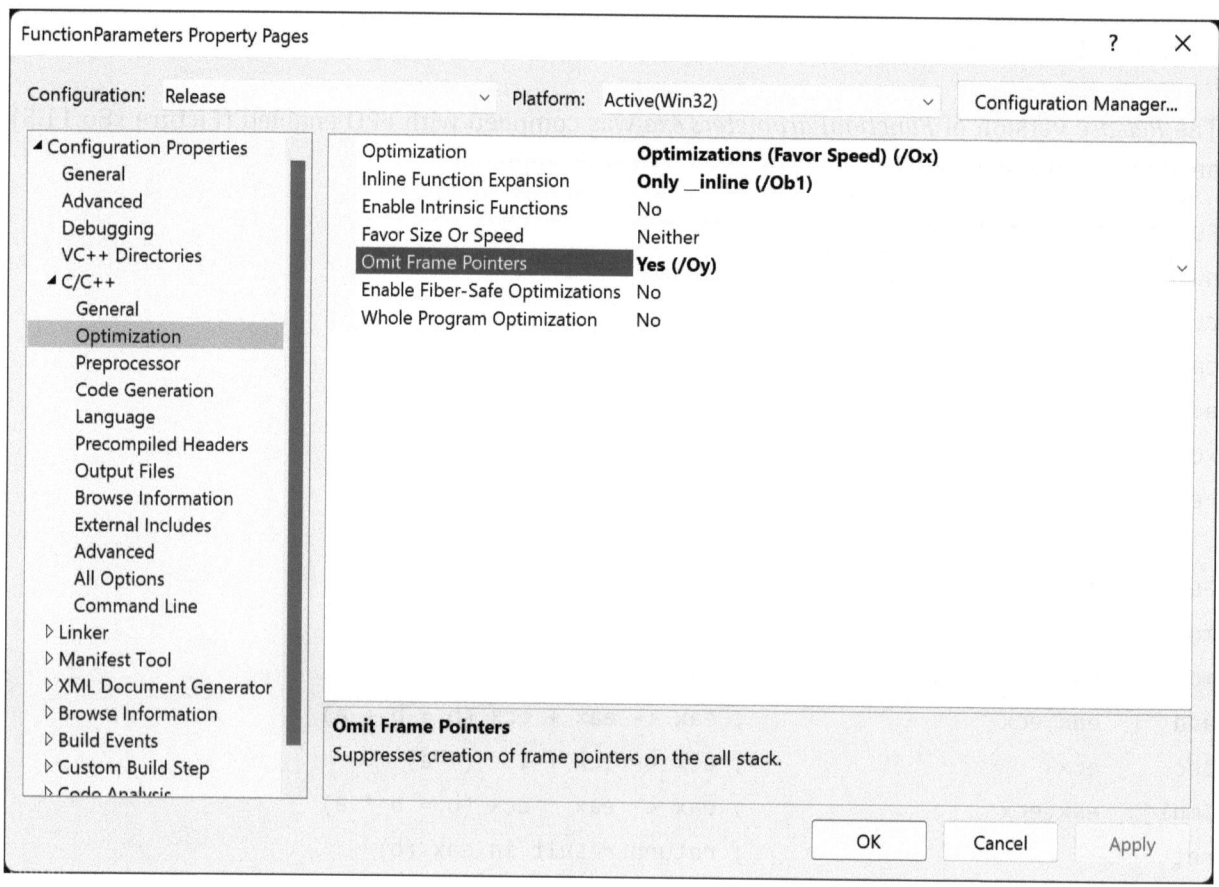

Picture x86.11.5

Cdecl Calling Convention

When looking at pictures and commented assembly language code, we saw that function parameters are passed from right to left, and the caller was responsible for adjusting the stack after calling the callee function. This arrangement is the so-called **cdecl** calling convention in C and C++. It allows calling functions with a variable number of parameters, for example, *printf* and *scanf*:

```
printf("result = %d", nVal);
```

Here is the corresponding stack memory layout:

```
EBP -> Previous EBP
       Return address
       The address of "" string
       The value of nVal variable
```

Another C code example and the following corresponding stack memory layout:

```
printf("left: %d right: %d top: %d bottom: %d", nLeft, nRight, nTop, nBottom);
```

```
EBP -> Previous EBP
       Return address
       The address of "" string
       The value of nLeft variable
       The value of nRight variable
       The value of nTop variable
       The value of nBottom variable
```

Parameter Mismatch Problem

To illustrate the importance of understanding stack memory layout, consider this typical interface mismatch problem. Function *main* calls *func* with two parameters:

```
// main.c
int main ()
{
    int locVar;
    func (1, 2);
    return 0;
}
```

The caller is expected the callee function *func* to see this stack memory layout:

```
EBP -> Previous EBP
       Return address
       1
       2
       locVar
```

However, the callee expects 3 parameters instead of 2:

```
// func.c
int func (int a, int b, int c)
{
    // code to use parameters
    return 0;
}
```

func code sees this stack memory layout:

```
EBP -> Previous EBP
       Return address
       a
       b
       c
```

We see that parameter **c** coincides with *locVar* local *main* function variable, and this is clearly a software defect (bug).

Chapter x86.12: More Instructions

CPU Flags Register

In addition to registers, the CPU also contains a special 32-bit EFLAGS register where certain bits are set or cleared in response to arithmetic and other operations. Separate machine instructions can manipulate some bit values, and their values affect code execution.

For example, the DF bit (Direction Flag) determines the direction of memory copy operations and can be set by STD and cleared by CLD instructions. It has the default value of 0, and its location is shown in Picture x86.12.1.

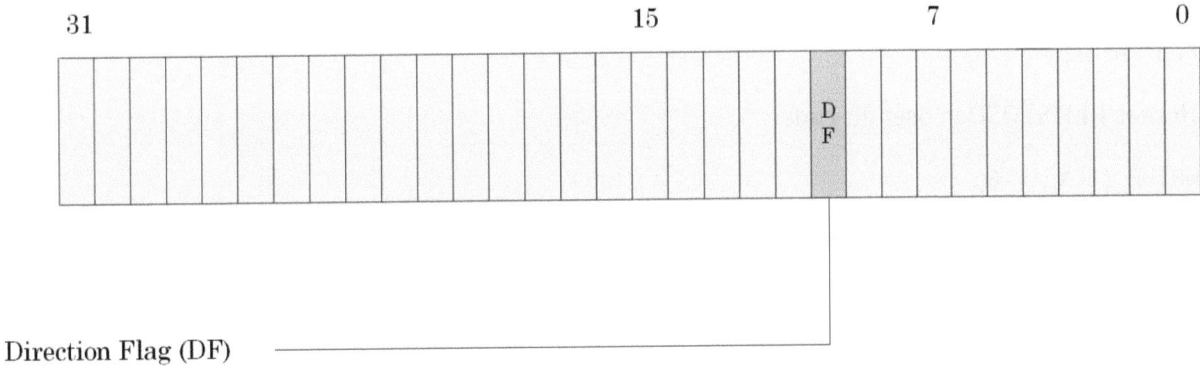

Picture x86.12.1

The Fastest Way to Fill Memory

This way (which may not be fastest on some CPUs) is done by STOSD instruction that stores a dword value from EAX into a memory location whose address is in the EDI register ("D" means destination). After the value from EAX is transferred to memory, the instruction increments EDI by 4, and the EDI register now points to the next DWORD in memory if the DF flag is 0. If the DF flag is 1, then the EDI value is decremented by 4, and EDI now points to the previous DWORD in memory.

If we prefix any instruction with the REP prefix, it causes the instruction to be repeated until the value in the ECX register is decremented to 0. For example, we can write very simple code that should theoretically zero "all memory" (practically, it traps because of access violation):

```
xor     eax, eax            ; fill with 0
mov     edi, 0              ; starting address or xor edi, edi
mov     ecx, 0xffffffff / 4 ; 0x3fffffff dwords
rep     stosd
```

Here is REP STOSD in pseudo-code:

```
WHILE (ECX != 0)
{
        [EDI] <- EAX

        IF DF = 0 THEN
                EDI <- EDI + 4
        ELSE
                EDI <- EDI - 4

        ECX <- ECX - 1
}
```

A simple example of erasing 16 bytes (4x4) is shown in Picture x86.12.2.

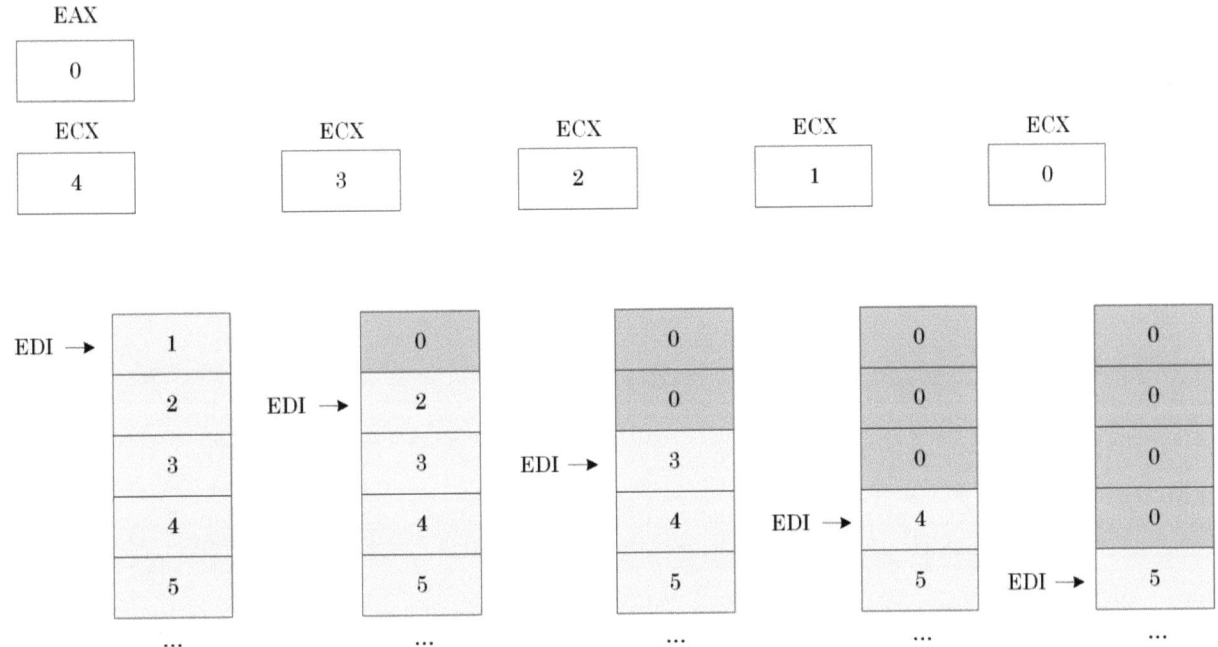

Picture x86.12.2

Testing for 0

ZF bit in EFLAGS register is set to 1 if the instruction result is 0 and cleared otherwise. This bit is affected by:

- Arithmetic instructions (for example, ADD, SUB, MUL)
- Logical compare instruction (TEST)
- "Arithmetical" compare instruction (CMP)

The location of the ZF bit is shown in Picture x86.12.3.

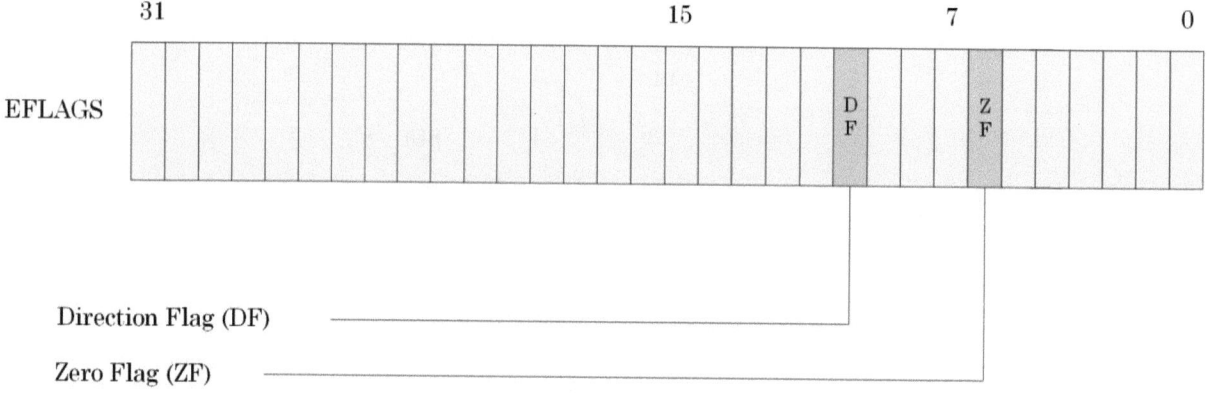

Picture x86.12.3

TEST - Logical Compare

This instruction computes bit-wise logical AND between both operands and sets flags (including ZF) according to the computed result (which is discarded):

```
TEST reg/mem, reg/imm
```

Examples:

```
TEST EDX, EDX
```

Suppose EDX register contains 4 (100_{bin})

```
100bin AND 100bin = 100bin    != 0 (ZF is cleared)

TEST EDX, 1
```

Suppose EDX contains 0 (0_{bin})

```
0bin AND 1bin = 0bin                == 0 (ZF is set)
```

Here is TEST instruction in pseudo-code (details not relevant to ZF bit are omitted):

```
TEMP <- OPERAND1 AND OPERAND2
IF TEMP = 0 THEN
      ZF <- 1
ELSE
      ZF <- 0
```

CMP – Compare Two Operands

This instruction compares the first operand with the second and sets flags (including ZF) according to the computed result (which is discarded). The comparison is performed by subtracting the second operand from the first (like SUB instruction: SUB EAX, 4).

```
CMP   reg/mem, reg/imm

CMP   reg, reg/mem/imm
```

Examples:

```
CMP   EDI, 0
```

Suppose EDI contains 0

```
0 - 0   == 0 (ZF is set)

CMP   EAX, 16
```

Suppose EAX contains 4_{hex}

4_{hex} - 16_{hex} = $FFFFFFEE_{hex}$!= 0 (ZF is cleared)

4_{dec} - 22_{dec} = -18_{dec}

Here is CMP instruction in pseudo-code (details not relevant to ZF bit are omitted):

```
TEMP <- OPERAND1 - OPERAND2
IF TEMP = 0 THEN
      ZF <- 1
ELSE
      ZF <- 0
```

CMP instruction is equivalent to this pseudo-code sequence:

```
TEMP <- OPERAND1
SUB   TEMP, OPERAND2
```

TEST or CMP?

These instructions are equivalent if we want to test for zero, but CMP instruction affects more flags:

```
TEST EAX, EAX
CMP  EAX, 0
```

CMP instruction is used to compare for inequality (TEST instruction cannot be used here):

```
CMP  EAX, 0  ; > 0 or < 0 ?
```

TEST instruction is used to see if individual bit is set:

```
TEST EAX, 2  ; 2 == 0010bin or in C language: if (var & 0x2)
```

Examples where EAX has the value of 2:

```
TEST EAX, 4  ; 0010bin AND 0100bin = 0000bin (ZF is set)
TEST EAX, 6  ; 0010bin AND 0110bin = 0010bin (ZF is cleared)
```

Conditional Jumps

Consider these two C or C++ code fragments:

```
if (a == 0)                     if (a != 0)
{                               {
   ++a;                            ++a;
}                               }
else                            else
{                               {
   --a;                            --a;
}                               }
```

CPU fetches instructions sequentially, so we must tell the CPU that we want to skip some instructions if some condition is (not) met, for example, if a != 0.

JNZ (jump if not zero) and JZ (jump if zero) test ZF flag and change EIP if ZF bit is cleared for JZN or set for JZ. The following assembly language code is equivalent to C/C++ code above:

```
        CMP     [A], 0                  MOV     EAX, [A]
        JNZ     label1                  TEST    EAX, EAX
        INC     [A]                     JZ      label1
        JMP     label2                  INC     EAX
label1: DEC     [A]                     JMP     label2
label2:                         label1: DEC     EAX
                                label2:
```

The Structure of Registers

32-bit registers have a 16-bit legacy structure that allows us to address their lower 16-bit and two 8-bit parts, as shown in Picture x86.12.4.

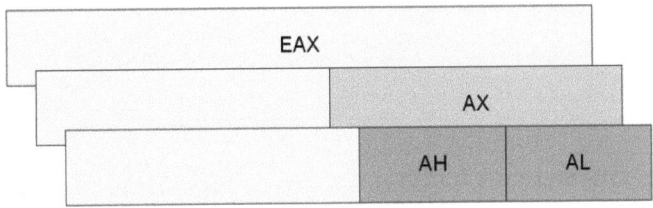

Picture x86.12.4

Function Return Value

Many functions return values via AL or EAX register. For example:

`int func();`

Return value is in EAX.

`bool func();`

Return value is in AL.

Note: bool values occupy one byte in memory.

Using Byte Registers

Suppose we have a byte value in the AL register, and we want to add this value to the ECX register. However, we don't know what values other parts of the full EAX register contain. We cannot use this instruction:

```
MOV    EBX, AL    ; operand size conflict
```

The proposed solution in pseudo-code:

```
EBX <- AL              or      EAX <- AL

ECX <- ECX + EBX               ECX <- ECX + EAX
```

We can only use MOV instructions that have the same operand size for both source and destination, for example:

```
MOV    BL, AL
MOV    byte ptr [b], AL    ; in C: static bool b = func()
```

For this task, there is a special MOVZX (Move with Zero eXtend) instruction that replaces the contents of the first operand with the contents of the second operand while filling the rest of the bits with zeros:

```
MOVZX reg, reg/mem
```

Therefore our solution for the task becomes very simple:

```
MOVZX EBX, AL
ADD    ECX, EBX
```

We can also reuse the EAX register:

```
MOVZX EAX, AL
ADD    ECX, EAX
```

Chapter x86.13: Function Pointer Parameters

"FunctionPointerParameters" Project

This project is our final project, and it can be downloaded from:

https://bitbucket.org/softwarediagnostics/pfwddr2/src/master/x86/Chapter13

The summary of the project source code:

```cpp
// FunctionPointerParameters.cpp
int main(int argc, char* argv[])
{
    int a, b;

    printf("Enter a and b: ");
    scanf("%d %d", &a, &b);

    if (arithmetic (a, &b))
    {
        printf("Result = %d", b);
    }

    return 0;
}

// Arithmetic.cpp
bool arithmetic (int a, int *b)
{
    if (!b)
    {
        return false;
    }

    *b = *b + a;
    ++a;
    *b = a * *b;

    return true;
}
```

Commented Disassembly

Here is the commented disassembly from *Debug* executable. FPO optimization was disabled.

```
FunctionPointerParameters!main:
push    ebp                              ; establishing stack frame
mov     ebp,esp                          ;
sub     esp,18h                          ; creating stack frame for locals
mov     eax,0CCCCCCCCh                   ; filling stack frame with 0xCC
mov     dword ptr [ebp-18h],eax          ;
mov     dword ptr [ebp-14h],eax          ;
mov     dword ptr [ebp-10h],eax          ;
mov     dword ptr [ebp-0Ch],eax          ;
mov     dword ptr [ebp-8],eax            ;
mov     dword ptr [ebp-4],eax            ;
push    offset FunctionPointerParameters!__xt_z+0x104 (004d1e50)
                                         ; address of "Enter a and b: " string
call    FunctionPointerParameters!ILT+3060(_printf) (00401bf9)
add     esp,4                            ; adjust stack pointer (1 parameter)
lea     eax,[ebp-14h]                    ; address of b
push    eax                              ;
lea     ecx,[ebp-8]                      ; address of a
push    ecx                              ;
push    offset FunctionPointerParameters!__xt_z+0x114 (004d1e60)
                                         ; address of "%d %d" string
call    FunctionPointerParameters!ILT+455(_scanf) (004011cc)
add     esp,0Ch                          ; adjust stack pointer (3 parameters,
                                         ;     3*4 = 12 bytes, 0xC in hexadecimal)
lea     edx,[ebp-14h]                    ; address of b
push    edx                              ;
mov     eax,dword ptr [ebp-8]            ; value of a
push    eax                              ;
call    FunctionPointerParameters!ILT+6155(?arithmeticYA_NHPAHZ) (00402810)
add     esp,8                            ; adjust stack pointer (2 parameters)
movzx   ecx,al                           ; bool result from arithmetic
test    ecx,ecx                          ; testing for zero
je      FunctionPointerParameters!main+0x67 (004087f7)
mov     edx,dword ptr [ebp-14h]          ; value of b
push    edx                              ;
```

```
push     offset FunctionPointerParameters!__xt_z+0x11c (004d1e68)
                                    ; address of "Result = %d" string
call     FunctionPointerParameters!ILT+3060(_printf) (00401bf9)
add      esp,8                      ; adjust stack pointer (2 variables)
004087f7:
xor      eax,eax                    ; return result 0
push     edx                        ; saving register ?
mov      ecx,ebp                    ; passing parameter via ecx
push     eax                        ; saving register ?
lea      edx,[FunctionPointerParameters!main+0x88 (00408818)]
                                    ; probably address of information
                                    ;    about stack frame
call     FunctionPointerParameters!ILT+7650(_RTC_CheckStackVars (00402de7)
pop      eax                        ; restoring registers
pop      edx
add      esp,18h                    ; adjusting stack pointer
cmp      ebp,esp                    ; ESP == EBP ?
call     FunctionPointerParameters!ILT+9020(__RTC_CheckEsp) (00403341)
mov      esp,ebp                    ; restoring previous stack pointer
pop      ebp                        ; restoring previous stack frame
ret                                 ; return
```

```
FunctionPointerParameters!arithmetic:
push    ebp
mov     ebp,esp
cmp     dword ptr [ebp+0Ch],0    ; &b == 0 ?
jne     FunctionPointerParameters!arithmetic+0xd (0040874d)
xor     al,al                    ; return bool value false (0)
jmp     FunctionPointerParameters!arithmetic+0x33 (00408773)
0040874d:
mov     eax,dword ptr [ebp+0Ch]  ; eax <- address of b
mov     ecx,dword ptr [eax]      ; ecx <- *b
add     ecx,dword ptr [ebp+8]    ; ecx <- ecx + [a]  (in C: t = t + a)
mov     edx,dword ptr [ebp+0Ch]  ; edx <- address of b
mov     dword ptr [edx],ecx      ; (in C: *b = t)
mov     eax,dword ptr [ebp+8]    ; eax <- [a]
add     eax,1                    ; (in C: ++a)
mov     dword ptr [ebp+8],eax    ; [a] <- eax
mov     ecx,dword ptr [ebp+0Ch]  ; ecx <- address of b
mov     edx,dword ptr [ebp+8]    ; edx <- [a]
imul    edx,dword ptr [ecx]      ; edx <- edx * [b]  (in C: t = a * *b)
mov     eax,dword ptr [ebp+0Ch]  ; eax <- address of b
mov     dword ptr [eax],edx      ; (in C: *b = t)
mov     al,1                     ; return bool value true (0)
00408773:
pop     ebp
ret
```

Dynamic Addressing of Local Variables

Here is the commented disassembly from *Release* executable. FPO optimization was enabled, and this provides an excellent example of dynamic variable addressing via the ESP register.

```
FunctionPointerParameters!main:
sub     esp,8               ; allocating room for local variables
push    offset FunctionPointerParameters!__xt_z+0xc (00419170)
                            ; address of "Enter a and b: "
call    FunctionPointerParameters!printf (00401090)
lea     eax,[esp+4]         ; address of b    ([ESP + 0 + 4])
push    eax                 ;
lea     eax,[esp+0Ch]       ; address of a    ([ESP + 4 + 8])
push    eax                 ;
push    offset FunctionPointerParameters!__xt_z+0x1c (00419180)
                            ; address of "%d %d"
call    FunctionPointerParameters!scanf (004010c0)
lea     eax,[esp+10h]       ; address of b    ([ESP + 0 + 0x10])
push    eax
push    dword ptr [esp+18h] ; value of a      ([ESP + 4 + 0x14])
call    FunctionPointerParameters!arithmetic (00401000)
add     esp,18h             ; adjusting stack after all pushes
test    al,al               ; al == 0 ?
je      FunctionPointerParameters!main+0x46 (00401066)
push    dword ptr [esp]     ; address of b    ([ESP + 0])
push    offset FunctionPointerParameters!__xt_z+0x24 (00419188)
                            ; address of "Result = %d"
call    FunctionPointerParameters!printf (00401090)
add     esp,8               ; adjust stack pointer (2 parameters)
00401066:
xor     eax,eax             ; return value 0
add     esp,8               ; adjust stack pointer (local variables)
ret
```

```
FunctionPointerParameters!arithmetic:
mov     edx,dword ptr [esp+8]     ; address of b
test    edx,edx                    ; &b == 0 ?
jne     FunctionPointerParameters!arithmetic+0xb (0040100b)
xor     al,al                      ; return value false (0)
ret
0040100b:
mov     ecx,dword ptr [edx]        ; ecx <- [b]  (in C: t = *b)
mov     eax,dword ptr [esp+4]      ; eax <- [a]
add     ecx,eax                    ; ecx <- ecx + [a] (in C: t = t + a)
inc     eax                        ; (in C: ++a)
imul    ecx,eax                    ; ecx <- ecx * [a] (in C: t = t * a)
mov     al,1                       ; return value true (1)
mov     dword ptr [edx],ecx        ; [b] <- ecx (in C: *b = t)
ret
```

Chapter x86.14: Summary of Code Disassembly Patterns

This final chapter summarizes various patterns we have encountered during the reading of this book.

Function Prolog/Epilog

Function prolog

```
push  ebp
mov   ebp,esp
```

Function epilog

```
mov   esp,ebp
pop   ebp
ret   [number]
```

In some old legacy code, this is equivalent to:

```
leave
ret   [number]
```

Knowing prolog can help identify situations when symbol files or function start addresses are not correct. For example, suppose you have the following stack trace:

```
func3+0x5F
func2+0x8F
func+0x20
```

If we disassemble *func2* function and see that it does not start with prolog we may assume that stack trace needs more attention:

```
0:000> u func2 func2+0x8F
add   ecx, 10
mov   eax, [ebx+10]
push  ebp
mov   ebp, esp
...
```

Passing Parameters

Local variable address

`[ebp - XXX]`

Function parameter address

`[ebp + XXX]`

Useful mnemonic: first push parameters (+, up) then use local variables (-, down).

Static/global variable address (or string constant)

`push 0x427034`

Local variable vs. local variable address

```
mov   reg,[ebp-XXX]
push  reg                  ; local variable
...
call  func


lea   reg,[ebp-XXX]
push  reg                  ; local variable address
...
call  func
```

LEA (Load Effective Address)

The following instruction

```
lea    eax,[ebp-0x8]
```

is equivalent to the following arithmetic sequence:

```
mov    eax,ebp
sub    eax,0x8
```

Accessing Parameters and Local Variables

Accessing DWORD parameter

```
mov    eax,[ebp+0x8]
add    eax,0x1
```

Accessing a pointer to a DWORD value

```
lea    eax,[ebp+0x8]
mov    eax,[eax]
add    eax,0x1
```

Accessing a local DWORD value

```
mov    eax,[ebp-0x8]
add    eax,0x1
```

Accessing a pointer to a DWORD local variable

```
lea    eax,[ebp-0x8]
mov    eax,[eax]
add    eax,0x1
```

Appendix x86: Using Docker Environment

With this edition, it is possible to use a Docker container image containing preinstalled WinDbg x86 with required chapter materials. However, the output may differ due to the absence of OS symbols.

```
D:\WinDbg.Docker.PFWDDR2>docker pull patterndiagnostics/windbg:10.0.22000.194-pfwddr2

D:\WinDbg.Docker.PFWDDR2>docker run -it patterndiagnostics/windbg:10.0.22000.194-pfwddr2

Microsoft Windows [Version 10.0.20348.587]
(c) Microsoft Corporation. All rights reserved.

C:\WinDbg> windbg32 x86\Chapter2\Debug\ArithmeticProjectC.exe

Microsoft (R) Windows Debugger Version 10.0.22000.194 X86
Copyright (c) Microsoft Corporation. All rights reserved.

CommandLine: x86\Chapter2\Debug\ArithmeticProjectC.exe

************* Path validation summary **************
Response                         Time (ms)     Location
OK                                             C:\WinDbg\mss
Symbol search path is: C:\WinDbg\mss
Executable search path is:
ModLoad: 00010000 000fa000   ArithmeticProjectC.exe
ModLoad: 77880000 77a28000   ntdll.dll
ModLoad: 77270000 77360000   C:\Windows\SysWOW64\KERNEL32.DLL
ModLoad: 75630000 75873000   C:\Windows\SysWOW64\KERNELBASE.dll
(5ec.5b8): Break instruction exception - code 80000003 (first chance)
eax=00000000 ebx=00d22000 ecx=b3230000 edx=00000000 esi=ffffffff edi=000100f8
eip=77935b11 esp=00baf64c ebp=00baf678 iopl=0         nv up ei pl zr na pe nc
cs=0023  ss=002b  ds=002b  es=002b  fs=0053  gs=002b             efl=00000246
ntdll!LdrInitShimEngineDynamic+0x6b1:
77935b11 cc              int     3

0:000> .sympath+ x86\Chapter2\Debug\
Symbol search path is: srv*;x86\Chapter2\Debug\
Expanded Symbol search path is:
cache*;SRV*https://msdl.microsoft.com/download/symbols;x86\chapter2\debug\

************* Path validation summary **************
Response                         Time (ms)     Location
Deferred                                       srv*
OK                                             x86\Chapter2\Debug\

0:000> bp ArithmeticProjectC!main
*** WARNING: Unable to verify checksum for ArithmeticProjectC.exe
```

```
0:000> g
Breakpoint 0 hit
eax=012559c8 ebx=00b5d000 ecx=00000001 edx=01256c30 esi=00fd1136 edi=00fd1136
eip=00fd7590 esp=00cffe98 ebp=00cffeb4 iopl=0         nv up ei pl nz na pe nc
cs=0023  ss=002b  ds=002b  es=002b  fs=0053  gs=002b              efl=00000206
ArithmeticProjectC!main:
00fd7590 55              push    ebp

0:000> uf main
ArithmeticProjectC!main:
00fd7590 55                      push    ebp
00fd7591 8bec                    mov     ebp,esp
00fd7593 c70548ef0a0101000000    mov     dword ptr [ArithmeticProjectC!a (010aef48)],1
00fd759d c7054cef0a0101000000    mov     dword ptr [ArithmeticProjectC!b (010aef4c)],1
00fd75a7 a14cef0a01              mov     eax,dword ptr [ArithmeticProjectC!b (010aef4c)]
00fd75ac 030548ef0a01            add     eax,dword ptr [ArithmeticProjectC!a (010aef48)]
00fd75b2 a34cef0a01              mov     dword ptr [ArithmeticProjectC!b (010aef4c)],eax
00fd75b7 8b0d48ef0a01            mov     ecx,dword ptr [ArithmeticProjectC!a (010aef48)]
00fd75bd 83c101                  add     ecx,1
00fd75c0 890d48ef0a01            mov     dword ptr [ArithmeticProjectC!a (010aef48)],ecx
00fd75c6 8b154cef0a01            mov     edx,dword ptr [ArithmeticProjectC!b (010aef4c)]
00fd75cc 0faf1548ef0a01          imul    edx,dword ptr [ArithmeticProjectC!a (010aef48)]
00fd75d3 89154cef0a01            mov     dword ptr [ArithmeticProjectC!b (010aef4c)],edx
00fd75d9 33c0                    xor     eax,eax
00fd75db 5d                      pop     ebp
00fd75dc c3                      ret

0:000> q
quit:
NatVis script unloaded from 'C:\Program Files (x86)\Windows
Kits\10\Debuggers\x86\Visualizers\atlmfc.natvis'
NatVis script unloaded from 'C:\Program Files (x86)\Windows
Kits\10\Debuggers\x86\Visualizers\ObjectiveC.natvis'
NatVis script unloaded from 'C:\Program Files (x86)\Windows
Kits\10\Debuggers\x86\Visualizers\concurrency.natvis'
NatVis script unloaded from 'C:\Program Files (x86)\Windows
Kits\10\Debuggers\x86\Visualizers\cpp_rest.natvis'
NatVis script unloaded from 'C:\Program Files (x86)\Windows
Kits\10\Debuggers\x86\Visualizers\stl.natvis'
NatVis script unloaded from 'C:\Program Files (x86)\Windows
Kits\10\Debuggers\x86\Visualizers\Windows.Data.Json.natvis'
NatVis script unloaded from 'C:\Program Files (x86)\Windows
Kits\10\Debuggers\x86\Visualizers\Windows.Devices.Geolocation.natvis'
NatVis script unloaded from 'C:\Program Files (x86)\Windows
Kits\10\Debuggers\x86\Visualizers\Windows.Devices.Sensors.natvis'
NatVis script unloaded from 'C:\Program Files (x86)\Windows
Kits\10\Debuggers\x86\Visualizers\Windows.Media.natvis'
NatVis script unloaded from 'C:\Program Files (x86)\Windows
Kits\10\Debuggers\x86\Visualizers\windows.natvis'
NatVis script unloaded from 'C:\Program Files (x86)\Windows
Kits\10\Debuggers\x86\Visualizers\winrt.natvis'

C:\WinDbg>exit

D:\WinDbg.Docker.PFWDDR2>
```

Chapter x64.1: Memory, Registers, and Simple Arithmetic

Memory and Registers inside an Idealized Computer

Computer memory consists of a sequence of memory cells, and each cell has a unique address (location). Every cell contains a "number". We refer to these "numbers" as contents at addresses (locations). Memory access is slower than arithmetic instructions, and there are so-called registers to speed up complex operations that require memory to store temporary results. We can also think about them as standalone memory cells. The name of a register is its address.

Address	Content		Register
Address (Location): 100	0		Register 1: 0
Address (Location): 101	0		Register 2: 10
Address (Location): 102	1		
Address (Location): 104	1		
Address (Location): 105	2		
Address (Location): 106	0		

Picture x64.1.1

Memory and Registers inside Intel 64-bit PC

Here addresses for memory locations containing integer values usually differ by 4 or 8, and we also show 2 registers called RAX and RCX. The first halves of them are called EAX and ECX.

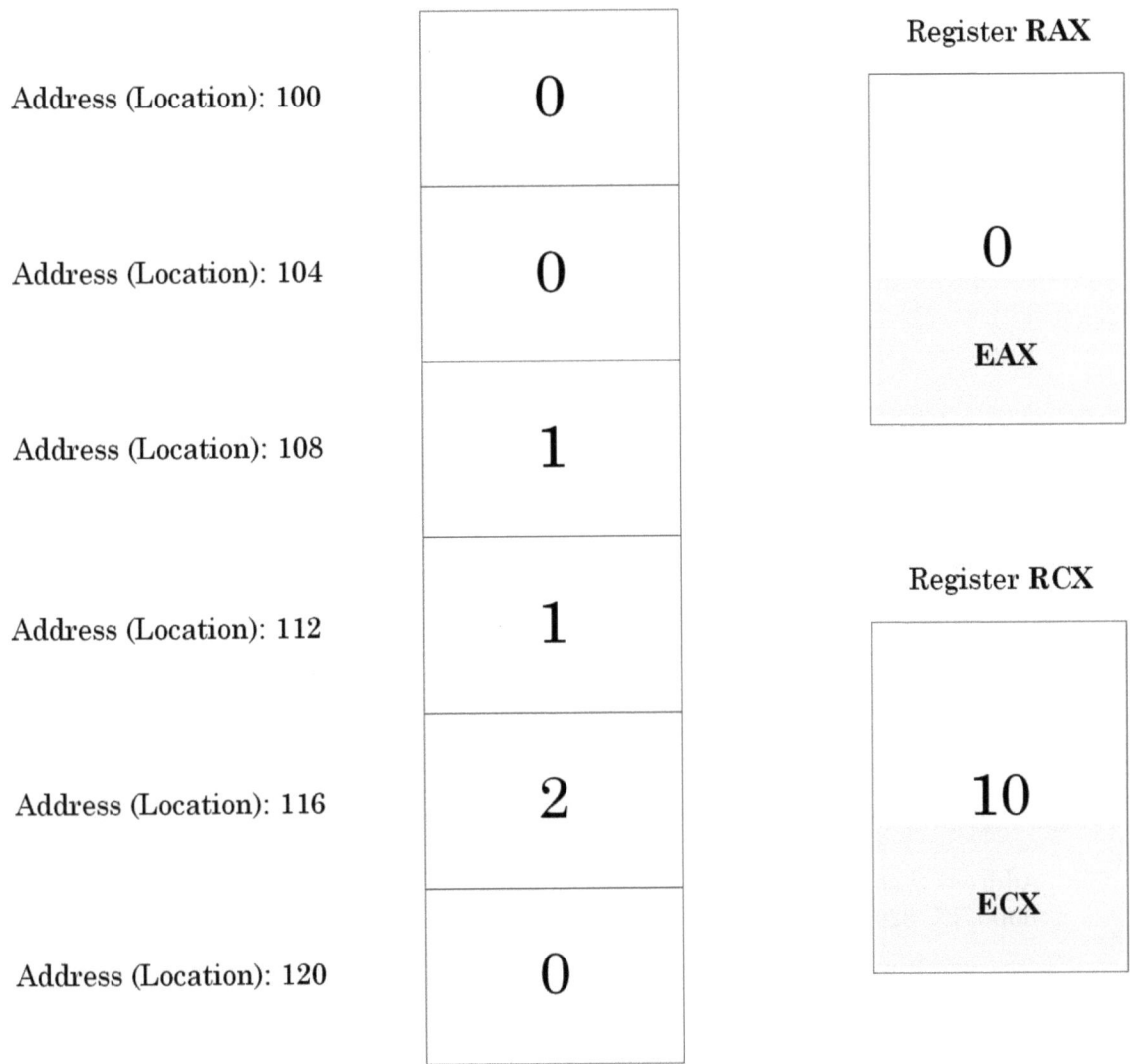

Picture x64.1.2

Because memory cells contain "numbers", we start with a simple arithmetic and ask a PC to compute the sum of two numbers to see how memory and registers change their values. We call our project "Arithmetic".

"Arithmetic" Project: Memory Layout and Registers

For our project, we have two memory addresses (locations) that we call "a" and "b". So we can think about "a" and "b" as names of their respective addresses (locations). Now we introduce a special notation where [a] means contents at the memory address (location) "a". If we use C or C++ language to write our project, we declare and define memory locations "a" and "b" as:

`static int a, b;`

By default, static memory locations are filled with zeroes when we load a program, and we can depict our initial memory layout after loading the program as shown in Picture x64.1.3. Addresses are twice as long in x64 Windows, and for readability, they are shown as split in half by '`' character.

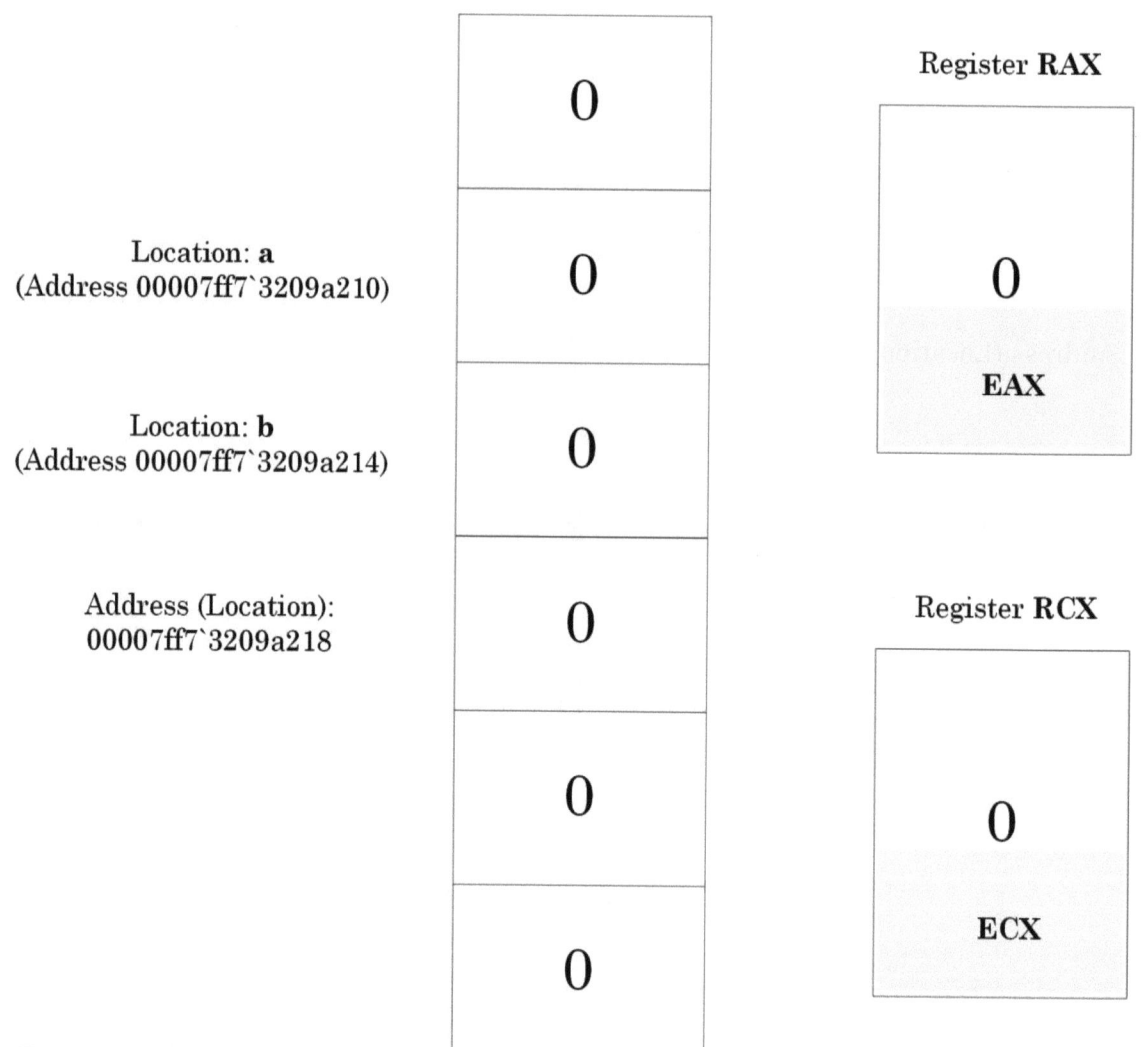

Picture x64.1.3

"Arithmetic" Project: A Computer Program

We can think of a computer program as a sequence of instructions for the manipulation of contents of memory cells and registers. For example, addition operation: add the contents of memory cell №12 to the contents of memory cell №14. In our pseudo-code, we can write:

[14] <- [14] + [12]

Our first program in pseudo-code is shown on the left of the table:

[a] <- 1 [b] <- 1 [b] <- [b] + [a] ; [b] = 2 [b] <- [b] * 2 ; [b] = 4	Here we put assembly instructions corresponding to pseudo-code.

'<-' means assignment when we replace the contents of a memory location (address) with the new value. ';' is a comment sign, and the rest of the line is a comment. '=' shows the current value at a memory location (address).

To remind, a code written in a high-level programming language is translated to a machine language by a compiler. However, the machine language can be readable if its digital codes are represented in some mnemonic system called assembly language. For example, **INC [a]**, to increment by one what is stored at a memory location **a.**

"Arithmetic" Project: Assigning Numbers to Memory Locations

We remind that "a" means location (address) of the memory cell, and it is also the name of the location (address) 00007ff7`3209a210 (see Picture x64.1.3). [a] means the contents (number) stored at the address "a".

If we use C or C++ language, "a" is called "the variable a", and we write the assignment as:

```
a = 1;
```

In Intel assembly language, we write:

```
mov   [a], 1
```

In WinDbg disassembly output, we see the following code where the variable "a" is prefixed by '!' after the name of the executable file (module) it belongs to (that is *ArithmeticProject.exe* in our case):

```
mov   dword ptr [ArithmeticProject!a (00007ff7`3209a210)],1
```

We show the translation of our pseudo code into assembly language in the right column:

`[a] <- 1`	`mov   dword ptr [a], 1`
`[b] <- 1`	`mov   dword ptr [b], 1`
`[b] <- [b] + [a]  ; [b] = 2`	
`[b] <- [b] * 2    ; [b] = 4`	

Notice "dword ptr" in front of memory references [a] and [b]. It is because "a" and "b" can point to both 32-bit (like EAX or ECX registers) and 64-bit (like RAX and RCX registers) memory cells. In the case of registers, it is clear from their names whether we use 64-bit RAX or 32-bit EAX. But in the case of memory addresses "a" and "b", it is unclear whether they refer to 64-bit or 32-bit cells. So we use "dword ptr" to disambiguate and show that we use 32-bit memory cells enough to hold integers from 0 to 4294967295.

After executing the first two assembly language instructions, we have the memory layout shown in Picture x64.1.4.

Chapter x64.1: Memory, Registers, and Simple Arithmetic   **181**

Location: **a** (Address 00007ff7`3209a210)	0
	1
Location: **b** (Address 00007ff7`3209a214)	1
Address (Location): 00007ff7`3209a218	0
	0
	0

Register **RAX**: 0 (EAX)

Register **RCX**: 0 (ECX)

Picture x64.1.4

Assigning Numbers to Registers

This operation is similar to memory assignments. We can write in pseudo-code

```
register <- 1 or register <- [a]
```

Note that we do not use brackets when we refer to register contents. The latter instruction means assigning (copying) the number at the location (address) "a" to a register.

In assembly language, we write:

```
mov    eax, 1    ; 1 is copied to the first half of RAX register

mov    rax, 1    ; full contents of RAX register are replaced with 1

mov    eax, dword ptr [a]

mov    rax, [a]
```

In WinDbg disassembly output, we see the following code:

```
mov    eax,dword ptr [ArithmeticProject!a (00007ff7`3209a210)]
```

"Arithmetic" Project: Adding Numbers to Memory Cells

Now let's look at the following pseudo-code statement in more detail:

```
[b] <- [b] + [a]
```

To recall, "a" and "b" mean the names of locations (addresses) 00007ff7`3209a210 and 00007ff7`3209a214 respectively (see Picture x64.1.4). [a] and [b] mean contents at addresses "a" and "b" respectively, simply some numbers stored there.

In C or C++ language, we write the following statement:

```
b = b + a; // or

b += a;
```

In assembly language, we use the instruction ADD. Due to limitations of AMD64 and Intel EM64T architecture, we cannot use both memory addresses in one step (instruction), for example, **add [b], [a]**. We can only use **add [b], register** to add the value stored in the **register** to the contents of memory cell **b**. Recall that a register is like a temporary memory cell itself here:

```
register <- [a]

[b] <- [b] + register
```

In assembly language we write:

```
mov   eax, dword ptr [a]

add   dword ptr [b], eax
```

In WinDbg disassembly output we see the following code:

```
mov   eax,dword ptr [ArithmeticProject!a (00007ff7`3209a210)]

add   dword ptr [ArithmeticProject!b (00007ff7`3209a214)],eax
```

Alternatively, we can use two registers:

```
register1 <- [a]

register2 <- [b]

registsr2 <- registsr2 + register1

[b] <- register2
```

"Arithmetic" Project: Adding Numbers to Memory Cells

In WinDbg disassembly output, we see the following code:

```
mov    eax,dword ptr [ArithmeticProject!a (00007ff7`3209a210)]
mov    ecx,dword ptr [ArithmeticProject!b (00007ff7`3209a214)]
add    ecx,eax
mov    dword ptr [ArithmeticProject!b (00007ff7`3209a214)],ecx
```

Now we can translate our pseudo-code into assembly language:

`[a] <- 1`	`mov    dword ptr [a], 1`
`[b] <- 1`	`mov    dword ptr [b], 1`
`[b] <- [b] + [a]  ; [b] = 2`	`mov    eax, dword ptr [a]`
`                  ; eax = 1`	`mov    ecx, dword ptr [b]`
`                  ; ecx = 2`	`add    ecx, eax`
	`mov    dword ptr [b], ecx`
`[b] <- [b] * 2    ; [b] = 4`	

After executing ADD and MOV instructions, we have the memory layout illustrated in Picture x64.1.5.

Chapter x64.1: Memory, Registers, and Simple Arithmetic

Location: **a**
(Address 00007ff7`3209a210)

Location: **b**
(Address 00007ff7`3209a214)

Address (Location):
00007ff7`3209a218

0
1
2
0
0
0

Register **RAX**

1
EAX

Register **RCX**

2
ECX

Picture x64.1.5

Incrementing/Decrementing Numbers in Memory and Registers

In pseudo-code it looks simple and means increment (decrement) a number stored at the location (address) "a":

```
[a] <- [a] + 1

[a] <- [a] - 1
```

In C or C++ language, we can write this using three possible ways:

```
a = a + 1; // or

++a; // or

a++;

b = b - 1; // or

--b; // or

b--;
```

In assembly language, we use instructions INC and DEC and write:

```
inc   [a]

inc   eax

dec   [a]

dec   eax
```

In WinDbg disassembly output, we see the same instruction:

```
inc   eax
```

or

```
add   eax, 1 // a compiler might decide to use ADD instead of INC
```

Now we add this additional increment to our pseudo-code and its assembly language translation (this is needed for subsequent multiplication explained later):

```
[a] <- 1                          mov   dword ptr [a], 1

[b] <- 1                          mov   dword ptr [b], 1

[b] <- [b] + [a]  ; [b] = 2       mov   eax, dword ptr [a]

                  ; eax = 1       mov   ecx, dword ptr [b]

                  ; ecx = 2       add   ecx, eax

                                  mov   dword ptr [b], ecx

eax <- eax + 1    ; eax = 2       add   eax, 1

[b] <- [b] * 2    ; [b] = 4
```

After the INC or ADD instruction execution, we have the memory layout illustrated in Picture x64.1.6.

188 Incrementing/Decrementing Numbers in Memory and Registers

	0	Register **RAX**
Location: **a** (Address 00007ff7`3209a210)	1	2
		EAX
Location: **b** (Address 00007ff7`3209a214)	2	
Address (Location): 00007ff7`3209a218	0	Register **RCX**
	0	2
	0	ECX

Picture x64.1.6

Multiplying Numbers

In pseudo-code we write:

`[b] <- [b] * 2`

This operation means we multiply the number at the location (address) "b" by 2.

In C or C++ language, we can write that using two ways:

`b = b * 2; // or`

`b *= 2;`

In assembly language, we use instruction IMUL (Integer MULtiply) and write:

`imul eax, dword ptr [b]`

`mov  dword ptr [b], eax`

The whole sequence means [b] <- eax * [b] and we have to put 2 into EAX (see previous section). Fortunately, we already have 2 in the EAX register. The result of the multiplication is put into the register EAX.

In WinDbg disassembly output, we see the following code:

`imul eax,dword ptr [ArithmeticProject!b (00007ff7`3209a214)]`

`mov  dword ptr [ArithmeticProject!b (00007ff7`3209a214)],eax`

Now we add two additional assembly instructions to our pseudo-code assembly language translation:

[a] <- 1	mov dword ptr [a], 1
[b] <- 1	mov dword ptr [b], 1
[b] <- [b] + [a] ; [b] = 2	mov eax, dword ptr [a]
; eax = 1	mov ecx, dword ptr [b]
; ecx = 2	add ecx, eax
	mov dword ptr [b], ecx
eax <- eax + 1 ; eax = 2	add eax, 1
[b] <- [b] * 2 ; eax = 4	imul eax, dword ptr [b]
; [b] = 4	mov dword ptr [b], eax

Multiplying Numbers

After executing IMUL and MOV instructions, we have the memory layout illustrated in Picture x64.1.7.

Location: **a**
(Address 00007ff7`3209a210)

Location: **b**
(Address 00007ff7`3209a214)

Address (Location):
00007ff7`3209a218

0
1
4
0
0
0

Register **RAX**

4
EAX

Register **RCX**

2
ECX

Picture x64.1.7

Chapter x64.2: Debug and Release Binaries

"Arithmetic" Project: C/C++ Program

Let's rewrite our "Arithmetic" program in C++. Corresponding assembly language instructions are put in comments:

```
int a, b;
int main(int argc, char* argv[])
{
    a = 1;              // mov   dword ptr [a], 1
    b = 1;              // mov   dword ptr [b], 1
    b = b + a;          // mov   eax, dword ptr [a]
                        // mov   ecx, dword ptr [b]
                        // add   ecx, eax
                        // mov   dword ptr [b], ecx
    ++a;                // add   eax, 1
                        // mov   dword ptr [a], eax
    b = a * b;          // imul  eax, dword ptr [b]
                        // mov   dword ptr [b], eax
                        // results: [a] = 2 and [b] = 4
    return 0;
}
```

If we compile and link the program in debug mode, we get the binary executable module which we can load in WinDbg and inspect assembly code.

Downloading and Configuring WinDbg Debugger

WinDbg from Debugging Tools for Windows or WinDbg Preview App can be installed from Microsoft website, or we can use WinDbg.org pointing to Microsoft download links as shown in Picture x64.2.1. In the book, we use WinDbg, but if you choose WinDbg Preview instead, there is no difference in debugger commands output. If you want to use a Docker environment, please check Appendix x64.

Pattern-Oriented Software Diagnostics

Software Diagnostics Institute

Software Diagnostics Library

Software Diagnostics Technology and Services

Memory Dump Analysis Anthology

Tables of Contents and Indexes of WinDbg Commands from all volumes

WinDbg Quick Links

Download Debugging Tools for Windows

Download WinDbg Preview

Debugging Tools for Windows Help

Debugging Tools for Windows Blog

Symbol Server (Microsoft):

srv*c:\mss*http://msdl.microsoft.com/download/symbols

Picture x64.2.1

For x64 chapters, we need to use x64 Windows and WinDbg (X64) for debugging 64-bit applications. After downloading and installing Debugging Tools, we start WinDbg (X64) as shown in Picture x64.2.2.

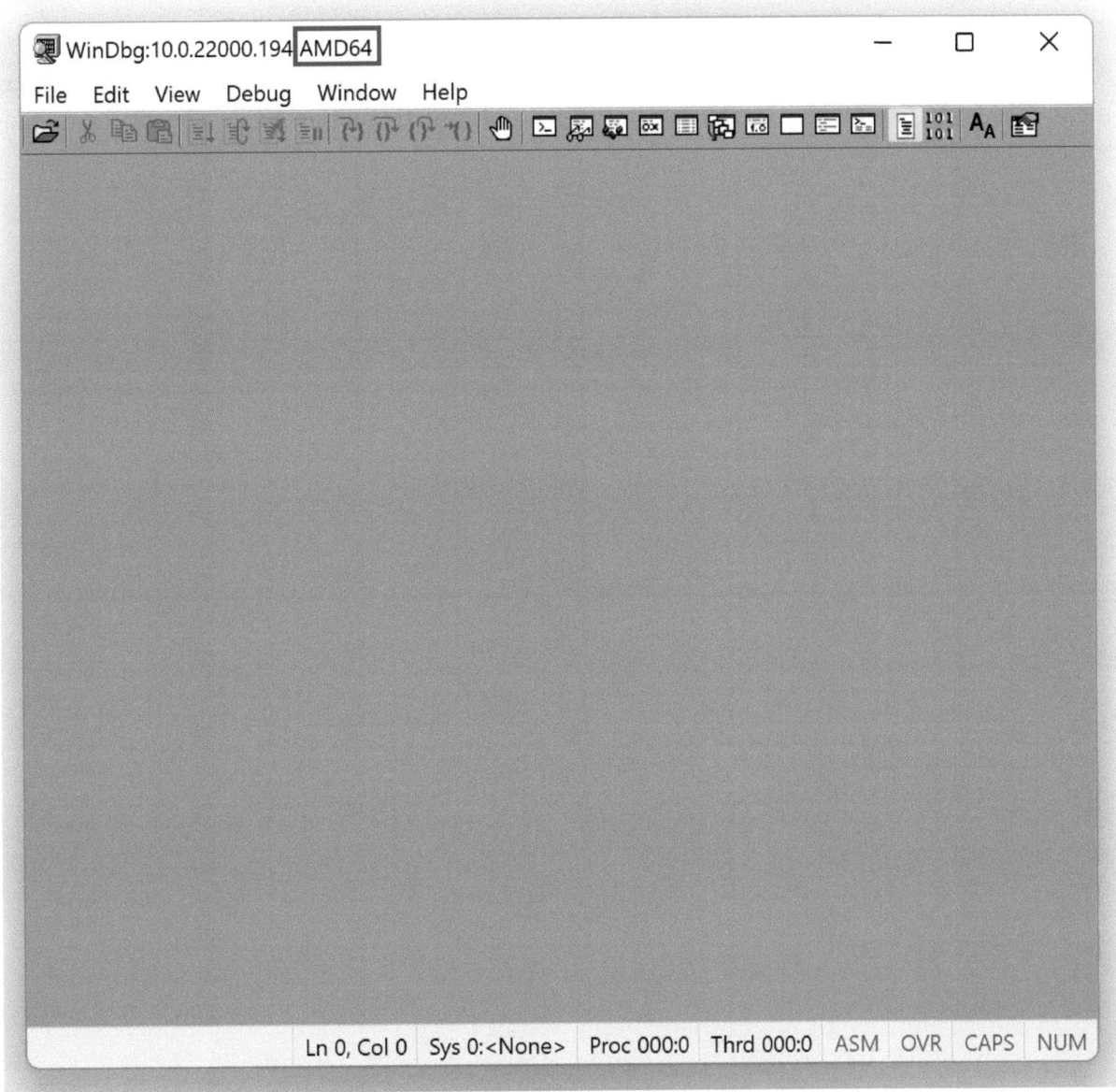

Picture x64.2.2

WinDbg Disassembly Output – Debug Executable

The *Debug* executable can be downloaded from the following location:

https://bitbucket.org/softwarediagnostics/pfwddr2/src/master/x64/Chapter2/

It is located under *Debug* subfolder. We run WinDbg and then load *ArithmeticProjectC.exe* (menu File\Open Executable...) as shown in Picture x64.2.3. The output, especially addresses, may differ for your Windows version.

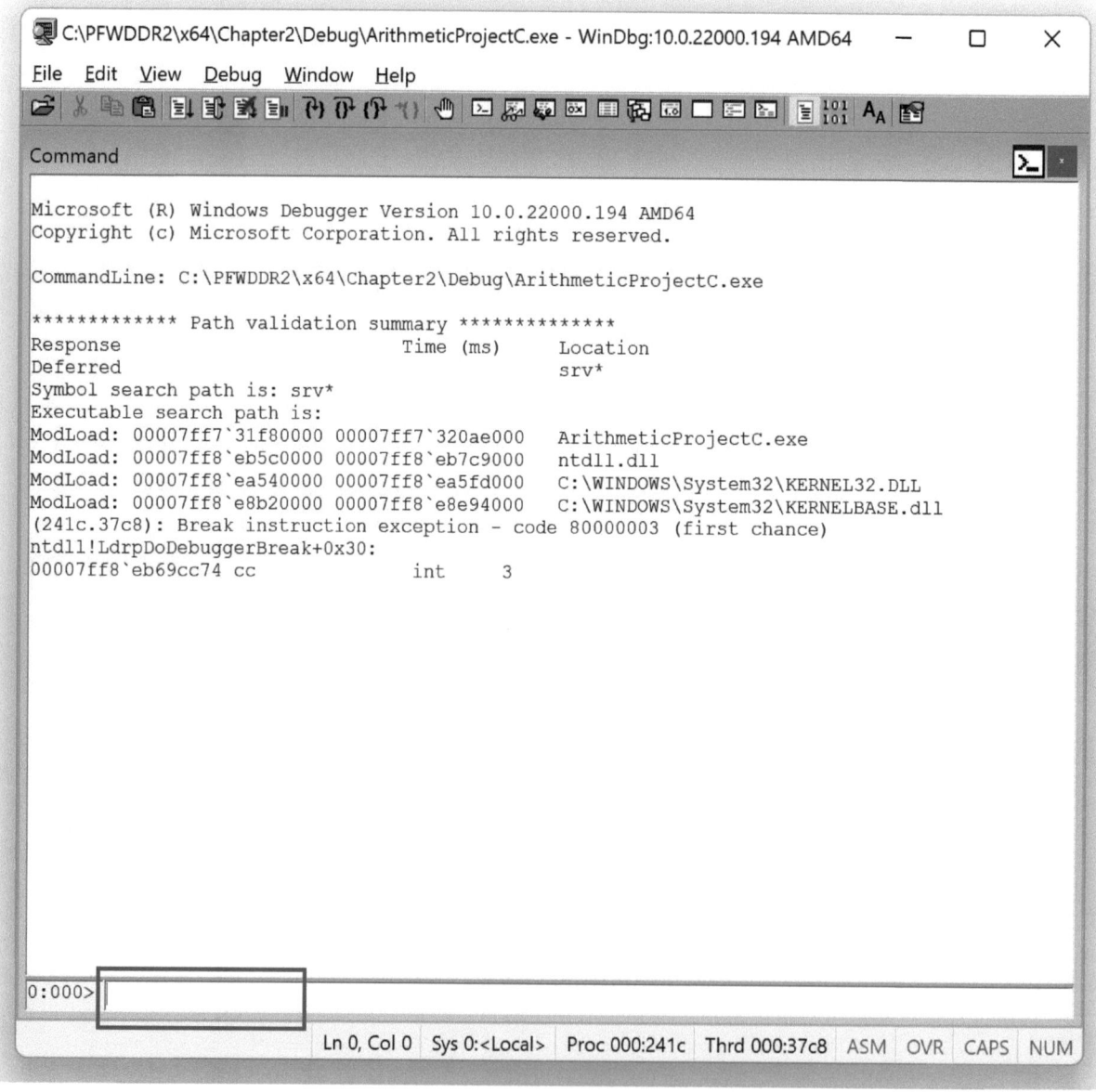

Picture x64.2.3

We see a command line window at the bottom where we can enter WinDbg commands. We also need symbol files for our project to interpret binary data in our own executable file. Fortunately, this symbol file (which has a *.PDB* file extension) is located in the same folder where the *.EXE* file resides, and we don't need a command to specify its path here (**.sympath+** <additional path>).

Next, we put a **b**reak**p**oint at our *main* C++ function, as shown in Picture x64.2.4, to allow the program execution to stop at that point and give us a chance to inspect memory and registers. Symbolic names/function names like "main" can be used instead of code memory locations after the symbol file is loaded into WinDbg. Showing symbolic names is one useful aspect of a symbol file: we can refer to a function name instead of identifying where the function code resides in memory. Since the *ArithmeticProjectC* executable module is not loaded yet, we specify the fully qualified name in *module!function* format (*ArithmeticProjectC!main*):

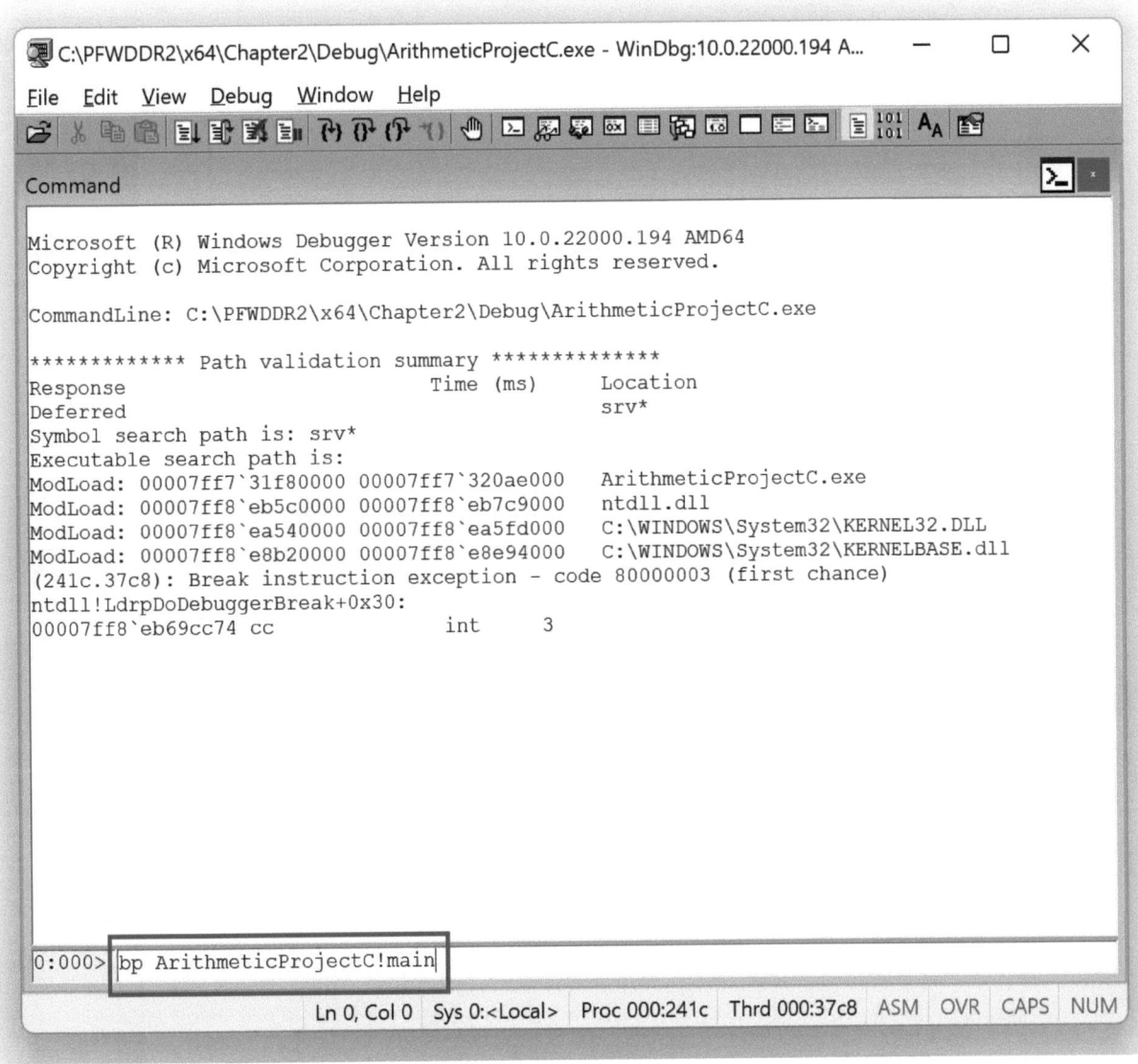

Picture x64.2.4

WinDbg Disassembly Output – Debug Executable

Then we start the program's execution (let it **g**o) as shown in Picture x64.2.5.

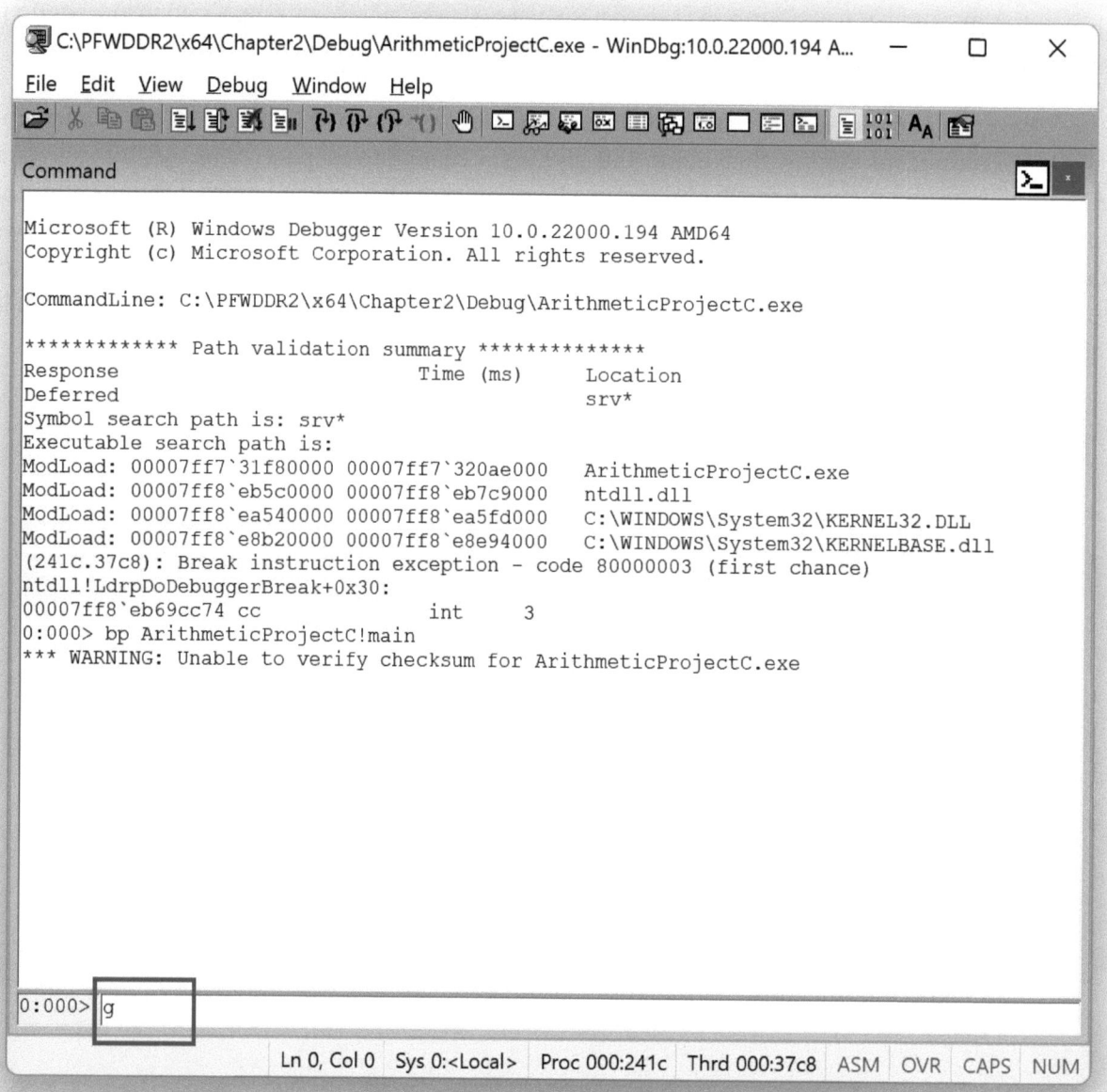

Picture x64.2.5

The program then stops at the previously set breakpoint, as shown in Picture x64.2.6.

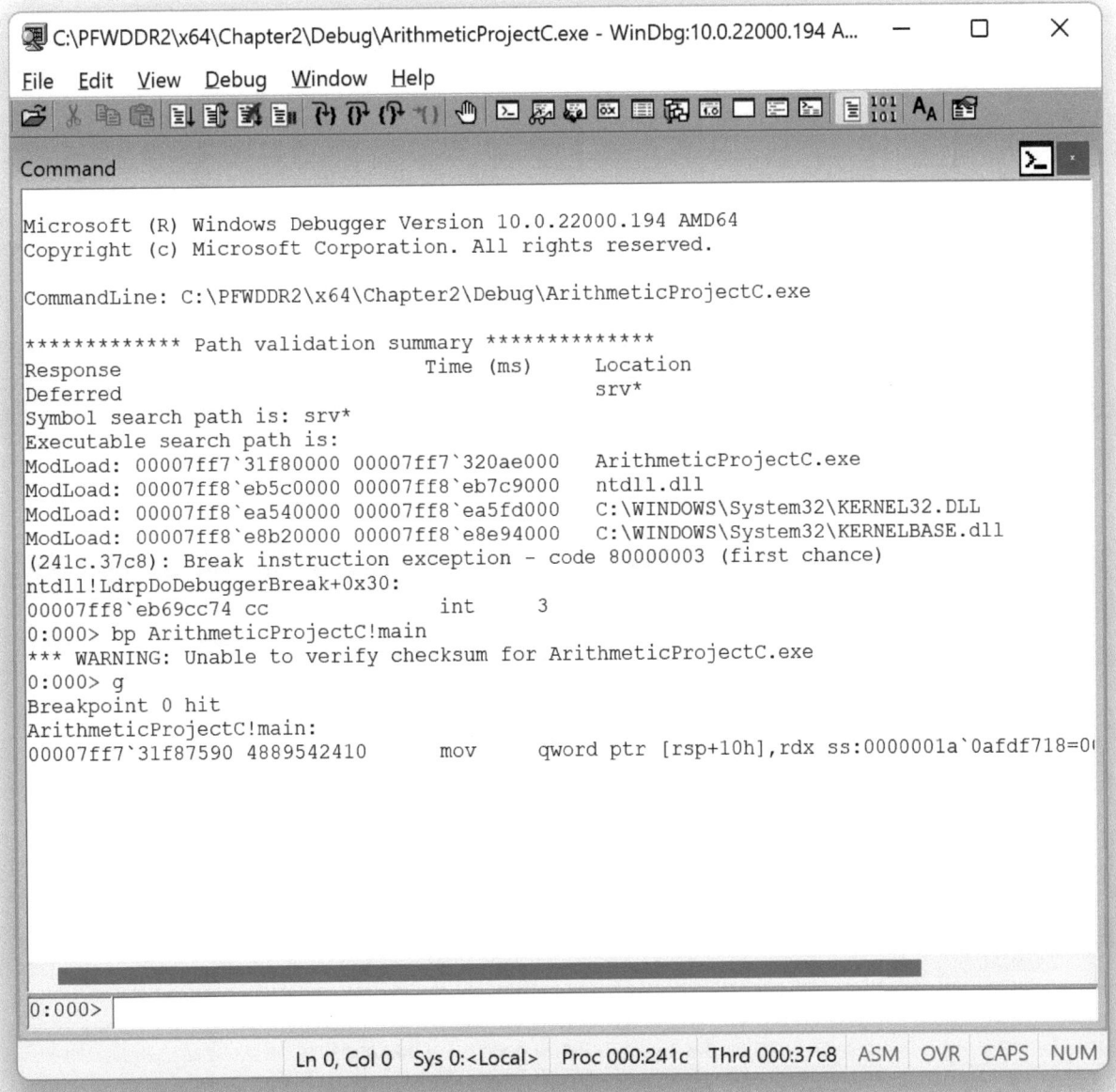

Picture x64.2.6

198 WinDbg Disassembly Output – Debug Executable

Now we **u**nassemble the *main* **f**unction as shown in Pictures x64.2.7 and x64.2.8.

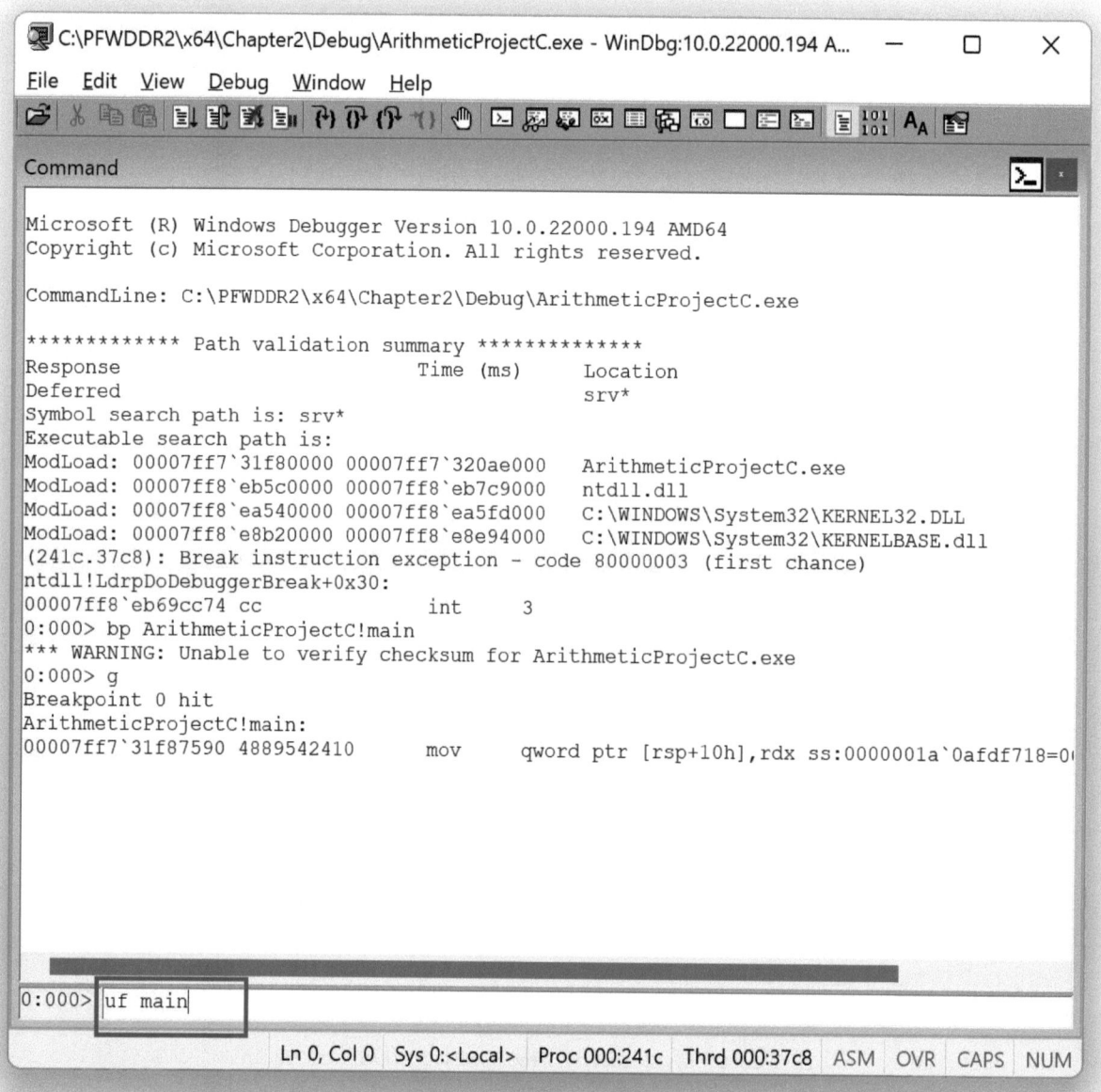

Picture x64.2.7

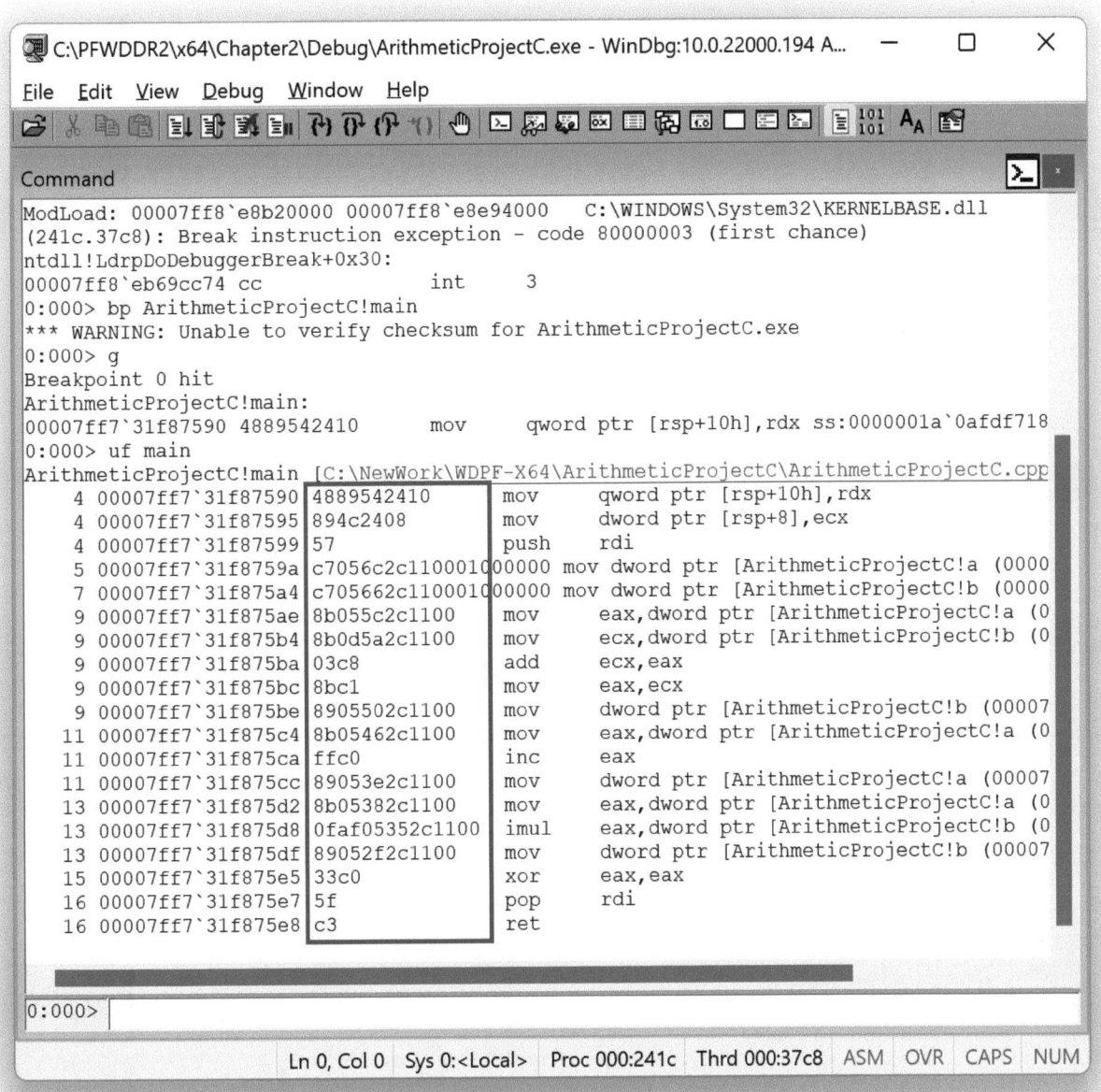

Picture x64.2.8

The middle column shows the binary code we are not interested in, and we opt not to include it in the future, as shown in Picture x64.2.9.

200 WinDbg Disassembly Output – Debug Executable

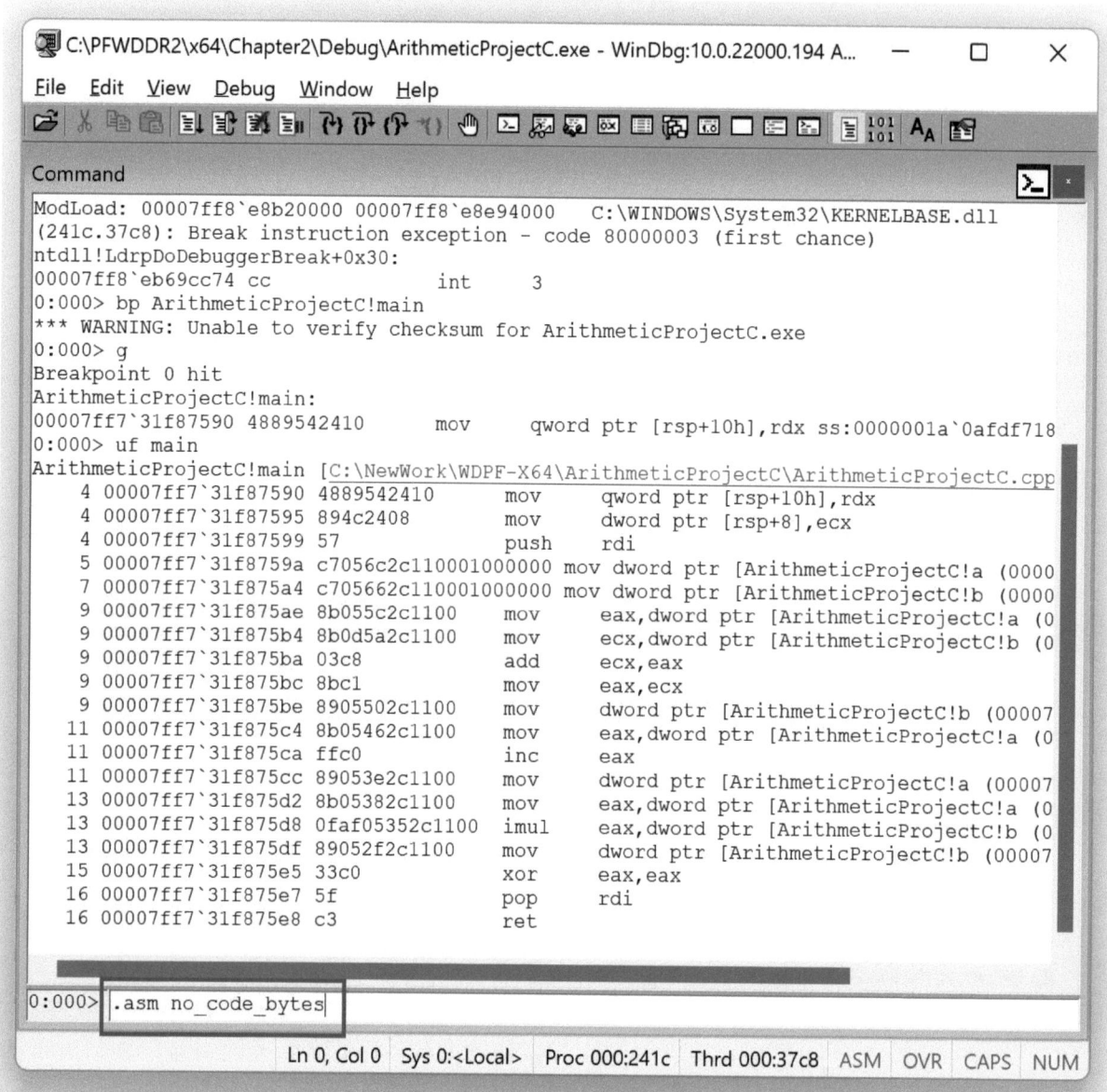

Picture x64.2.9

We repeat our disassembly command, as shown in Picture x64.2.10.

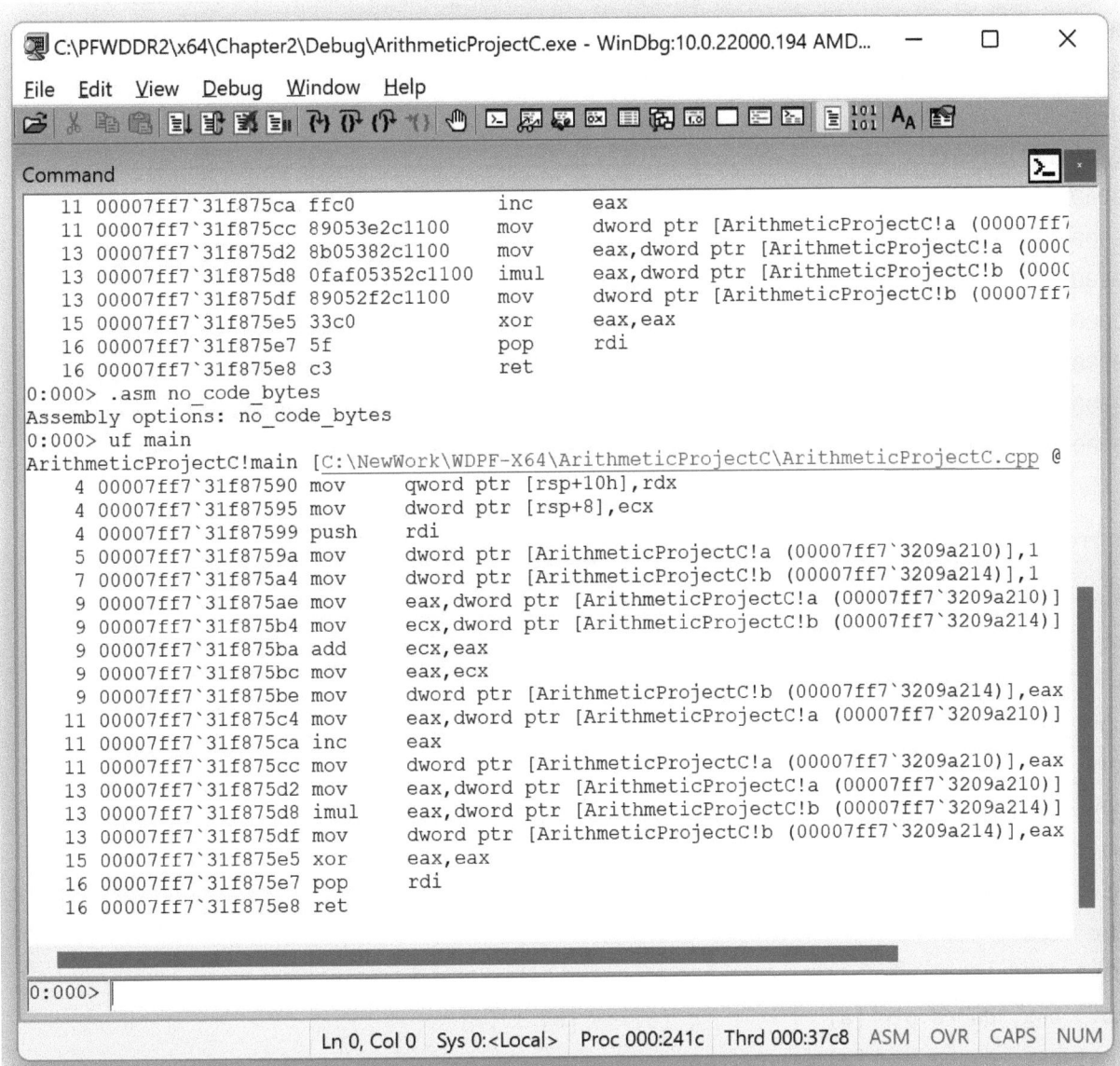

Picture x64.2.10

We repeat the part of the formatted disassembly output here that corresponds to our C++ code where we removed source code line numbers:

```
00007ff7`31f8759a mov     dword ptr [ArithmeticProjectC!a (00007ff7`3209a210)],1
00007ff7`31f875a4 mov     dword ptr [ArithmeticProjectC!b (00007ff7`3209a214)],1
00007ff7`31f875ae mov     eax,dword ptr [ArithmeticProjectC!a (00007ff7`3209a210)]
00007ff7`31f875b4 mov     ecx,dword ptr [ArithmeticProjectC!b (00007ff7`3209a214)]
00007ff7`31f875ba add     ecx,eax
00007ff7`31f875bc mov     eax,ecx
00007ff7`31f875be mov     dword ptr [ArithmeticProjectC!b (00007ff7`3209a214)],eax
00007ff7`31f875c4 mov     eax,dword ptr [ArithmeticProjectC!a (00007ff7`3209a210)]
00007ff7`31f875ca inc     eax
00007ff7`31f875cc mov     dword ptr [ArithmeticProjectC!a (00007ff7`3209a210)],eax
00007ff7`31f875d2 mov     eax,dword ptr [ArithmeticProjectC!a (00007ff7`3209a210)]
00007ff7`31f875d8 imul    eax,dword ptr [ArithmeticProjectC!b (00007ff7`3209a214)]
00007ff7`31f875df mov     dword ptr [ArithmeticProjectC!b (00007ff7`3209a214)],eax
```

We can directly translate it to bare assembly code we used in the previous chapter and put corresponding pseudo-code in comments:

```
mov   dword ptr [a], 1          ; [a] <- 1
mov   dword ptr [b], 1          ; [b] <- 1
mov   eax, dword ptr [a]        ; [b] <- [b] + [a]
mov   ecx, dword ptr [b]        ;
add   ecx, eax                  ;
mov   eax, ecx                  ;
mov   dword ptr [b], eax        ;
mov   eax, dword ptr [a]        ; [a] <- [a] + 1
inc   eax                       ;
mov   dword ptr [a], eax        ;
mov   eax, dword ptr [a]        ; [b] <- [b] * [a]
imul  eax, dword ptr [b]        ;
mov   dword ptr [b], eax        ;
```

WinDbg Disassembly Output – Release Executable

If we repeat the same procedure for an executable located under *Release* subfolder we get the following output:

```
ArithmeticProjectC!main:
00007ff6`6f8b1000 mov dword ptr [ArithmeticProjectC!a (00007ff6`6f8caa70)],2
00007ff6`6f8b100a xor     eax,eax
00007ff6`6f8b100c mov dword ptr [ArithmeticProjectC!b (00007ff6`6f8caa74)],4
00007ff6`6f8b1016 ret
```

This corresponds to the following pseudo-code:

```
mov    dword ptr [a], 2    ; [a] <- 2
mov    dword ptr [b], 4    ; [b] <- 4
```

What happened to all our assembly code in this *Release* executable? If we observe, this code seems to be directly placing the result into [b]. Why is this happening? The answer lies in compiler optimization. When the code is compiled in Release mode, the Visual C++ compiler can calculate the final result from the simple C source code itself and generate code only necessary to update corresponding memory locations.

Chapter x64.3: Number Representations

Numbers and Their Representations

Imagine ourselves a herder in ancient times trying to count his sheep. We have a certain number of stones (twelve):

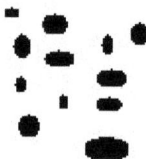

However, we can only count up to three and arrange the total into groups of three:

The last picture is a representation (a kind of notation) of the number of stones. We have one group of three groups of three stones plus a separate group of three stones. If we could count up to ten, we would see a different representation of the same number of stones. We would have one group of ten stones and another group of two stones.

Decimal Representation (Base Ten)

Let's now see how twelve stones are represented in arithmetic notation if we can count up to ten. We have one group of ten numbers plus two:

$12_{dec} = \mathbf{1} * 10 + \mathbf{2}$ or $\mathbf{1} * 10^1 + \mathbf{2} * 10^0$

Here is another exercise with one hundred and twenty-three stones. We have **1** group of ten by ten stones, another group of **2** groups of ten stones and the last group of **3** stones:

$\mathbf{123}_{dec} = \mathbf{1} * 10*10 + \mathbf{2} * 10 + \mathbf{3}$ or $\mathbf{1} * 10^2 + \mathbf{2} * 10^1 + \mathbf{3} * 10^0$

We can formalize it in the following summation notation:

$N_{dec} = a_n*10^n + a_{n-1}*10^{n-1} + \ldots + a_2*10^2 + a_1*10^1 + a_0*10^0$ $0 <= a_i <= 9$

Using the summation symbol, we have this formula:

$$N_{dec} = \sum_{i=0}^{n} a_i*10^i$$

Ternary Representation (Base Three)

Now we come back to our herder's example of twelve stones. We have **1** group of three by three stones, **1** group of three stones, and an empty (**0**) group (which is not empty if we have only one stone or thirteen stones instead of twelve). We can write down the number of groups sequentially: **110**. Therefore **110** is a ternary representation (notation) of twelve stones, and it is equivalent to 12 written in decimal notation:

$12_{dec} = 1*3^2 + 1*3^1 + 0*3^0$

$N_{dec} = a_n*3^n + a_{n-1}*3^{n-1} + ... + a_2*3^2 + a_1*3^1 + a_0*3^0 \qquad a_i = 0 \text{ or } 1 \text{ or } 2$

$$N_{dec} = \sum_{i=0}^{n} a_i*3^i$$

Binary Representation (Base Two)

In the case of counting up to 2, we have more groups for twelve stones: **1100**. Therefore **1100** is a binary representation (notation) for 12 in decimal notation:

$12_{dec} = 1*2^3 + 1*2^2 + 0*2^1 + 0*2^0$

$123_{dec} = 1*2^6 + 1*2^5 + 1*2^4 + 1*2^3 + 0*2^2 + 1*2^1 + 1*2^0$ or 1111011_2

$N_{dec} = a_n*2^n + a_{n-1}*2^{n-1} + ... + a_2*2^2 + a_1*2^1 + a_0*2^0 \qquad a_i = 0 \text{ or } 1$

$N_{dec} = \sum_{i=0}^{n} a_i*2^i$

Hexadecimal Representation (Base Sixteen)

If we can count up to sixteen, twelve stones fit in one group, but we need more symbols: **A**, **B**, **C**, **D**, **E**, and **F** for ten, eleven, twelve, thirteen, fourteen, and fifteen respectively:

12_{dec} = C in hexadecimal representation (notation)

$123_{dec} = 7B_{hex}$

$123_{dec} = 7*16^1 + 11*16^0$

$$N_{dec} = \sum_{i=0}^{n} a_i * 16^i$$

Why are Hexadecimals Used?

Consider this number written in binary notation: 110001010011_2. Its equivalent in decimal notation is 3155:

$3155_{dec} = 1*2^{11} + 1*2^{10} + 0*2^9 + 0*2^8 + 0*2^7 + 1*2^6 + 0*2^5 + 1*2^4 + 0*2^3 + 0*2^2 + 1*2^1 + 1*2^0$

Now we divide the binary number digits into groups of four and write them down in decimal and hexadecimal notation:

1100_01010011

12$_{dec}$ **5**$_{dec}$ **3**$_{dec}$

C$_{hex}$ **5**$_{hex}$ **3**$_{hex}$

We see that hexadecimal notation is more compact because every four binary digit group number corresponds to one hexadecimal number. Table x64.3.1 lists hexadecimal equivalents for every four binary digit combination.

In WinDbg and other debuggers, memory addresses are displayed in hexadecimal notation.

Why are Hexadecimals Used?

Binary	Decimal	Hexadecimal
0000	0	0
0001	1	1
0010	2	2
0011	3	3
0100	4	4
0101	5	5
0110	6	6
0111	7	7
1000	8	8
1001	9	9
1010	10	A
1011	11	B
1100	12	C
1101	13	D
1110	14	E
1111	15	F

Table x64.3.1

Chapter x64.4: Pointers

A Definition

The concept of a pointer is one of the most important to understand thoroughly to master Windows debugging. By definition, a pointer is a memory cell or a processor register that contains the address of another memory cell, as shown in Picture x64.4.1. It has its own address as any memory cell. Sometimes, a pointer is called an indirect address (vs. direct address, the address of a memory cell). Iteratively, we can define another level of indirection and introduce a pointer to a pointer as a memory cell or a processor register that contains the address of another memory cell, that contains the address of another memory cell, and so on.

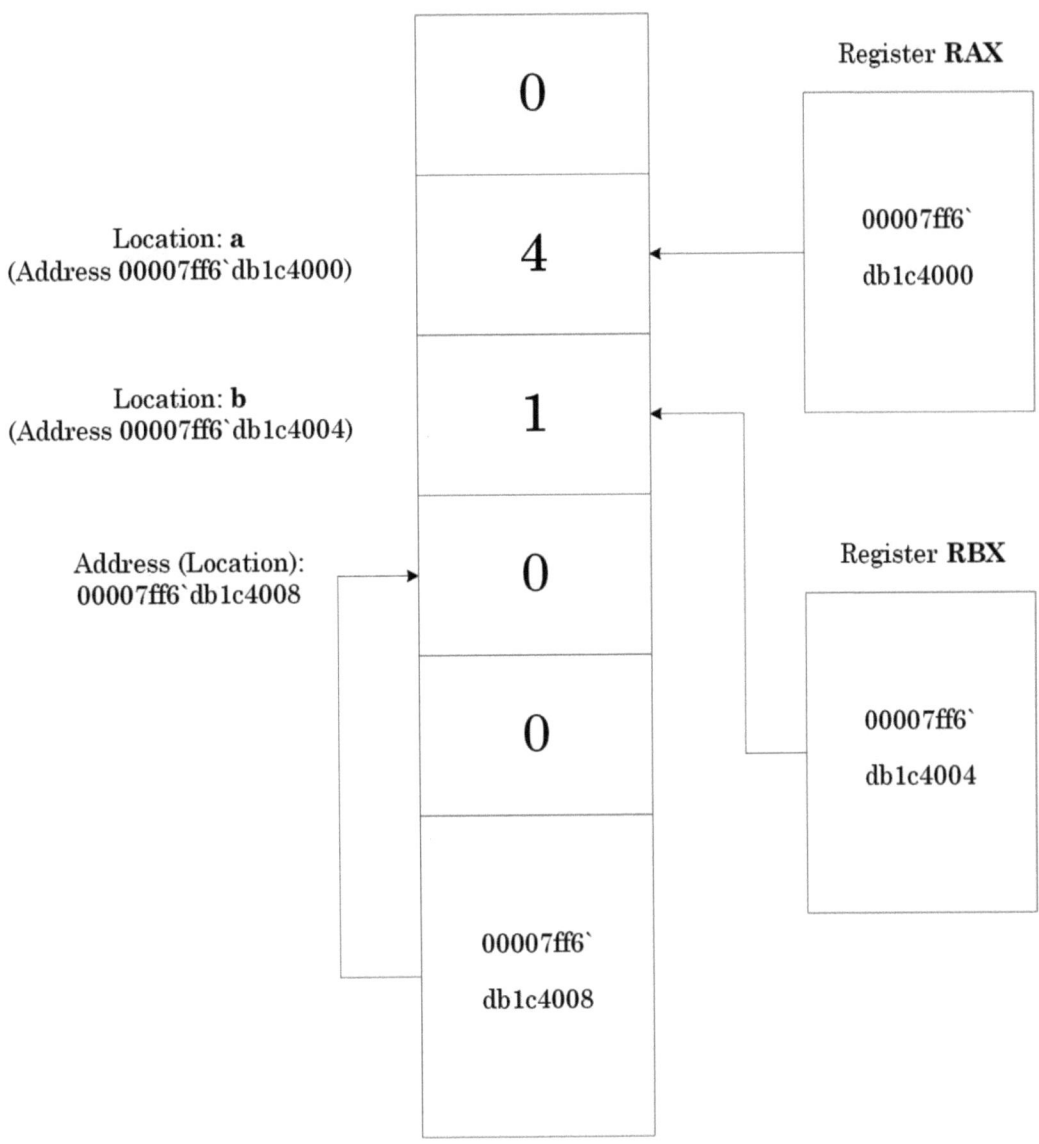

Picture x64.4.1

"Pointers" Project: Memory Layout and Registers

In our debugging project, we have two memory addresses (locations), "a" and "b". We can think about "a" and "b" as names of addresses (locations). We remind that notation [a] means contents at the memory address (location) "a".

We also have the registers RAX and RBX as pointers to "a" and "b". These registers contain addresses of "a" and "b", respectively. The notation [RAX] means contents of a memory cell whose address is in the register RAX.

In C and C++ languages, we declare and define pointers to "a" and "b" as:

int *a, *b;

Our project memory layout before program execution is shown in Picture x64.4.2. Addresses always occupy 64-bit memory cells or full 64-bit registers like RAX or RBX (they cannot fit in EAX or EBX or a 32-bit memory cell).

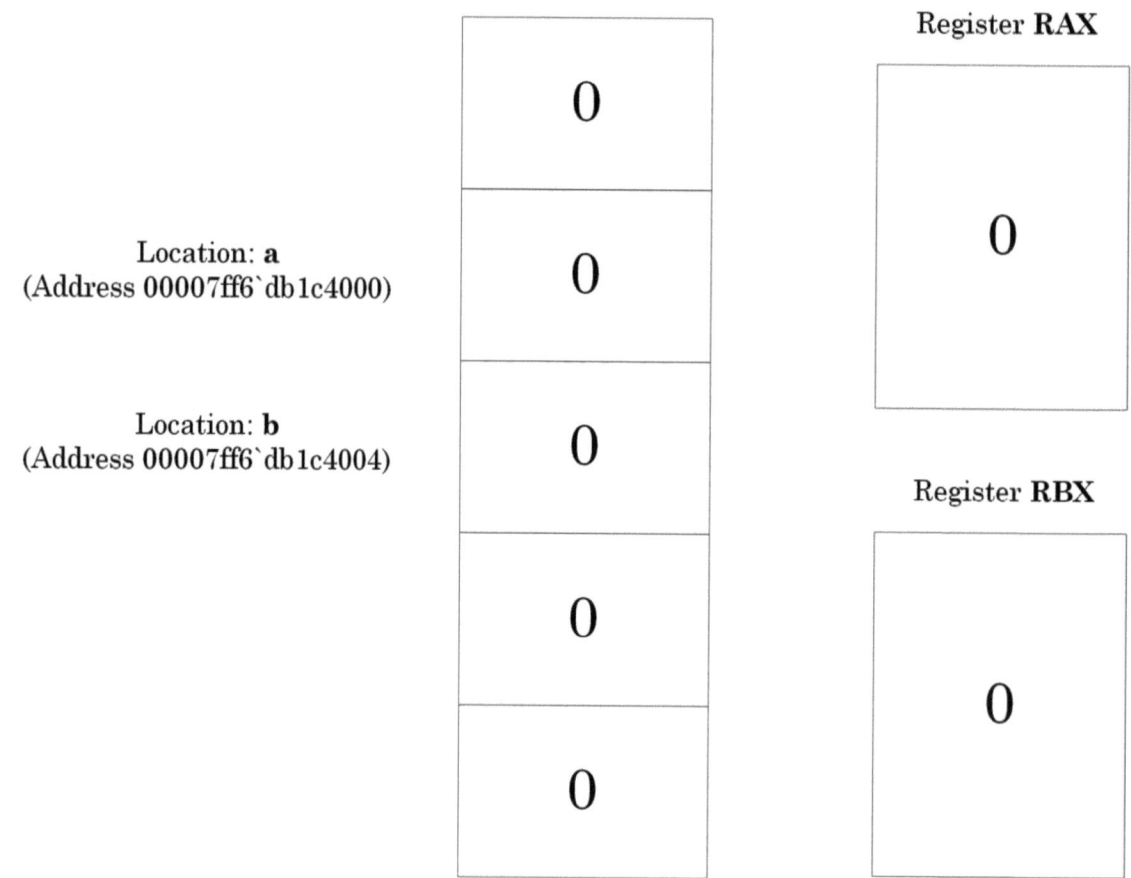

Picture x64.4.2

"Pointers" Project: Calculations

To understand pointers better from a low-level assembly language perspective, we perform our old arithmetic calculations from Chapter x64.1 using pointers to memory instead of direct memory addresses:

```
rax <- address a
[rax] <- 1              ; [a] = 1
rbx <- address b
[rbx] <- 1              ; [b] = 1
[rbx] <- [rbx] + [rax]
                        ; [b] = 2
[rbx] <- [rbx] * 2
                        ; [b] = 4
```

Using Pointers to Assign Numbers to Memory Cells

First, the following sequence of pseudo-code instructions means that we interpret the contents of the RAX register as the address of a memory cell and then assign a value to that memory cell:

```
rax <- address a

[rax] <- 1
```

In C language, it is called "dereferencing a pointer" and we write:

```
int a;

int *pa;    // declaration and definition of a pointer

*pa = 1;    // get a memory cell (dereference a pointer)
            // and assign a value to it
```

In assembly language, we write:

```
Lea  rax, a ; load the address a into rax

mov  dword ptr [rax], 1 ; use rax as a pointer
```

Again, we see the "dword ptr" prefix because integers occupy 32-bit memory cells: in x64 Windows, memory cells to contain integers are half the size of memory cells to contain addresses (32-bit vs. 64-bit).

In WinDbg disassembly output, we would see something like this:

```
00007ff6`db1c1010 lea     rax,[PointersProject!a (00007ff6`db1c4000)]

00007ff6`db1c1017 mov     dword ptr [rax],1
```

The project for this chapter can be downloaded from

https://bitbucket.org/softwarediagnostics/pfwddr2/src/master/x64/Chapter4/

We can load the executable into WinDbg and disassemble its *main* function as described in Chapter x64.2. From now on, we do not see screenshots of WinDbg windows but the output from the command window instead.

First, we load *PointersProject.exe* using File\Open Executable... menu option in WinDbg and get the following output (the output, especially addresses, may differ for your Windows version):

```
Microsoft (R) Windows Debugger Version 10.0.22000.194 AMD64
Copyright (c) Microsoft Corporation. All rights reserved.


CommandLine: C:\PFWDDR2\x64\Chapter4\PointersProject.exe

************* Path validation summary **************
Response                         Time (ms)     Location
Deferred                                       srv*
Symbol search path is: srv*
Executable search path is:
ModLoad: 00007ff6`db1c0000 00007ff6`db1c6000   PointersProject.exe
ModLoad: 00007ff8`eb5c0000 00007ff8`eb7c9000   ntdll.dll
ModLoad: 00007ff8`ea540000 00007ff8`ea5fd000   C:\WINDOWS\System32\KERNEL32.DLL
ModLoad: 00007ff8`e8b20000 00007ff8`e8e94000   C:\WINDOWS\System32\KERNELBASE.dll
(3b54.4110): Break instruction exception - code 80000003 (first chance)
ntdll!LdrpDoDebuggerBreak+0x30:
00007ff8`eb69cc74 cc              int     3
```

We also allow the output of registers:

```
0:000> .prompt_allow +reg
Allow the following information to be displayed at the prompt:
(Other settings can affect whether the information is actually displayed)
   sym - Symbol for current instruction
   dis - Disassembly of current instruction
    ea - Effective address for current instruction
   reg - Register state
   src - Source info for current instruction
Do not allow the following information to be displayed at the prompt:
  None
```

Then we put a breakpoint to the *main* function and run the program until WinDbg breaks in:

```
0:000> bp PointersProject!main
*** WARNING: Unable to verify checksum for PointersProject.exe
```

```
0:000> g
Breakpoint 0 hit
rax=00007ff6db1c1005 rbx=0000000000000000 rcx=0000008ec8bee000
rdx=00007ff6db1c1005 rsi=0000000000000000 rdi=0000000000000000
rip=00007ff6db1c1010 rsp=0000008ec892fab8 rbp=0000000000000000
 r8=0000008ec8bee000  r9=00007ff6db1c1005 r10=00007ff8ea5d7c90
r11=0000000000000000 r12=0000000000000000 r13=0000000000000000
r14=0000000000000000 r15=0000000000000000
iopl=0         nv up ei pl zr na po nc
cs=0033  ss=002b  ds=002b  es=002b  fs=0053  gs=002b             efl=00000246
PointersProject!main:
00007ff6`db1c1010 488d05e92f0000  lea     rax,[PointersProject!a (00007ff6`db1c4000)]
```

For visual clarity, we disable the output of binary codes before disassembling *main* function:

```
0:000> .asm no_code_bytes
Assembly options: no_code_bytes
```

```
0:000> uf main
PointersProject!main [C:\NewWork\WDPF-X64\PointersProject\PointersProject.asm @ 12]:
   12 00007ff6`db1c1010 lea     rax,[PointersProject!a (00007ff6`db1c4000)]
   15 00007ff6`db1c1017 mov     dword ptr [rax],1
   17 00007ff6`db1c101d lea     rbx,[PointersProject!b (00007ff6`db1c4004)]
   18 00007ff6`db1c1024 mov     dword ptr [rbx],1
   20 00007ff6`db1c102a mov     eax,dword ptr [rax]
   21 00007ff6`db1c102c add     dword ptr [rbx],eax
   23 00007ff6`db1c102e inc     eax
   25 00007ff6`db1c1030 imul    eax,dword ptr [rbx]
   26 00007ff6`db1c1033 mov     dword ptr [rbx],eax
   28 00007ff6`db1c1035 ret
```

Now, we examine variables "a" and "b" to verify the memory layout shown previously in Picture x64.4.2 using the **dd** (**d**ump **d**ouble word) WinDbg command:

```
0:000> dd PointersProject!a L1
00007ff6`db1c4000  00000000
```

```
0:000> dd PointersProject!b L1
00007ff6`db1c4004  00000000
```

We also clear values of RAX and RBX registers in accordance with Picture x64.4.2:

```
0:000> r rax = 0
```

```
0:000> r rbx = 0
```

We can verify registers by using the **r** WinDbg command:

```
0:000> r
rax=0000000000000000 rbx=0000000000000000 rcx=0000008ec8bee000
rdx=00007ff6db1c1005 rsi=0000000000000000 rdi=0000000000000000
rip=00007ff6db1c1010 rsp=0000008ec892fab8 rbp=0000000000000000
 r8=0000008ec8bee000  r9=00007ff6db1c1005 r10=00007ff8ea5d7c90
r11=0000000000000000 r12=0000000000000000 r13=0000000000000000
r14=0000000000000000 r15=0000000000000000
iopl=0         nv up ei pl zr na po nc
cs=0033  ss=002b  ds=002b  es=002b  fs=0053  gs=002b             efl=00000246
PointersProject!main:
00007ff6`db1c1010 lea     rax,[PointersProject!a (00007ff6`db1c4000)]
```

Now we execute the first four instructions that correspond to our pseudo-code using the **t** WinDbg command (the output of the **t** command also shows the instruction to be executed next):

rax <- address a	lea rax, a
[rax] <- 1 ; [a] = 1	mov dword ptr [rax], 1
rbx <- address b	lea rbx, b
[rbx] <- 1 ; [b] = 1	mov dword ptr [rbx], 1
[rbx] <- [rbx] + [rax]	
; [b] = 2	
[rbx] <- [rbx] * 2	
; [b] = 4	

```
0:000> t
rax=00007ff6db1c4000 rbx=0000000000000000 rcx=0000008ec8bee000
rdx=00007ff6db1c1005 rsi=0000000000000000 rdi=0000000000000000
rip=00007ff6db1c1017 rsp=0000008ec892fab8 rbp=0000000000000000
 r8=0000008ec8bee000  r9=00007ff6db1c1005 r10=00007ff8ea5d7c90
r11=0000000000000000 r12=0000000000000000 r13=0000000000000000
r14=0000000000000000 r15=0000000000000000
iopl=0         nv up ei pl zr na po nc
cs=0033  ss=002b  ds=002b  es=002b  fs=0053  gs=002b             efl=00000246
PointersProject!main+0x7:
00007ff6`db1c1017 mov     dword ptr [rax],1    ds:00007ff6`db1c4000=00000000

0:000> t
rax=00007ff6db1c4000 rbx=0000000000000000 rcx=0000008ec8bee000
rdx=00007ff6db1c1005 rsi=0000000000000000 rdi=0000000000000000
rip=00007ff6db1c101d rsp=0000008ec892fab8 rbp=0000000000000000
 r8=0000008ec8bee000  r9=00007ff6db1c1005 r10=00007ff8ea5d7c90
r11=0000000000000000 r12=0000000000000000 r13=0000000000000000
r14=0000000000000000 r15=0000000000000000
iopl=0         nv up ei pl zr na po nc
cs=0033  ss=002b  ds=002b  es=002b  fs=0053  gs=002b             efl=00000246
PointersProject!main+0xd:
00007ff6`db1c101d lea     rbx,[PointersProject!b (00007ff6`db1c4004)]

0:000> t
rax=00007ff6db1c4000 rbx=00007ff6db1c4004 rcx=0000008ec8bee000
rdx=00007ff6db1c1005 rsi=0000000000000000 rdi=0000000000000000
rip=00007ff6db1c1024 rsp=0000008ec892fab8 rbp=0000000000000000
 r8=0000008ec8bee000  r9=00007ff6db1c1005 r10=00007ff8ea5d7c90
r11=0000000000000000 r12=0000000000000000 r13=0000000000000000
r14=0000000000000000 r15=0000000000000000
iopl=0         nv up ei pl zr na po nc
cs=0033  ss=002b  ds=002b  es=002b  fs=0053  gs=002b             efl=00000246
PointersProject!main+0x14:
00007ff6`db1c1024 mov     dword ptr [rbx],1    ds:00007ff6`db1c4004=00000000
```

```
0:000> t
rax=00007ff6db1c4000 rbx=00007ff6db1c4004 rcx=0000008ec8bee000
rdx=00007ff6db1c1005 rsi=0000000000000000 rdi=0000000000000000
rip=00007ff6db1c102a rsp=0000008ec892fab8 rbp=0000000000000000
 r8=0000008ec8bee000  r9=00007ff6db1c1005 r10=00007ff8ea5d7c90
r11=0000000000000000 r12=0000000000000000 r13=0000000000000000
r14=0000000000000000 r15=0000000000000000
iopl=0         nv up ei pl zr na po nc
cs=0033  ss=002b  ds=002b  es=002b  fs=0053  gs=002b             efl=00000246
PointersProject!main+0x1a:
00007ff6`db1c102a mov     eax,dword ptr [rax]    ds:00007ff6`db1c4000=00000001
```

We also see that the values of "a" and "b" have changed as expected:

```
0:000> dd PointersProject!a L1
00007ff6`db1c4000  00000001
```

```
0:000> dd PointersProject!b L1
00007ff6`db1c4004  00000001
```

All this corresponds to a memory layout shown in Picture x64.4.3.

220 Using Pointers to Assign Numbers to Memory Cells

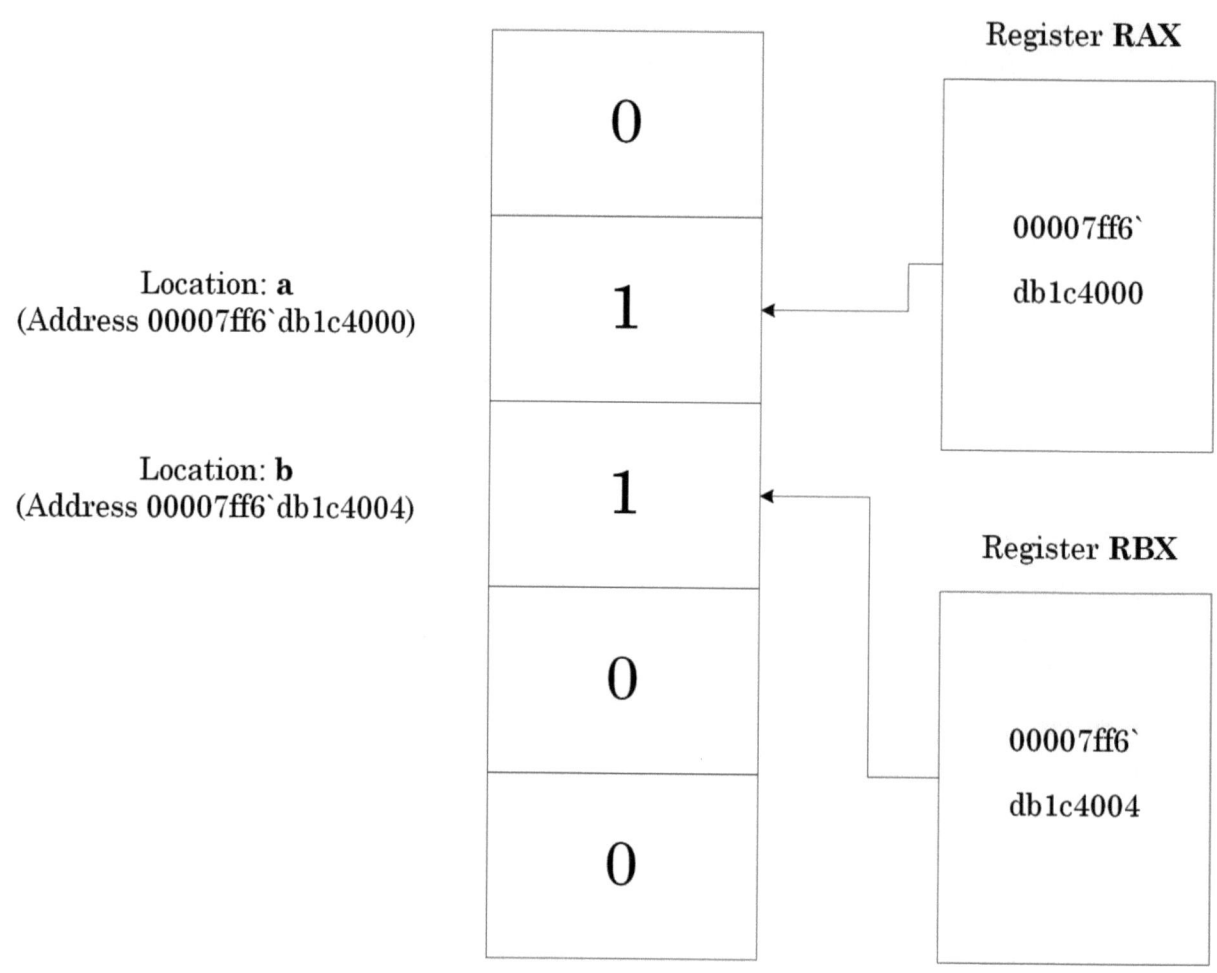

Picture x64.4.3

Adding Numbers Using Pointers

Now we look at the next pseudo-code statement:

```
[rbx] <- [rbx] + [rax]
```

Recall that [rax] and [rbx] mean contents of memory cells whose addresses (locations) are stored in RAX and RBX CPU registers. The statement above is equivalent to the following C or C++ language expression where the '*' operator means to get memory contents pointed to by **pa** or **pb** pointer (also called pointer dereference):

```
*pb = *pb + *pa;
```

In assembly language, we use the instruction ADD for the '+' operator, but we cannot use both memory addresses in one step instruction:

```
add   [rbx], [rax]
```

We can only use one memory reference, and therefore, we need to employ another register as a temporary variable:

```
register <- [rax]
[rbx] <- [rbx] + register
```

In assembly language, we write this sequence of instructions:

```
mov   eax, dword ptr [rax]
add   dword ptr [rbx], eax
```

In WinDbg disassembly output, we see these instructions indeed:

```
00007ff6`db1c102a mov     eax,dword ptr [rax]
00007ff6`db1c102c add     dword ptr [rbx],eax
```

We add them to our pseudo-code table:

`rax <- address a`	`lea    rax, a`
`[rax] <- 1        ; [a] = 1`	`mov    dword ptr [rax], 1`
`rbx <- address b`	`lea    rbx, b`
`[rbx] <- 1        ; [b] = 1`	`mov    dword ptr [rbx], 1`
`[rbx] <- [rbx] + [rax]`	**`mov    eax, dword ptr [rax]`**
`                  ; [b] = 2`	**`add    dword ptr [rbx], eax`**
`[rbx] <- [rbx] * 2`	
`                  ; [b] = 4`	

Now, we execute these two instructions (we remind that the output of the **t** command shows the next instruction to be executed when we use the **t** command again):

```
[From the previous output]
rax=00007ff6db1c4000 rbx=00007ff6db1c4004 rcx=0000008ec8bee000
rdx=00007ff6db1c1005 rsi=0000000000000000 rdi=0000000000000000
rip=00007ff6db1c102a rsp=0000008ec892fab8 rbp=0000000000000000
 r8=0000008ec8bee000  r9=00007ff6db1c1005 r10=00007ff8ea5d7c90
r11=0000000000000000 r12=0000000000000000 r13=0000000000000000
r14=0000000000000000 r15=0000000000000000
iopl=0         nv up ei pl zr na po nc
cs=0033  ss=002b  ds=002b  es=002b  fs=0053  gs=002b             efl=00000246
PointersProject!main+0x1a:
00007ff6`db1c102a mov     eax,dword ptr [rax]    ds:00007ff6`db1c4000=00000001

0:000> t
rax=0000000000000001 rbx=00007ff6db1c4004 rcx=0000008ec8bee000
rdx=00007ff6db1c1005 rsi=0000000000000000 rdi=0000000000000000
rip=00007ff6db1c102c rsp=0000008ec892fab8 rbp=0000000000000000
 r8=0000008ec8bee000  r9=00007ff6db1c1005 r10=00007ff8ea5d7c90
r11=0000000000000000 r12=0000000000000000 r13=0000000000000000
r14=0000000000000000 r15=0000000000000000
iopl=0         nv up ei pl zr na po nc
cs=0033  ss=002b  ds=002b  es=002b  fs=0053  gs=002b             efl=00000246
PointersProject!main+0x1c:
```

```
00007ff6`db1c102c add     dword ptr [rbx],eax      ds:00007ff6`db1c4004=00000001
```

```
0:000> t
rax=0000000000000001 rbx=00007ff6db1c4004 rcx=0000008ec8bee000
rdx=00007ff6db1c1005 rsi=0000000000000000 rdi=0000000000000000
rip=00007ff6db1c102e rsp=0000008ec892fab8 rbp=0000000000000000
 r8=0000008ec8bee000  r9=00007ff6db1c1005 r10=00007ff8ea5d7c90
r11=0000000000000000 r12=0000000000000000 r13=0000000000000000
r14=0000000000000000 r15=0000000000000000
iopl=0         nv up ei pl nz na pe nc
cs=0033  ss=002b  ds=002b  es=002b  fs=0053  gs=002b             efl=00000202
PointersProject!main+0x1e:
00007ff6`db1c102e inc     eax
```

We also check the memory location of the **b** variable to see that it has really changed its value:

```
0:000> dd PointersProject!b L1
00007ff6`db1c4004  00000002
```

All this corresponds to a memory layout shown in Picture x64.4.4.

224 Adding Numbers Using Pointers

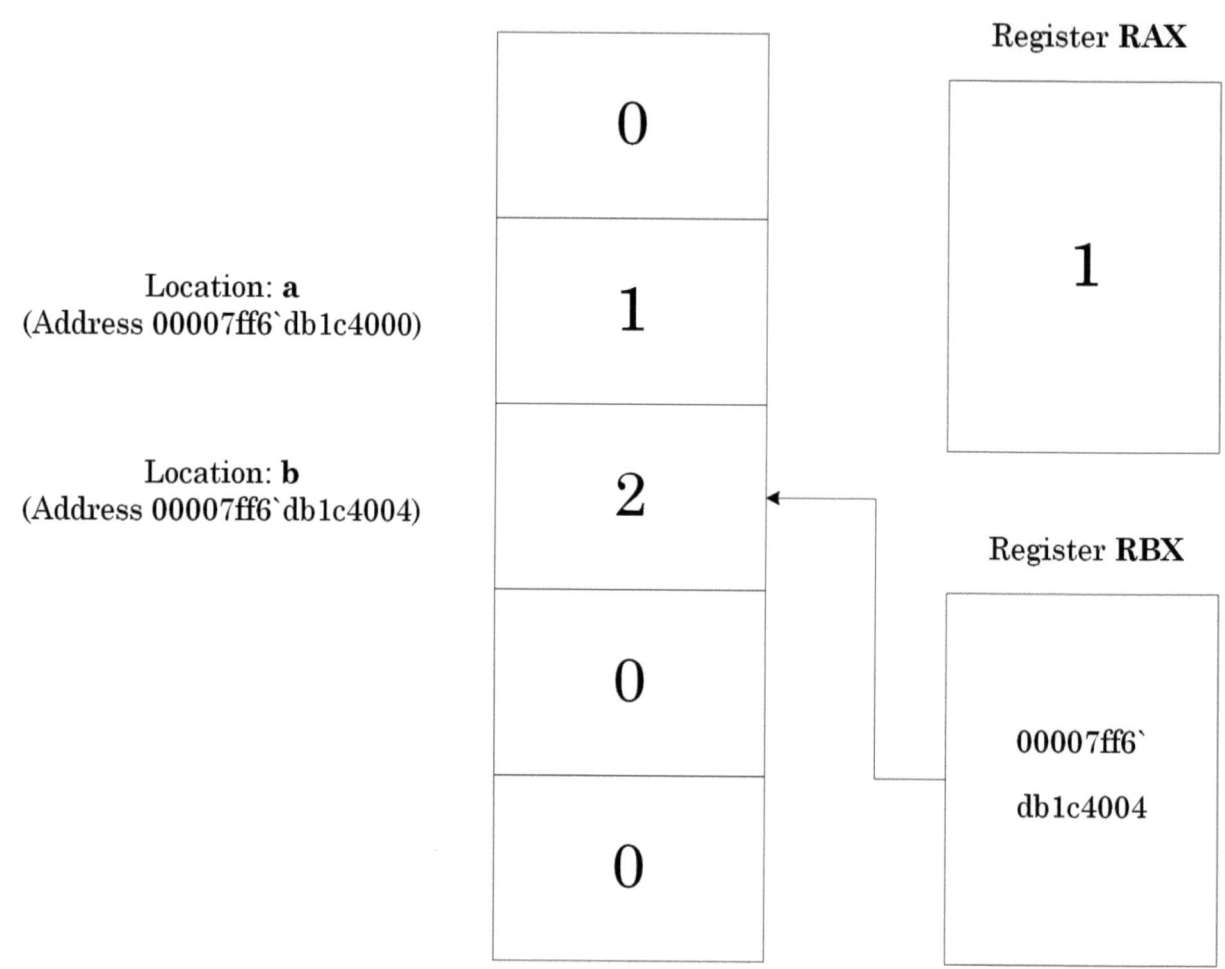

Picture x64.4.4

Multiplying Numbers Using Pointers

Our next pseudo-code statement does multiplication:

[rbx] <- [rbx] * 2

This statement means that we multiply the contents of the memory whose address is stored in the RBX register by 2. In C or C++ language, we write a similar expression as the addition statement we have seen in the previous section (note that we have two distinct meanings of '*' operator, pointer dereference and multiplication):

*pb = *pb * 2; // or

*pb *= 2;

The latter is a shorthand notation. In assembly language, we use instruction IMUL (Integer MULtiply):

imul eax, dword ptr [rbx]

This instruction is equivalent to the following pseudo-code:

eax <- eax * [rbx]

Therefore, we have to put 2 into the EAX register, but we already have 1 in EAX, so we use INC EAX instruction before IMUL to increment EAX by 1.

In WinDbg disassembly output, we would see this:

```
00007ff6`db1c102e inc     eax
00007ff6`db1c1030 imul    eax,dword ptr [rbx]
00007ff6`db1c1033 mov     dword ptr [rbx],eax
```

We add instructions to our pseudo-code table:

`rax <- address a`	`lea    rax, a`
`[rax] <- 1       ; [a] = 1`	`mov    dword ptr [rax], 1`
`rbx <- address b`	`lea    rbx, b`
`[rbx] <- 1       ; [b] = 1`	`mov    dword ptr [rbx], 1`
`[rbx] <- [rbx] + [rax]`	`mov    eax, dword ptr [rax]`
`                 ; [b] = 2`	`add    dword ptr [rbx], eax`
`[rbx] <- [rbx] * 2`	`inc    eax`
`                 ; [b] = 4`	`imul   eax, dword ptr [rbx]`
	`mov    dword ptr [rbx], eax`

Now we execute these three instructions (we remind that the output of the **t** command shows the next instruction to be executed when we use the **t** command again):

```
[From the previous output]
rax=0000000000000001 rbx=00007ff6db1c4004 rcx=0000008ec8bee000
rdx=00007ff6db1c1005 rsi=0000000000000000 rdi=0000000000000000
rip=00007ff6db1c102e rsp=0000008ec892fab8 rbp=0000000000000000
 r8=0000008ec8bee000  r9=00007ff6db1c1005 r10=00007ff8ea5d7c90
r11=0000000000000000 r12=0000000000000000 r13=0000000000000000
r14=0000000000000000 r15=0000000000000000
iopl=0         nv up ei pl nz na pe nc
cs=0033  ss=002b  ds=002b  es=002b  fs=0053  gs=002b             efl=00000202
PointersProject!main+0x1e:
00007ff6`db1c102e inc     eax
```

```
0:000> t
rax=0000000000000002 rbx=00007ff6db1c4004 rcx=0000008ec8bee000
rdx=00007ff6db1c1005 rsi=0000000000000000 rdi=0000000000000000
rip=00007ff6db1c1030 rsp=0000008ec892fab8 rbp=0000000000000000
 r8=0000008ec8bee000  r9=00007ff6db1c1005 r10=00007ff8ea5d7c90
r11=0000000000000000 r12=0000000000000000 r13=0000000000000000
r14=0000000000000000 r15=0000000000000000
iopl=0         nv up ei pl nz na pe nc
cs=0033  ss=002b  ds=002b  es=002b  fs=0053  gs=002b             efl=00000202
PointersProject!main+0x20:
00007ff6`db1c1030 imul    eax,dword ptr [rbx]    ds:00007ff6`db1c4004=00000002
```

```
0:000> t
rax=0000000000000004 rbx=00007ff6db1c4004 rcx=0000008ec8bee000
rdx=00007ff6db1c1005 rsi=0000000000000000 rdi=0000000000000000
rip=00007ff6db1c1033 rsp=0000008ec892fab8 rbp=0000000000000000
 r8=0000008ec8bee000  r9=00007ff6db1c1005 r10=00007ff8ea5d7c90
r11=0000000000000000 r12=0000000000000000 r13=0000000000000000
r14=0000000000000000 r15=0000000000000000
iopl=0         nv up ei pl nz na pe nc
cs=0033  ss=002b  ds=002b  es=002b  fs=0053  gs=002b             efl=00000202
PointersProject!main+0x23:
00007ff6`db1c1033 mov     dword ptr [rbx],eax    ds:00007ff6`db1c4004=00000002
```

```
0:000> t
rax=0000000000000004 rbx=00007ff6db1c4004 rcx=0000008ec8bee000
rdx=00007ff6db1c1005 rsi=0000000000000000 rdi=0000000000000000
rip=00007ff6db1c1035 rsp=0000008ec892fab8 rbp=0000000000000000
 r8=0000008ec8bee000  r9=00007ff6db1c1005 r10=00007ff8ea5d7c90
r11=0000000000000000 r12=0000000000000000 r13=0000000000000000
r14=0000000000000000 r15=0000000000000000
iopl=0         nv up ei pl nz na pe nc
cs=0033  ss=002b  ds=002b  es=002b  fs=0053  gs=002b             efl=00000202
PointersProject!main+0x25:
00007ff6`db1c1035 ret
```

We again check the memory location of the **b** variable to see that it has really changed its value:

```
0:000> dd PointersProject!b L1
00007ff6`db1c4004  00000004
```

228 Multiplying Numbers Using Pointers

All this corresponds to a memory layout shown in Picture x64.4.5.

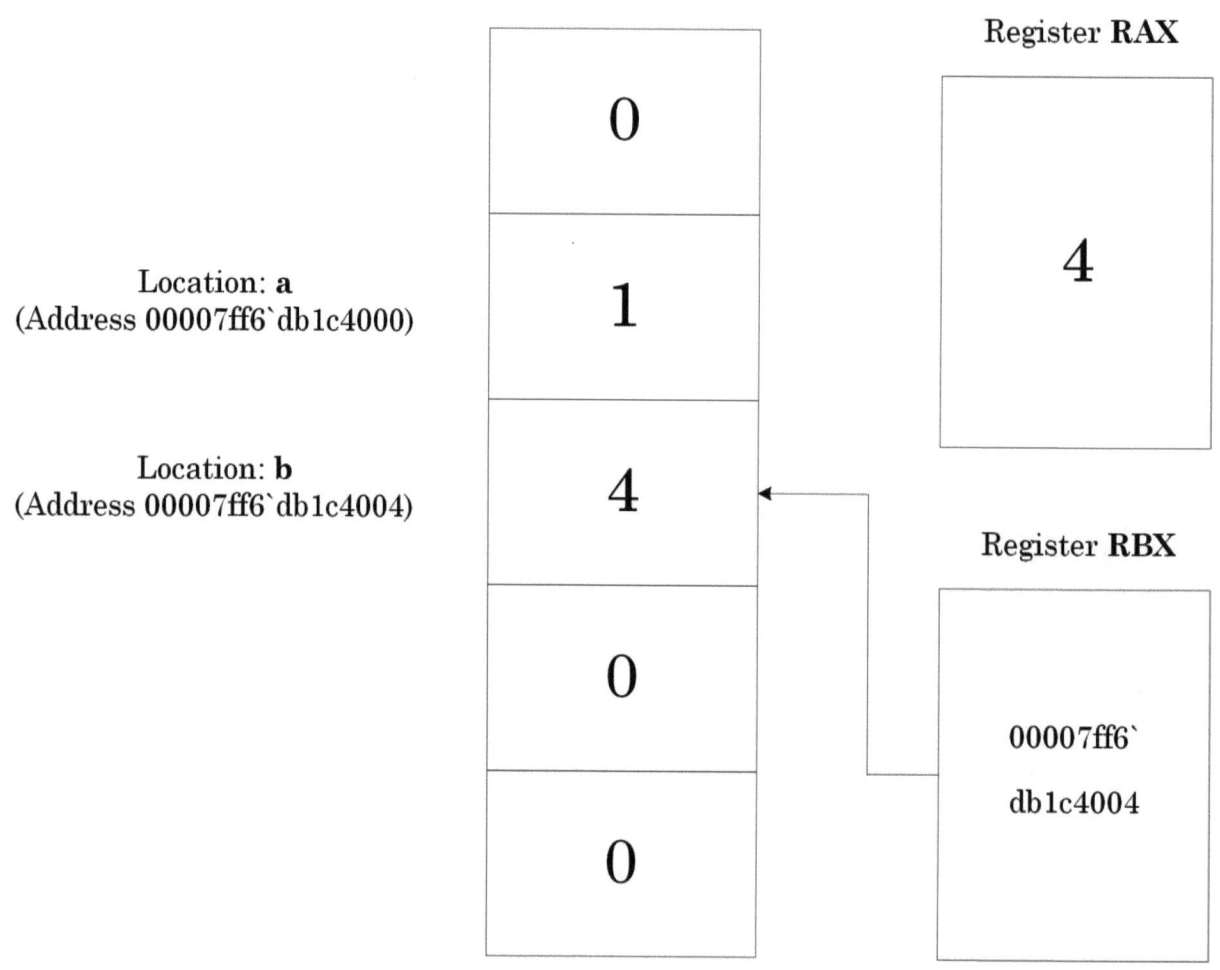

Picture x64.4.5

Chapter x64.5: Bytes, Words, and Double Words

Using Hexadecimal Numbers

If we want to use hexadecimal numbers in C language we prefix them with **0x**, for example:

```
a = 12;    // 12_dec

a = 0xC;   // C_hex
```

In WinDbg disassembly output, and when entering commands, numbers are interpreted as hexadecimal by default, although we can still prefix them with **0x**. If we want a number to be interpreted as decimal, we prefix it with **0n**, for example:

```
mov  [a], 0n12

mov  [a], C

mov  [a], 0xC
```

or the suffix '**h**' is used to disambiguate between decimal and hexadecimal, for example:

```
mov  [a], 52h
```

Byte Granularity

Picture x64.5.1 shows the difference between bytes, words, double words, and quad words in terms of byte granularity. We see that each successive size is double the previous.

Byte	Byte							
Word	Byte	Byte						
Double Word	Byte	Byte	Byte	Byte				
Quad Word	Byte	Byte	Byte	Byte	Byte	Byte	Byte	Byte

Picture x64.5.1

Bit Granularity

Every byte consists of 8 bits. Every bit has a value of 0 or 1. Here are some examples of bytes, words, double words, and quad words shown as bit strings (we can also see clearly the correspondence between 4-bit sequences and hexadecimal numbers, Table x64.3.1):

- Byte

    C/C++: unsigned char, uint8_t (C++11), char8_t (C++20)

    Windows definitions: BYTE, UCHAR

    8 bits

    Values 0_{dec} - 255_{dec} or 0_{hex} - FF_{hex}

    Example: 12_{dec} 00001100_{bin} $0C_{hex}$

- Word

    C/C++: unsigned short, uint16_t (C++11)

    Windows definitions: USHORT, WORD

    16 bits

    Values 0_{dec} - 65535_{dec} or 0_{hex} - $FFFF_{hex}$

    Example: 0000000000001100_{bin} $000C_{hex}$

- Double word

    C/C++ (ILP32, int, long, and pointer are 32-bit):

    unsigned int, unsigned, unsigned long, uint32_t (C++11)

    Windows definitions (Win32 API): DWORD, UINT, ULONG

    32 bits

    Values 0_{dec} - 4294967295_{dec} or 0_{hex} - $FFFFFFFF_{hex}$

    Example: $00000000000000000000000000001100_{bin}$

      $0000000C_{hex}$

- Quad word

    C / C++: unsigned long long, uint64_t (C++11)

    Windows definitions: unsigned _int64, QWORD, ULONG_PTR

    64 bits

    Values 0_{dec} - $18446744073709551615_{dec}$ or

    0_{hex} - $FFFFFFFFFFFFFFFF_{hex}$

    Example: $0000000000000000000000000000000000000000000000000000000000001100_{bin}$

    $000000000000000C_{hex}$

Memory Layout

The minimum addressable element of memory is a byte. The maximum addressable element is a **double word** or **dword** on 32-bit machines and a **quad word** or **qword** on 64-bit machines. All general registers are 32-bit on 32-bit processors or presented as such when the 32-bit mode is emulated on 64-bit processors and can contain double word values. Picture x64.5.2 shows a typical memory layout, and Picture x64.5.3 shows the byte layout of some general CPU registers.

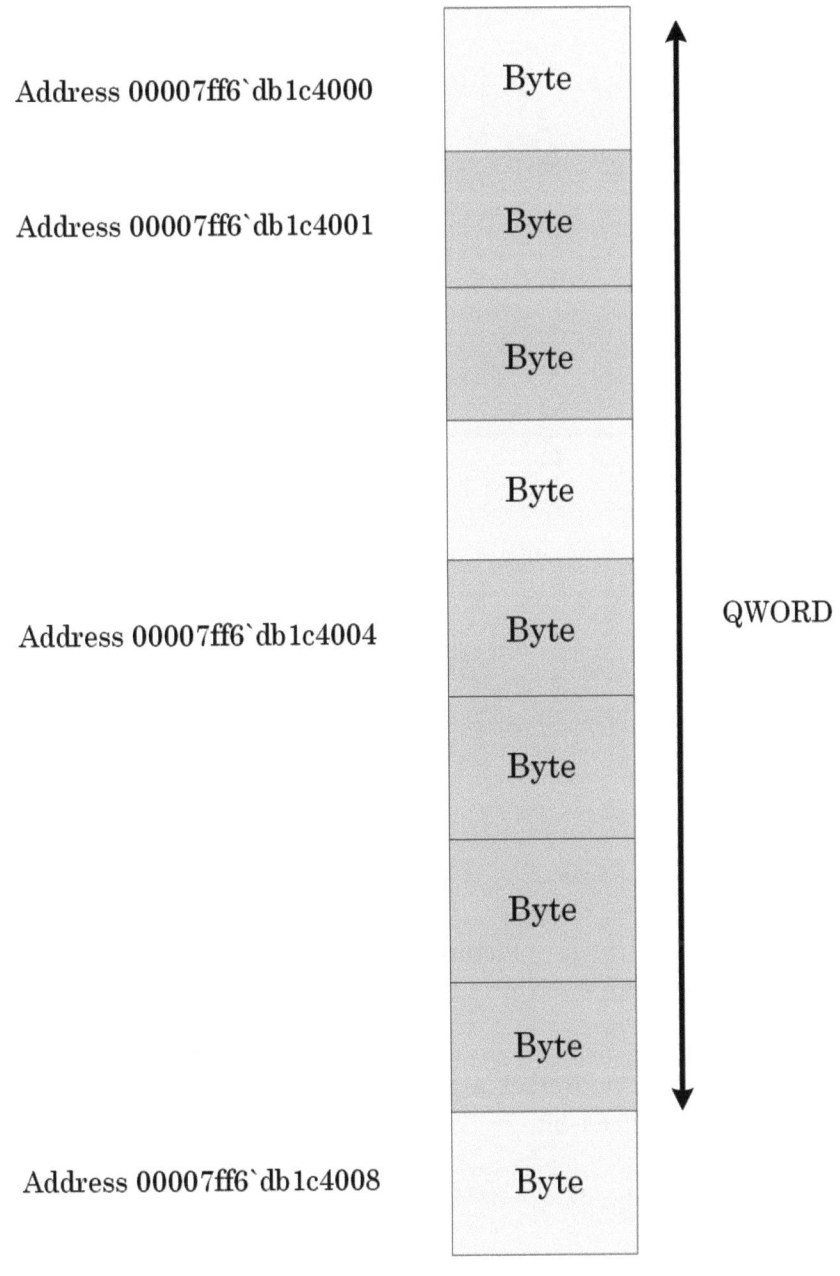

Picture x64.5.2

Memory Layout

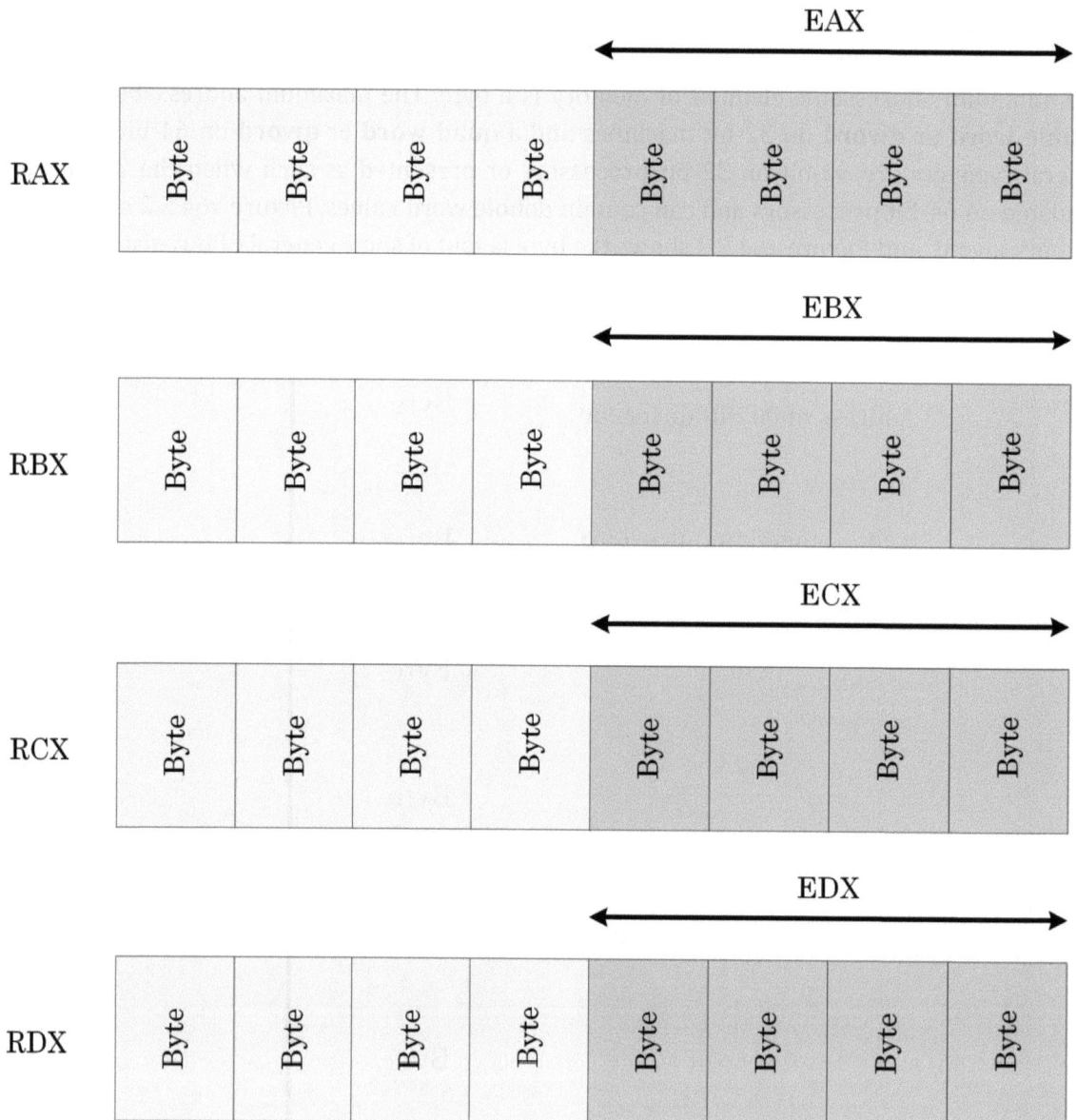

Picture x64.5.3

Remember that memory addresses are always 64-bit, and memory addresses of 32-bit memory cells like integers are also 64-bit.

Chapter x64.6: Pointers to Memory

Pointers Revisited

The pointer is a memory cell or a register that contains the address of another memory cell. Memory pointers have their own addresses because they are memory cells too. On 32-bit Windows, pointers are always 32-bit. On 64-bit Windows, pointers are 64-bit except in emulation mode when executing 32-bit applications and services.

Addressing Types

As seen in Chapter x64.5, memory cells can be of one byte, one word, double word, or quad word sizes. Therefore, we can have a pointer to a byte (**byte ptr**), a pointer to a word (**word ptr**), a pointer to a double word (**dword ptr**), and a pointer to a quad word (**qword ptr**). For example, WinDbg disassembly output in Chapter x64.4 has **dword ptr** prefixes in instructions involving pointers to memory that hold 32-bit (dword size) values.

Here are some illustrated examples:

```
mov   byte ptr [rax], 0xFF
```

The layout of memory before instruction execution is shown in Picture x64.6.1, and the layout of memory after execution is shown in Picture x64.6.2.

```
mov   word ptr [rax], 0xFF
```

```
mov   dword ptr [rax], 0xFF
```

The layout of memory before instruction execution is shown in Picture x64.6.3, and the layout of memory after execution is shown in Picture x64.6.4. We can see that, although we specify just one byte 0xFF as a source operand to MOV instruction, it replaces all other 3 bytes of a double word in memory because we specify the destination as a pointer to 4 bytes, and 0xFF is really 0x000000FF as a double word. So we need to specify the **dword ptr** prefix to disambiguate moving a double word value from moving a byte value. Because we have 64-bit (quad word) registers, we need to specify the **qword ptr** prefix to disambiguate moving a quad word value from moving a byte value. In the following equivalent instruction, we don't need to specify the **qword ptr** prefix:

```
mov   [rax], 0x00000000000000FF
```

However, if we want to move a double word value only, we need to specify the **dword ptr** prefix:

```
mov   dword ptr [rax], 0xFF
```

This is equivalent to:

```
mov   dword ptr [rax], 0x000000FF
```

Picture x64.6.5 shows a summary of various addressing modes.

Chapter x64.6: Pointers to Memory

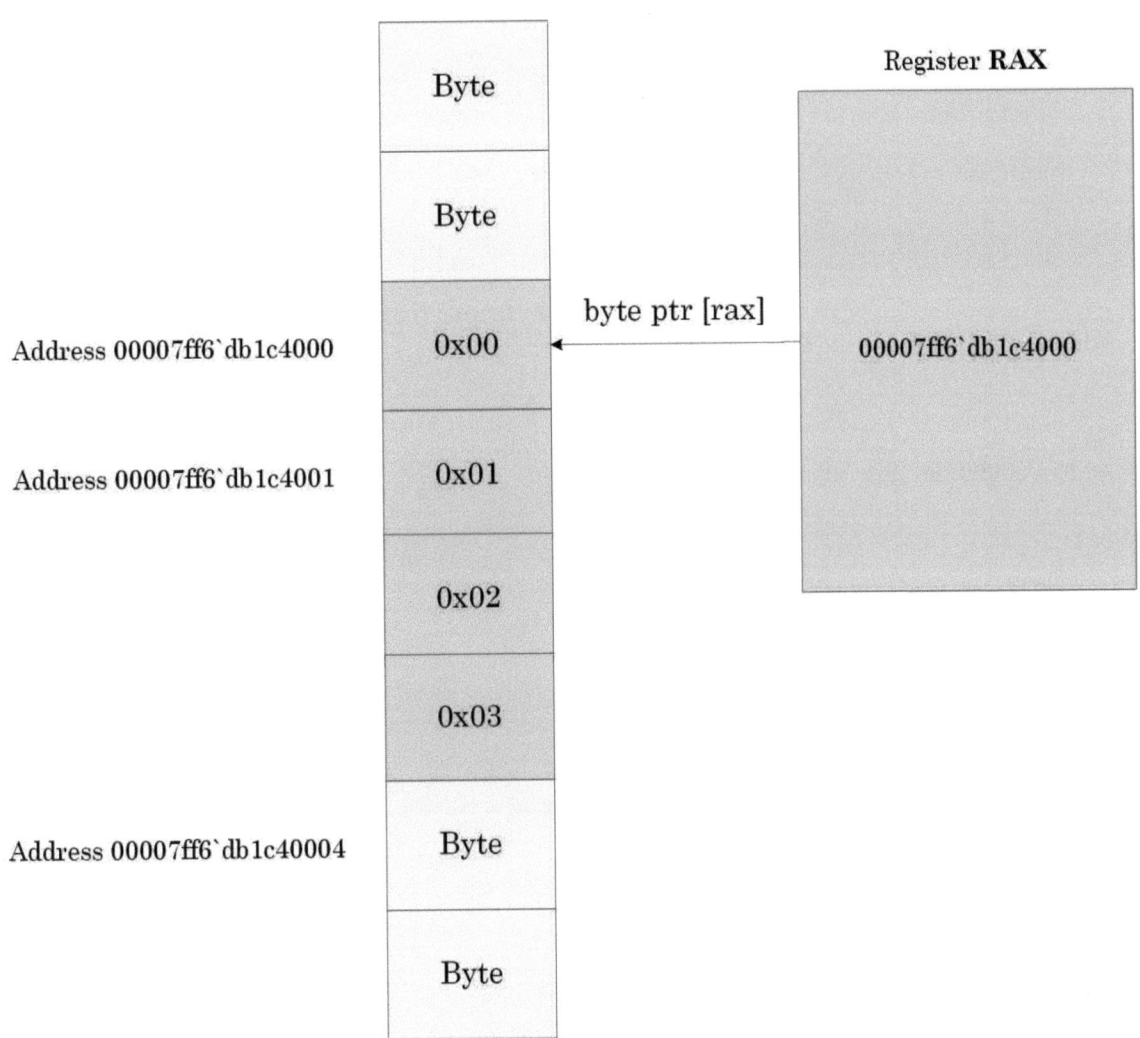

Picture x64.6.1

238 Addressing Types

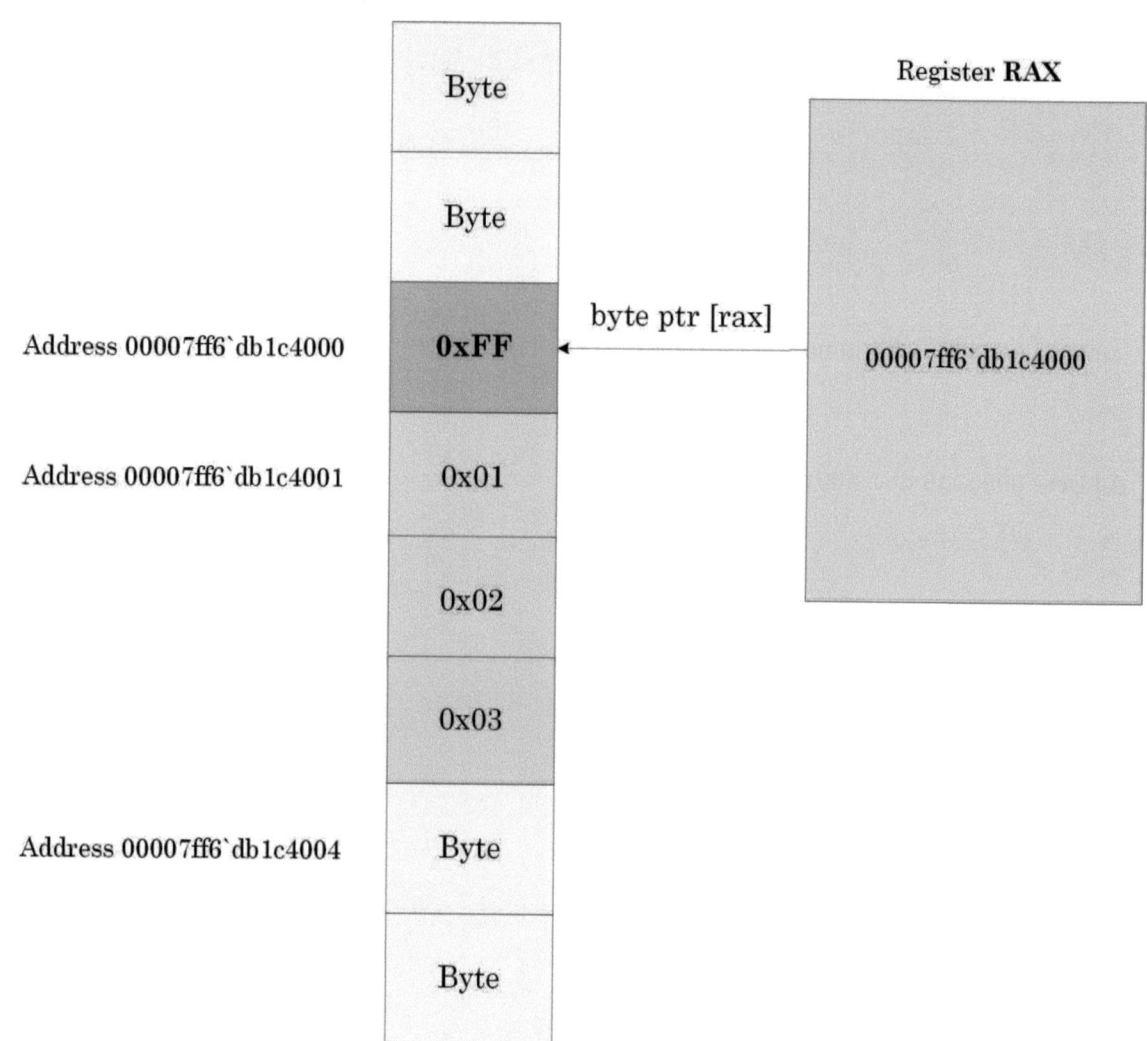

Picture x64.6.2

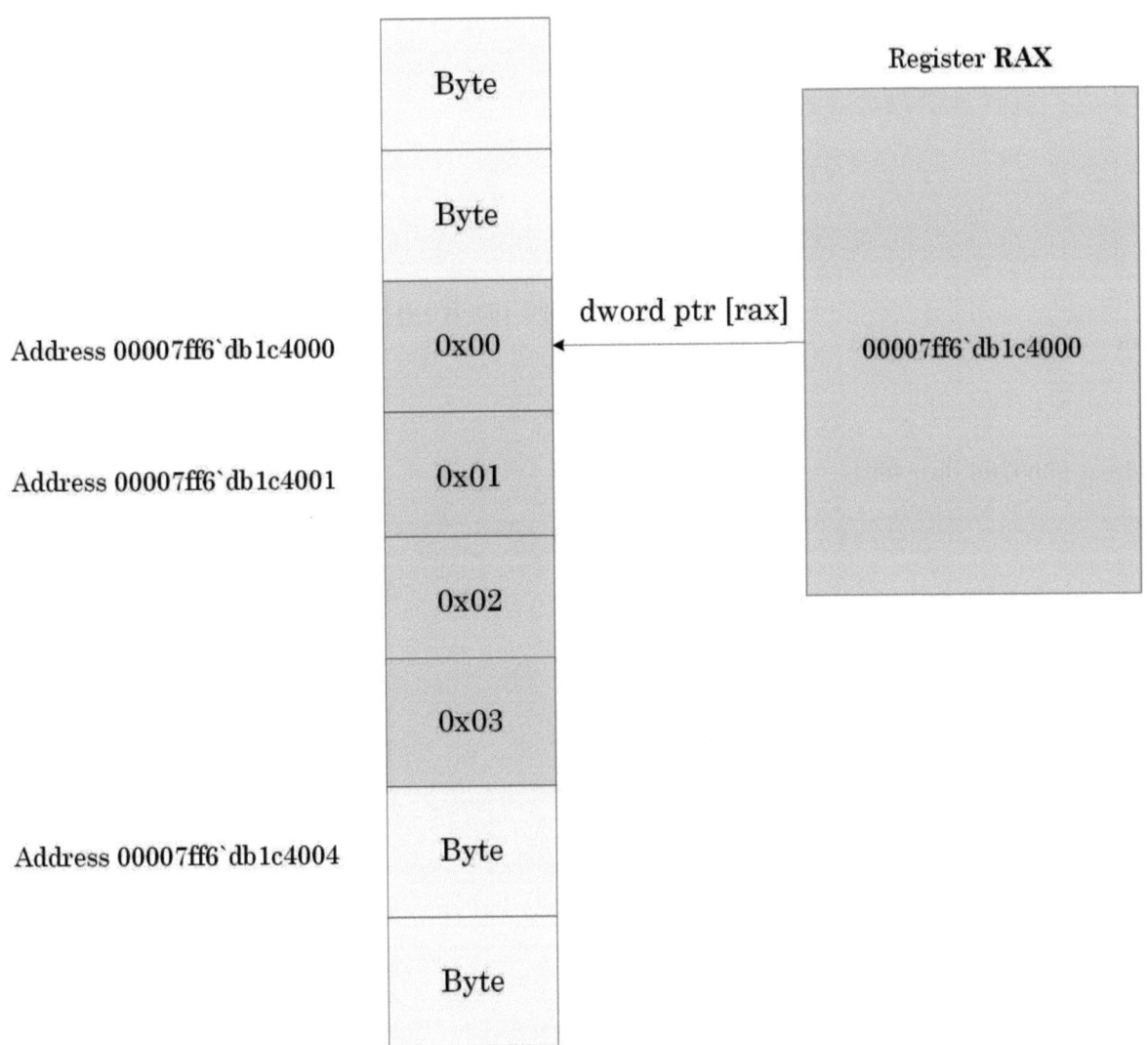

Picture x64.6.3

240 Addressing Types

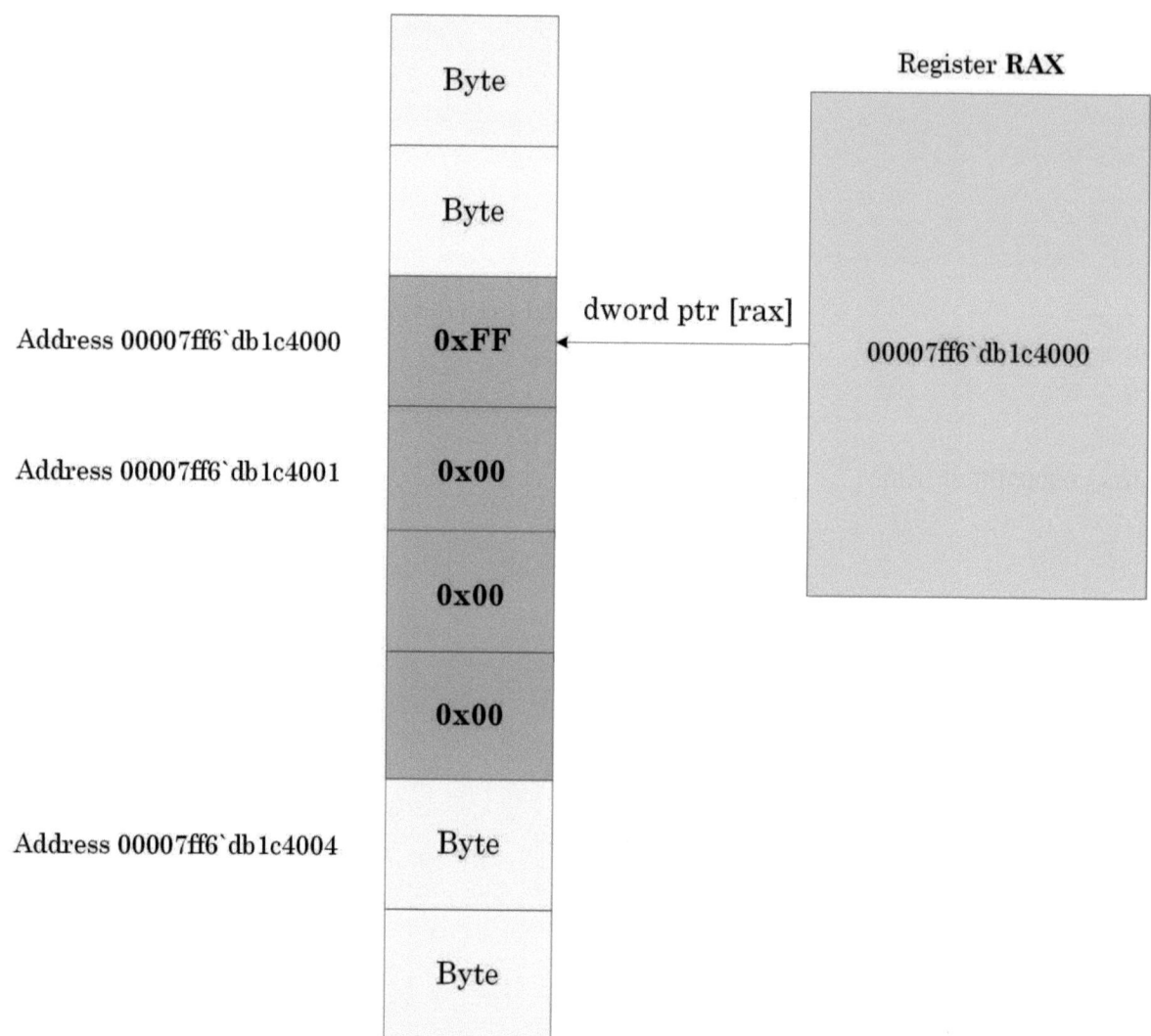

Picture x64.6.4

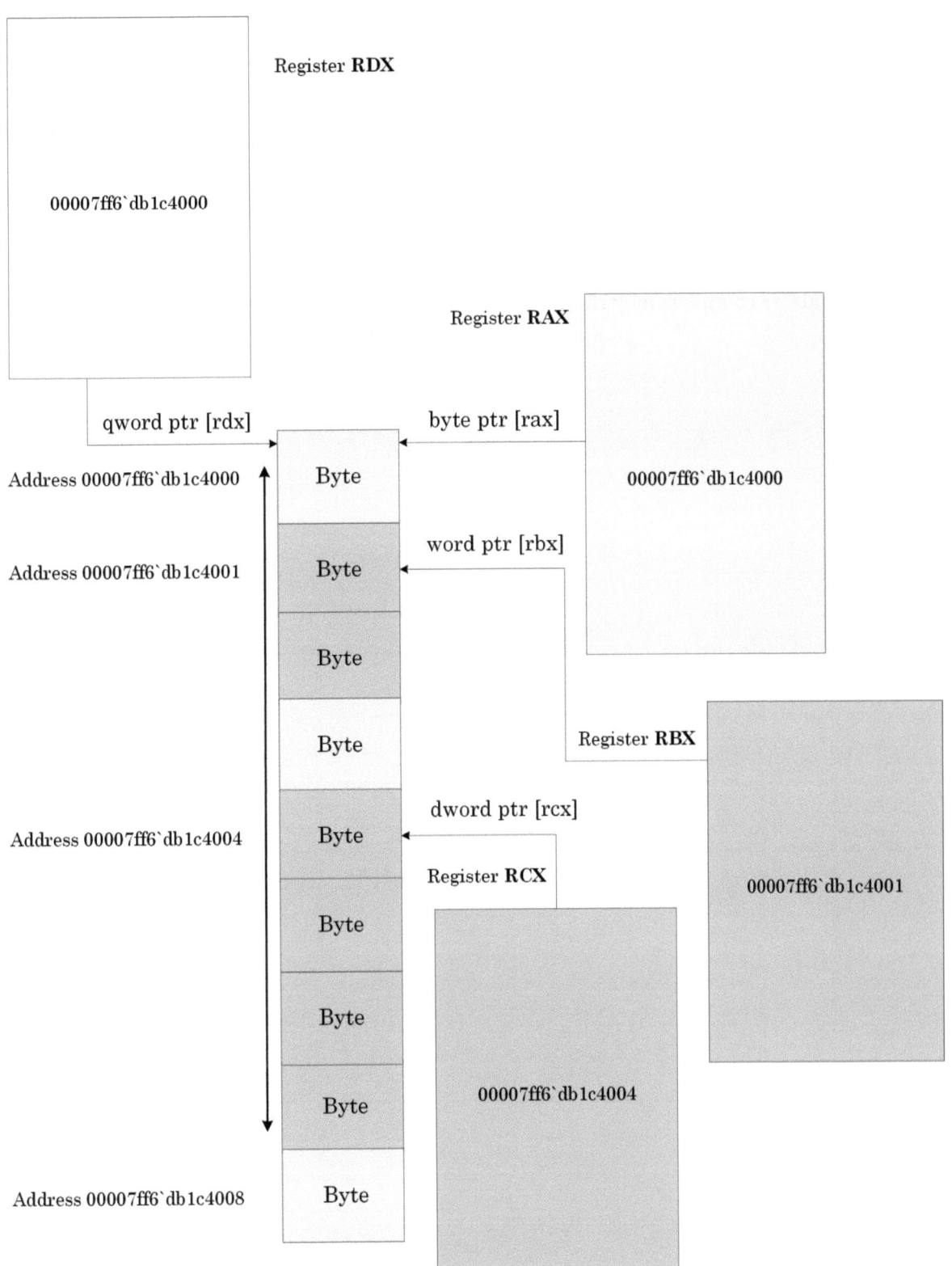

Picture x64.6.5

Registers Revisited

RAX, RBX, RCX, and RDX 64-bit registers can be used as pointers to memory. They contain x86 32-bit registers EAX, EBX, ECX, and EDX. These 32-bit parts contain old 16-bit registers AX, BX, CX, and DX (each can hold a word). RCX register was often used as a loop counter, R(Counter)X, in assembly language corresponding to simple loops in C and C++ code

```
for (int i = 0; i < N ; ++i)
```

but modern C and C++ compilers may choose to use any other register or even a memory location for such a purpose.

NULL Pointers

Addresses 0x00000000`00000000 – 0x00000000`0000FFFF are specifically made inaccessible on Windows. The following code will force an application crash or BSOD if executed inside a driver:

```
mov   rax, 0xF
mov   [rax], 1   ; Access violation
```

Invalid Pointers

There are different kinds of invalid pointers that cause an access violation when we try to dereference them:

- NULL pointers
- Pointers to inaccessible memory
- Pointers to read-only memory when writing

Other pointers may or may not cause an access violation, and some of them are discussed in subsequent chapters:

- Pointers pointing to "random" memory
- Uninitialized pointers having random values inherited from past code execution
- Dangling pointers

The last pointers are similar to pointers pointing to "random" memory locations and arise when we forget to set pointer variables to zero (NULL) after disposing (deallocating) of the memory they point to. By nullifying pointers, we indicate that they no longer point to memory.

Variables as Pointers

Suppose we have two memory addresses (locations) "a" and "b" declared and defined in C and C++ as:

`int a, b;`

These are normal variables "a" and "b". In addition, we can have another two memory addresses (locations) "pa" and "pb" declared and defined in C and C++ as:

`int *pa, *pb;`

Here **pa** is a pointer to an *int* or, in other words, the memory cell **pa** contains the address of another memory cell that contains an integer value.

Pointer Initialization

In order to have pointers to point to memory we need to initialize them with corresponding memory addresses. Here is typical C or C++ code that does what we need:

```
int a;              // uninitialized variable

int *pa;            // uninitialized pointer

pa = &a;            // [pa] now contains the address a

int b = 12;         // initialized variable

int *pb = &b;       // initialized pointer
```

We see that pointers are also variables and can change their values, effectively pointing to different memory locations during program execution.

Note: Initialized and Uninitialized Data

A bit of additional information about initialized and uninitialized variables that is useful to know: an executable program on Windows is divided into different sections. One of them is called **.data**, where all global and static variables (including pointers) are put.

Consider this C or C++ data definition:

```
int array[1000000]; // size 4,000,000 bytes or 3.8Mb
```

We would expect the size of the .EXE file to be about 4Mb. However, the program size on a disk is only 32Kb. It is because the uninitialized array contains only information about its size. When we launch the program, this array is recreated from its size information and filled with zeroes. The size of the program in memory becomes about 4Mb.

In the case of the initialized array, the program size on disk is 4.7Mb:

```
int array[1000000] = { 12 };
```

This is because the array was put into a **.data** section and contains the following sequence of integers { 12, 0, 0, 0, 0 ... }.

More Pseudo Notation

We remind that **[a]** means contents of memory at the address **a**, **dword ptr [rax]** means contents of a 32-bit memory cell at the address stored in the RAX register (here, RAX is a pointer).

We also introduce an additional notation to employ in this chapter, and subsequent chapters: ***[pa]** means contents at the address stored at the address **pa** and is called dereferencing a pointer whose address is **pa**. The corresponding C code is similar:

```
int *pa = &a;

int b = *pa;
```

"MemoryPointers" Project: Memory Layout

This project is very similar to the "Pointers" project from Chapter x64.4. We have this data declaration and definition in C or C++ language:

int a, b;

int *pa, *pb = &b;

The project code corresponds to the following pseudo-code and assembly language:

[pa] <- address a		lea rax, a
		mov [pa],rax
*[pa] <- 1	; [a] = 1	mov rax, [pa]
		mov dword ptr [rax], 1
*[pb] <- 1	; [b] = 1	mov rbx, [pb]
		mov dword ptr [rbx], 1
*[pb] <- *[pb] + *[pa]	; [b]=2	mov ecx, dword ptr [rax]
		add ecx, dword ptr [rbx]
		mov dword ptr [rbx], ecx

The project for this chapter can be downloaded from:

https://bitbucket.org/softwarediagnostics/pfwddr2/src/master/x64/Chapter6/

We can load the executable into WinDbg and disassemble its *main* function as described in Chapter x64.2 or Chapter x64.4.

First, we load *MemoryPointers.exe* using File\Open Executable… menu option in WinDbg and get the following output (the output, especially addresses, may differ for your Windows version):

"MemoryPointers" Project: Memory Layout

```
Microsoft (R) Windows Debugger Version 10.0.22000.194 AMD64
Copyright (c) Microsoft Corporation. All rights reserved.

CommandLine: C:\PFWDDR2\x64\Chapter6\MemoryPointers.exe

************* Path validation summary **************
Response                     Time (ms)     Location
Deferred                                   srv*
Symbol search path is: srv*
Executable search path is:
ModLoad: 00007ff6`66ab0000 00007ff6`66ab6000   MemoryPointers.exe
ModLoad: 00007ff8`eb5c0000 00007ff8`eb7c9000   ntdll.dll
ModLoad: 00007ff8`ea540000 00007ff8`ea5fd000   C:\WINDOWS\System32\KERNEL32.DLL
ModLoad: 00007ff8`e8b20000 00007ff8`e8e94000   C:\WINDOWS\System32\KERNELBASE.dll
(3968.6884): Break instruction exception - code 80000003 (first chance)
ntdll!LdrpDoDebuggerBreak+0x30:
00007ff8`eb69cc74 cc              int     3
```

We allow the output of registers:

```
0:000> .prompt_allow +reg
Allow the following information to be displayed at the prompt:
(Other settings can affect whether the information is actually displayed)
    sym - Symbol for current instruction
    dis - Disassembly of current instruction
     ea - Effective address for current instruction
    reg - Register state
    src - Source info for current instruction
Do not allow the following information to be displayed at the prompt:
  None
```

Then we put a breakpoint to the *main* function and run the program until WinDbg breaks in:

```
0:000> bp MemoryPointers!main
*** WARNING: Unable to verify checksum for MemoryPointers.exe
```

For visual clarity, we disable the output of binary codes:

```
0:000> .asm no_code_bytes
Assembly options: no_code_bytes
```

```
0:000> g
Breakpoint 0 hit
rax=00007ff666ab1005 rbx=0000000000000000 rcx=000000a3e515d000
rdx=00007ff666ab1005 rsi=0000000000000000 rdi=0000000000000000
rip=00007ff666ab1010 rsp=000000a3e52ff7d8 rbp=0000000000000000
 r8=000000a3e515d000  r9=00007ff666ab1005 r10=00007ff8ea5d7c90
r11=0000000000000000 r12=0000000000000000 r13=0000000000000000
r14=0000000000000000 r15=0000000000000000
iopl=0         nv up ei pl zr na po nc
cs=0033  ss=002b  ds=002b  es=002b  fs=0053  gs=002b             efl=00000246
MemoryPointers!main:
00007ff6`66ab1010 lea     rax,[MemoryPointers!a (00007ff6`66ab4000)]
```

We disassemble the *main* function:

```
0:000> uf main
MemoryPointers!main [C:\NewWork\WDPF-X64\MemoryPointers\MemoryPointers.asm @ 14]:
   14 00007ff6`66ab1010 lea     rax,[MemoryPointers!a (00007ff6`66ab4000)]
   17 00007ff6`66ab1017 mov     qword ptr [MemoryPointers!pa (00007ff6`66ab4008)],rax
   19 00007ff6`66ab101e mov     rax,qword ptr [MemoryPointers!pa (00007ff6`66ab4008)]
   20 00007ff6`66ab1025 mov     dword ptr [rax],1
   22 00007ff6`66ab102b mov     rbx,qword ptr [MemoryPointers!pb (00007ff6`66ab4010)]
   23 00007ff6`66ab1032 mov     dword ptr [rbx],1
   25 00007ff6`66ab1038 mov     ecx,dword ptr [rax]
   26 00007ff6`66ab103a add     ecx,dword ptr [rbx]
   28 00007ff6`66ab103c mov     dword ptr [rbx],ecx
   30 00007ff6`66ab103e ret
```

Then we clear RAX, RBX, and RCX registers to set up a memory layout that is easy to follow:

```
0:000> r rax = 0
```

```
0:000> r rbx = 0
```

```
0:000> r rcx = 0
```

"MemoryPointers" Project: Memory Layout

```
0:000> r
rax=0000000000000000 rbx=0000000000000000 rcx=0000000000000000
rdx=00007ff666ab1005 rsi=0000000000000000 rdi=0000000000000000
rip=00007ff666ab1010 rsp=000000a3e52ff7d8 rbp=0000000000000000
 r8=000000a3e515d000  r9=00007ff666ab1005 r10=00007ff8ea5d7c90
r11=0000000000000000 r12=0000000000000000 r13=0000000000000000
r14=0000000000000000 r15=0000000000000000
iopl=0         nv up ei pl zr na po nc
cs=0033  ss=002b  ds=002b  es=002b  fs=0053  gs=002b             efl=00000246
MemoryPointers!main:
00007ff6`66ab1010 lea     rax,[MemoryPointers!a (00007ff6`66ab4000)]
```

We check the values and addresses of **a**, **b**, **pa**, and **pb** variables:

```
0:000> dd MemoryPointers!a L1
00007ff6`66ab4000  00000000
```

```
0:000> dd MemoryPointers!b L1
00007ff6`66ab4004  00000000
```

For pointers we use **dq** (**d**ump **q**uad word) WinDbg command:

```
0:000> dq MemoryPointers!pa L1
00007ff6`66ab4008  00000000`00000000
```

```
0:000> dq MemoryPointers!pb L1
00007ff6`66ab4010  00007ff6`66ab4004
```

These values correspond to the memory layout before executing the first LEA instruction, and it is shown in Picture x64.6.6.

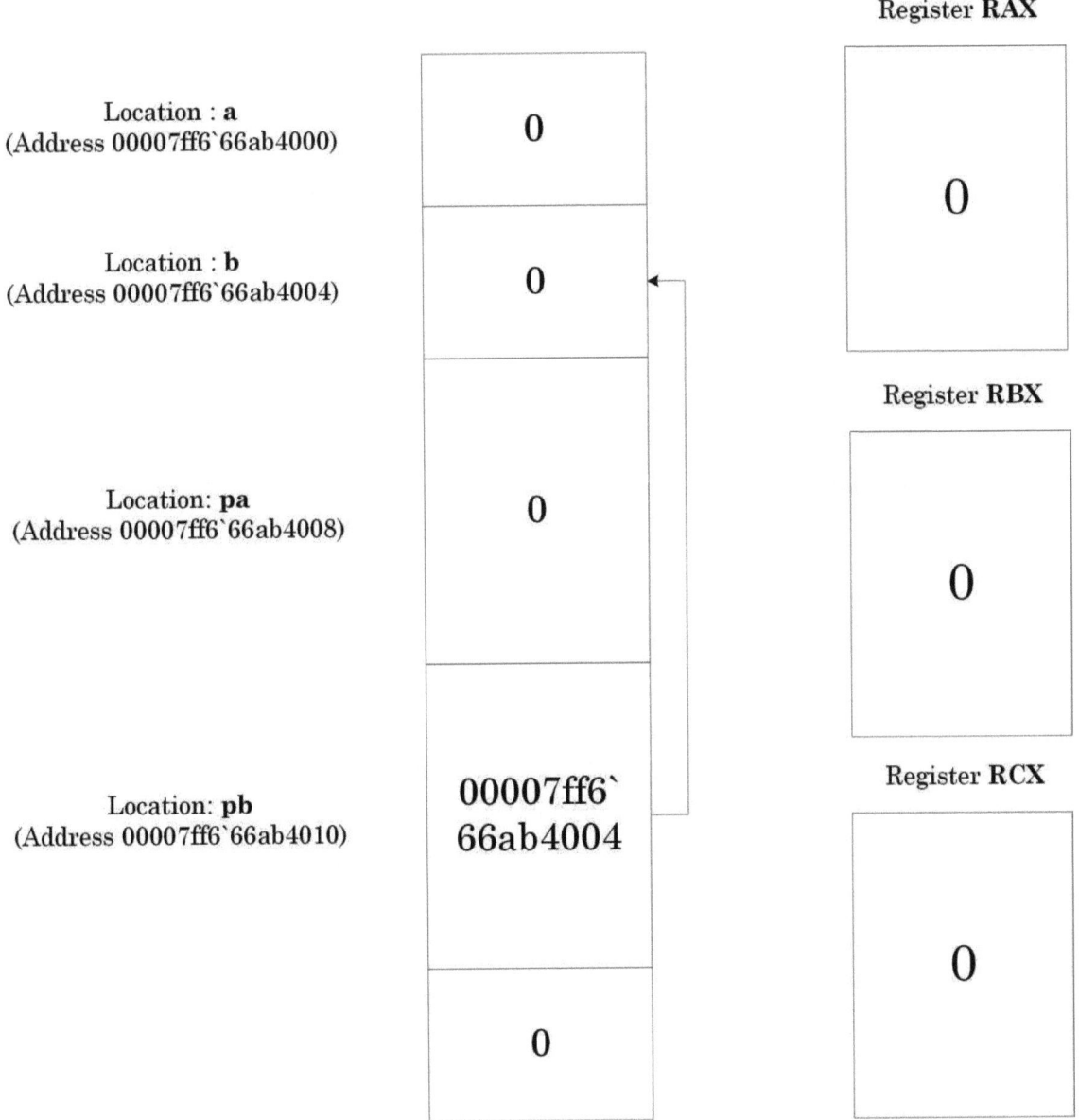

Picture x64.6.6

We then execute our code step by step (changes are in bold):

```
0:000> t; t
rax=00007ff666ab4000 rbx=0000000000000000 rcx=0000000000000000
rdx=00007ff666ab1005 rsi=0000000000000000 rdi=0000000000000000
rip=00007ff666ab101e rsp=000000a3e52ff7d8 rbp=0000000000000000
 r8=000000a3e515d000  r9=00007ff666ab1005 r10=00007ff8ea5d7c90
r11=0000000000000000 r12=0000000000000000 r13=0000000000000000
r14=0000000000000000 r15=0000000000000000
iopl=0         nv up ei pl zr na po nc
cs=0033  ss=002b  ds=002b  es=002b  fs=0053  gs=002b             efl=00000246
MemoryPointers!main+0xe:
00007ff6`66ab101e mov     rax,qword ptr [MemoryPointers!pa (00007ff6`66ab4008)]
ds:00007ff6`66ab4008={MemoryPointers!a (00007ff6`66ab4000)}
```

```
0:000> dq MemoryPointers!pa L1
00007ff6`66ab4008  00007ff6`66ab4000
```

```
0:000> t; t
rax=00007ff666ab4000 rbx=0000000000000000 rcx=0000000000000000
rdx=00007ff666ab1005 rsi=0000000000000000 rdi=0000000000000000
rip=00007ff666ab102b rsp=000000a3e52ff7d8 rbp=0000000000000000
 r8=000000a3e515d000  r9=00007ff666ab1005 r10=00007ff8ea5d7c90
r11=0000000000000000 r12=0000000000000000 r13=0000000000000000
r14=0000000000000000 r15=0000000000000000
iopl=0         nv up ei pl zr na po nc
cs=0033  ss=002b  ds=002b  es=002b  fs=0053  gs=002b             efl=00000246
MemoryPointers!main+0x1b:
00007ff6`66ab102b mov     rbx,qword ptr [MemoryPointers!pb (00007ff6`66ab4010)]
ds:00007ff6`66ab4010={MemoryPointers!b (00007ff6`66ab4004)}
```

```
0:000> dd MemoryPointers!a L1
00007ff6`66ab4000  00000001
```

We can also use @ prefix before a register to interpret its value as a pointer and dereference it:

```
0:000> dd @rax L1
00007ff6`66ab4000  00000001
```

```
0:000> t; t
rax=00007ff666ab4000 rbx=00007ff666ab4004 rcx=0000000000000000
rdx=00007ff666ab1005 rsi=0000000000000000 rdi=0000000000000000
rip=00007ff666ab1038 rsp=000000a3e52ff7d8 rbp=0000000000000000
 r8=000000a3e515d000  r9=00007ff666ab1005 r10=00007ff8ea5d7c90
r11=0000000000000000 r12=0000000000000000 r13=0000000000000000
r14=0000000000000000 r15=0000000000000000
iopl=0         nv up ei pl zr na po nc
cs=0033  ss=002b  ds=002b  es=002b  fs=0053  gs=002b             efl=00000246
MemoryPointers!main+0x28:
00007ff6`66ab1038 mov     ecx,dword ptr [rax]    ds:00007ff6`66ab4000=00000001

0:000> dd MemoryPointers!b L1
00007ff6`66ab4004  00000001

0:000> dd @rbx L1
00007ff6`66ab4004  00000001

0:000> t
rax=00007ff666ab4000 rbx=00007ff666ab4004 rcx=0000000000000001
rdx=00007ff666ab1005 rsi=0000000000000000 rdi=0000000000000000
rip=00007ff666ab103a rsp=000000a3e52ff7d8 rbp=0000000000000000
 r8=000000a3e515d000  r9=00007ff666ab1005 r10=00007ff8ea5d7c90
r11=0000000000000000 r12=0000000000000000 r13=0000000000000000
r14=0000000000000000 r15=0000000000000000
iopl=0         nv up ei pl zr na po nc
cs=0033  ss=002b  ds=002b  es=002b  fs=0053  gs=002b             efl=00000246
MemoryPointers!main+0x2a:
00007ff6`66ab103a add     ecx,dword ptr [rbx]    ds:00007ff6`66ab4004=00000001
```

```
0:000> t
rax=00007ff666ab4000 rbx=00007ff666ab4004 rcx=0000000000000002
rdx=00007ff666ab1005 rsi=0000000000000000 rdi=0000000000000000
rip=00007ff666ab103c rsp=000000a3e52ff7d8 rbp=0000000000000000
 r8=000000a3e515d000  r9=00007ff666ab1005 r10=00007ff8ea5d7c90
r11=0000000000000000 r12=0000000000000000 r13=0000000000000000
r14=0000000000000000 r15=0000000000000000
iopl=0         nv up ei pl nz na pe nc
cs=0033  ss=002b  ds=002b  es=002b  fs=0053  gs=002b             efl=00000202
MemoryPointers!main+0x2c:
00007ff6`66ab103c mov     dword ptr [rbx],ecx    ds:00007ff6`66ab4004=00000001
```

```
0:000> t
rax=00007ff666ab4000 rbx=00007ff666ab4004 rcx=0000000000000002
rdx=00007ff666ab1005 rsi=0000000000000000 rdi=0000000000000000
rip=00007ff666ab103e rsp=000000a3e52ff7d8 rbp=0000000000000000
 r8=000000a3e515d000  r9=00007ff666ab1005 r10=00007ff8ea5d7c90
r11=0000000000000000 r12=0000000000000000 r13=0000000000000000
r14=0000000000000000 r15=0000000000000000
iopl=0         nv up ei pl nz na pe nc
cs=0033  ss=002b  ds=002b  es=002b  fs=0053  gs=002b             efl=00000202
MemoryPointers!main+0x2e:
00007ff6`66ab103e ret
```

```
0:000> dd MemoryPointers!b L1
00007ff6`66ab4004  00000002
```

```
0:000> dd @rbx L1
00007ff6`66ab4004  00000002
```

Final memory layout and registers are shown in Picture x64.6.7.

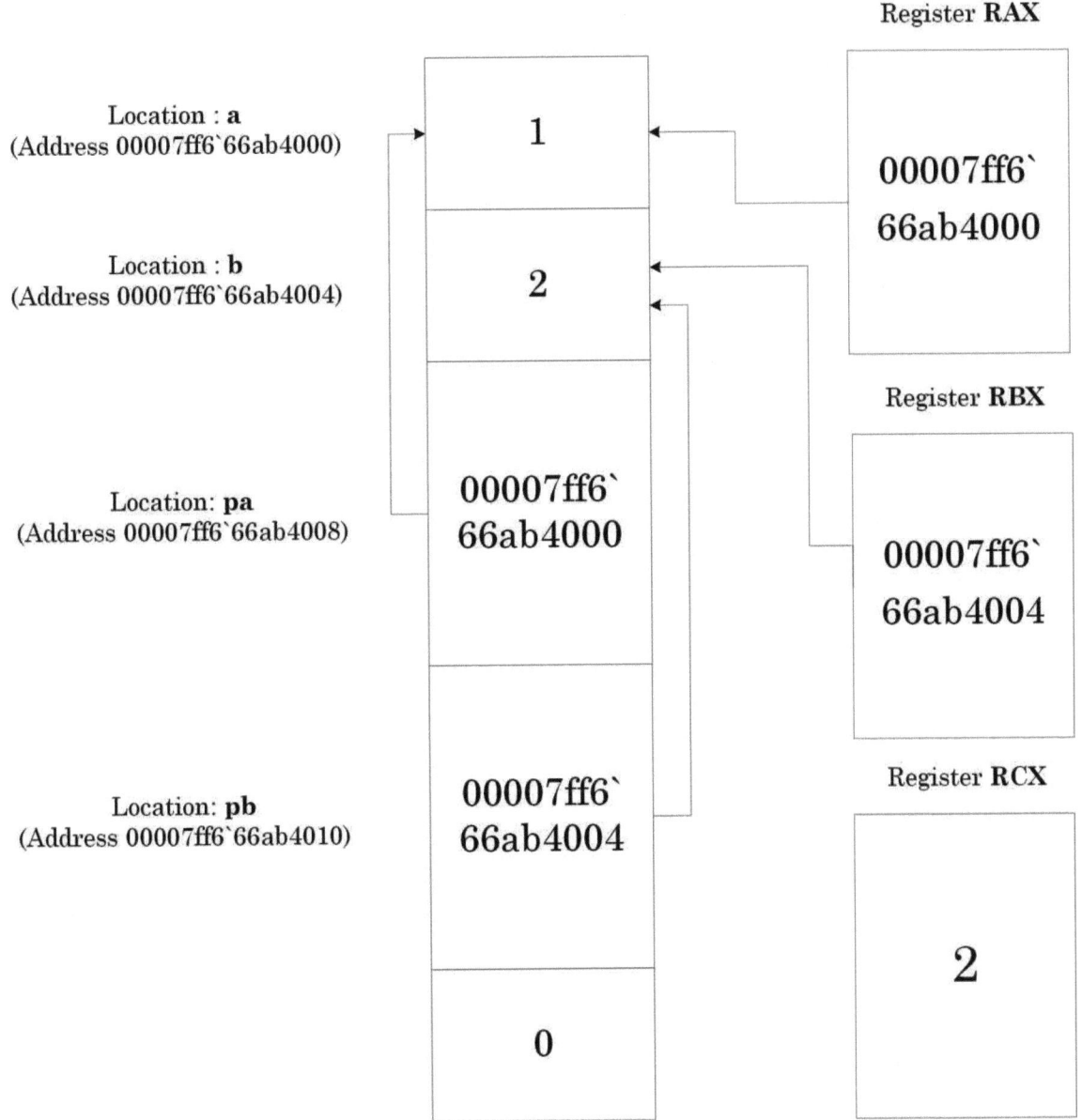

Picture x64.6.7

Chapter x64.7: Logical Instructions and EIP

Instruction Format

We have seen that assembly language instructions have uniform format:

Opcode *operand*

Opcode *destination_operand, source_operand*

Operands can be registers (reg), memory reference (mem) or some number, called immediate value (imm). Typical notational examples:

```
inc   mem/reg
dec   mem/reg
add   mem/reg, reg/imm
add   reg, mem/imm
```

and some concrete assembly language examples:

```
inc   dword ptr [rax]
dec   byte ptr [a]
add   byte ptr [rax], 10
add   rax, qword ptr [a]
```

Logical Shift Instructions

In addition to arithmetic instructions, there are so-called logical shift instructions that just shift a bit string to the left or the right.

Shift to the left:

```
11111111   ->   11111110    ; shift by 1

11111110   ->   11110000    ; shift by 3

shl   mem/reg, imm/reg

shl   rax, 1

shl   byte ptr [rax], 2
```

Shift to the right:

```
11111111   ->   01111111    ; shift by 1

01111111   ->   00001111    ; shift by 3

shr   mem/reg, imm/reg

shr   rax, 1

shr   byte ptr [rax], 2
```

Logical Operations

Here we recall logical operations and corresponding truth tables you probably learned earlier. Here we abbreviate True as T and False as F.

AND

```
1 and 1 = 1    T and T = T
1 and 0 = 0    T and F = F
0 and 1 = 0    F and T = F
0 and 0 = 0    F and F = F
```

OR

```
1 or 1 = 1     T or T = T
1 or 0 = 1     T or F = T
0 or 1 = 1     F or T = T
0 or 0 = 0     F or F = F
```

Zeroing Memory or Registers

There are several ways to put a zero value into a register or a memory location:

1. Move a value:

```
mov   dword ptr [a], 0

mov   rax, 0

mov   eax, 0
```

2. Use XOR (Exclusive OR) logical operation:

```
xor   rax, rax

xor   eax, eax
```

XOR

```
1 xor 1 = 0      T xor T = F

1 xor 0 = 1      T xor F = T

0 xor 1 = 1      F xor T = T

0 xor 0 = 0      F xor F = F
```

This operation clears its destination operand because the source operand is the same, and the same bits are cleared.

Instruction Pointer

Consider these two execution steps from the previous chapter project:

```
0:000> t
rax=00007ff666ab4000 rbx=00007ff666ab4004 rcx=0000000000000002
rdx=00007ff666ab1005 rsi=0000000000000000 rdi=0000000000000000
rip=00007ff666ab103c rsp=000000a3e52ff7d8 rbp=0000000000000000
 r8=000000a3e515d000  r9=00007ff666ab1005 r10=00007ff8ea5d7c90
r11=0000000000000000 r12=0000000000000000 r13=0000000000000000
r14=0000000000000000 r15=0000000000000000
iopl=0         nv up ei pl nz na pe nc
cs=0033  ss=002b  ds=002b  es=002b  fs=0053  gs=002b             efl=00000202
MemoryPointers!main+0x2c:
00007ff6`66ab103c mov     dword ptr [rbx],ecx    ds:00007ff6`66ab4004=00000001

0:000> t
rax=00007ff666ab4000 rbx=00007ff666ab4004 rcx=0000000000000002
rdx=00007ff666ab1005 rsi=0000000000000000 rdi=0000000000000000
rip=00007ff666ab103e rsp=000000a3e52ff7d8 rbp=0000000000000000
 r8=000000a3e515d000  r9=00007ff666ab1005 r10=00007ff8ea5d7c90
r11=0000000000000000 r12=0000000000000000 r13=0000000000000000
r14=0000000000000000 r15=0000000000000000
iopl=0         nv up ei pl nz na pe nc
cs=0033  ss=002b  ds=002b  es=002b  fs=0053  gs=002b             efl=00000202
MemoryPointers!main+0x2e:
00007ff6`66ab103e ret
```

When MOV instruction at 00007ff6`66ab103c address is being executed, the CPU register RIP points to the next instruction at 00007ff6`66ab103e address to be executed. It is shown in Picture x64.7.1.

Chapter x64.7: Logical Instructions and EIP

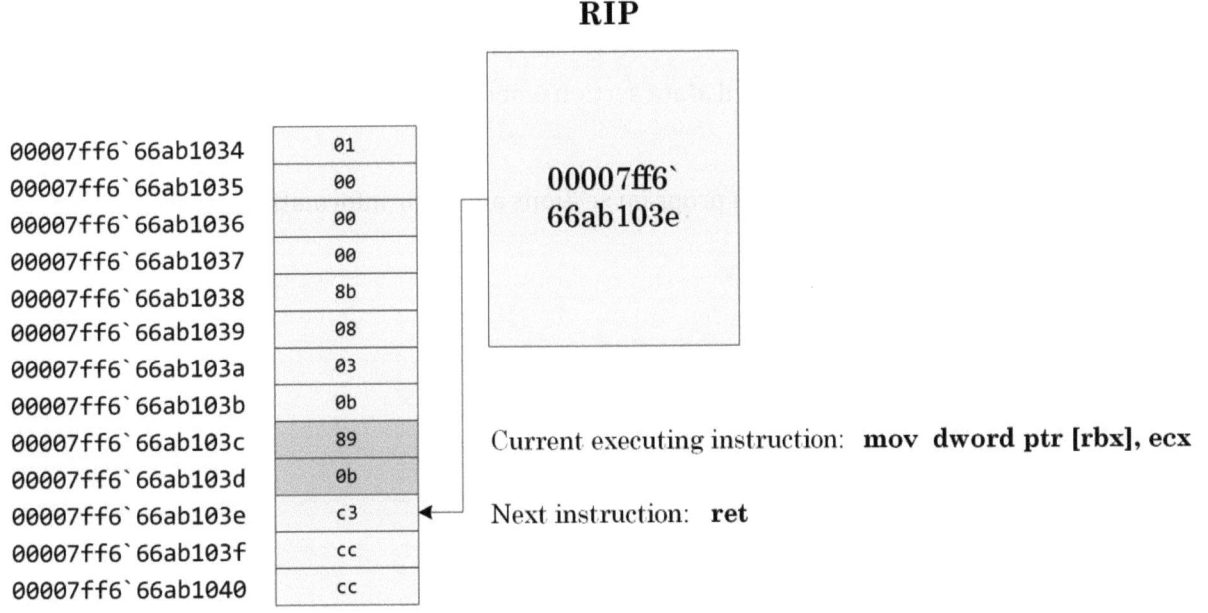

Picture x64.7.1

Note: Code Section

Recall that in Chapter x64.6 we discussed **.data** section where program data is put. The program code is put into **.text** section.

The **!dh** WinDbg command lists various program sections and their information:

```
0:000> !dh MemoryPointers
```

```
File Type: EXECUTABLE IMAGE
FILE HEADER VALUES
    8664 machine (X64)
       4 number of sections
62515299 time date stamp Sat Apr  9 10:32:09 2022

       0 file pointer to symbol table
       0 number of symbols
      F0 size of optional header
      22 characteristics
            Executable
            App can handle >2gb addresses

OPTIONAL HEADER VALUES
     20B magic #
   14.31 linker version
    1200 size of code
     800 size of initialized data
       0 size of uninitialized data
    1005 address of entry point
    1000 base of code
         ----- new -----
00007ff666ab0000 image base
    1000 section alignment
     200 file alignment
       3 subsystem (Windows CUI)
    6.00 operating system version
    0.00 image version
    6.00 subsystem version
    6000 size of image
     400 size of headers
```

```
               0 checksum
0000000000100000 size of stack reserve
0000000000001000 size of stack commit
0000000000100000 size of heap reserve
0000000000001000 size of heap commit
```
[Skipped]

```
SECTION HEADER #1
    .text name
    104E virtual size
    1000 virtual address
    1200 size of raw data
     400 file pointer to raw data
       0 file pointer to relocation table
       0 file pointer to line numbers
       0 number of relocations
       0 number of line numbers
60000020 flags
         Code
         (no align specified)
         Execute Read
```
[Skipped]

```
SECTION HEADER #3
    .data name
     11C virtual size
    4000 virtual address
     200 size of raw data
    1A00 file pointer to raw data
       0 file pointer to relocation table
       0 file pointer to line numbers
       0 number of relocations
       0 number of line numbers
C0000040 flags
         Initialized Data
         (no align specified)
         Read Write
```
[Skipped]

Chapter x64.8: Reconstructing a Program with Pointers

Example of Disassembly Output: No Optimization

The ability to reconstruct approximate C or C++ code from code disassembly is very important in memory dump analysis and debugging.

The project for this chapter can be downloaded from:

https://bitbucket.org/softwarediagnostics/pfwddr2/src/master/x64/Chapter8/

The executable is located under *Debug* subfolder. We load it into WinDbg and disassemble its *main* function.

First, we load *PointersAsVariables.exe* using File\Open Executable... menu option in WinDbg and get the following output (the output, especially addresses, may differ for your Windows version):

```
Microsoft (R) Windows Debugger Version 10.0.22000.194 AMD64
Copyright (c) Microsoft Corporation. All rights reserved.

CommandLine: C:\PFWDDR2\x64\Chapter8\Debug\PointersAsVariables.exe

************* Path validation summary **************
Response                         Time (ms)     Location
Deferred                                       srv*
Symbol search path is: srv*
Executable search path is:
ModLoad: 00007ff7`46010000 00007ff7`4613e000   PointersAsVariables.exe
ModLoad: 00007ff8`eb5c0000 00007ff8`eb7c9000   ntdll.dll
ModLoad: 00007ff8`ea540000 00007ff8`ea5fd000   C:\WINDOWS\System32\KERNEL32.DLL
ModLoad: 00007ff8`e8b20000 00007ff8`e8e94000   C:\WINDOWS\System32\KERNELBASE.dll
(7a04.83d8): Break instruction exception - code 80000003 (first chance)
ntdll!LdrpDoDebuggerBreak+0x30:
00007ff8`eb69cc74 cc              int     3
```

We allow the output of registers:

```
0:000> .prompt_allow +reg
Allow the following information to be displayed at the prompt:
(Other settings can affect whether the information is actually displayed)
   sym - Symbol for current instruction
   dis - Disassembly of current instruction
    ea - Effective address for current instruction
```

```
    reg - Register state
    src - Source info for current instruction
Do not allow the following information to be displayed at the prompt:
  None
```

Then we put a breakpoint to the *main* function and run the program until WinDbg breaks in:

```
0:000> bp PointersAsVariables!main
*** WARNING: Unable to verify checksum for PointersAsVariables.exe


0:000> .asm no_code_bytes
Assembly options: no_code_bytes


0:000> g
Breakpoint 0 hit
rax=0000000000000001 rbx=0000000000000000 rcx=0000000000000001
rdx=0000015931079d90 rsi=0000000000000000 rdi=0000000000000000
rip=00007ff746017590 rsp=00000031ed93f798 rbp=0000000000000000
 r8=000001593107d1c0  r9=0000000000000000 r10=0000000000000000
r11=00000031ed93f740 r12=0000000000000000 r13=0000000000000000
r14=0000000000000000 r15=0000000000000000
iopl=0         nv up ei pl nz na pe nc
cs=0033  ss=002b  ds=002b  es=002b  fs=0053  gs=002b             efl=00000202
PointersAsVariables!main:
00007ff7`46017590 mov     qword ptr [rsp+10h],rdx
ss:00000031`ed93f7a8=00007ff746043233
```

Next, we disassemble our *main* function (we removed source code line numbers from the output):

```
0:000> uf main
PointersAsVariables!main [C:\NewWork\WDPF-X64\PointersAsVariables\PointersAsVariables.cpp @ 5]:
00007ff7`46017590 mov     qword ptr [rsp+10h],rdx
00007ff7`46017595 mov     dword ptr [rsp+8],ecx
00007ff7`46017599 push    rdi
00007ff7`4601759a lea     rax,[PointersAsVariables!a (00007ff7`4612a210)]
00007ff7`460175a1 mov     qword ptr [PointersAsVariables!pa (00007ff7`4612a218)],rax
00007ff7`460175a8 lea     rax,[PointersAsVariables!b (00007ff7`4612a214)]
00007ff7`460175af mov     qword ptr [PointersAsVariables!pb (00007ff7`4612a220)],rax
00007ff7`460175b6 mov     rax,qword ptr [PointersAsVariables!pa (00007ff7`4612a218)]
00007ff7`460175bd mov     dword ptr [rax],1
00007ff7`460175c3 mov     rax,qword ptr [PointersAsVariables!pb (00007ff7`4612a220)]
00007ff7`460175ca mov     dword ptr [rax],1
00007ff7`460175d0 mov     rax,qword ptr [PointersAsVariables!pb (00007ff7`4612a220)]
00007ff7`460175d7 mov     eax,dword ptr [rax]
00007ff7`460175d9 mov     rcx,qword ptr [PointersAsVariables!pa (00007ff7`4612a218)]
00007ff7`460175e0 add     eax,dword ptr [rcx]
00007ff7`460175e2 mov     rcx,qword ptr [PointersAsVariables!pb (00007ff7`4612a220)]
00007ff7`460175e9 mov     dword ptr [rcx],eax
00007ff7`460175eb mov     rax,qword ptr [PointersAsVariables!pb (00007ff7`4612a220)]
00007ff7`460175f2 mov     eax,dword ptr [rax]
00007ff7`460175f4 shl     eax,1
00007ff7`460175f6 mov     rcx,qword ptr [PointersAsVariables!pb (00007ff7`4612a220)]
00007ff7`460175fd mov     dword ptr [rcx],eax
00007ff7`460175ff xor     eax,eax
00007ff7`46017601 pop     rdi
00007ff7`46017602 ret
```

Reconstructing C/C++ Code: Part 1

Now we go from instruction to instruction highlighted in bold on the previous page and try to reconstruct pseudo-code which is shown as comments to assembly language code.

```
lea     rax,[PointersAsVariables!a (00007ff7`4612a210)]
; rax   <- address of a
mov     qword ptr [PointersAsVariables!pa (00007ff7`4612a218)],rax
; [pa]  <- rax
lea     rax,[PointersAsVariables!b (00007ff7`4612a214)]
; rax   <- address of b
mov     qword ptr [PointersAsVariables!pb (00007ff7`4612a220)],rax
; [pb]  <- rax
mov     rax,qword ptr [PointersAsVariables!pa (00007ff7`4612a218)]
; rax   <- [pa]
mov     dword ptr [rax],1
; [rax] <- 1
mov     rax,qword ptr [PointersAsVariables!pb (00007ff7`4612a220)]
; rax   <- [pb]
mov     dword ptr [rax],1
; [rax] <- 1
mov     rax,qword ptr [PointersAsVariables!pb (00007ff7`4612a220)]
; rax   <- [pb]
mov     eax,dword ptr [rax]
; eax   <- [rax]
mov     rcx,qword ptr [PointersAsVariables!pa (00007ff7`4612a218)]
; rcx   <- [pa]
add     eax,dword ptr [rcx]
; eax   <- eax + [rcx]
mov     rcx,qword ptr [PointersAsVariables!pb (00007ff7`4612a220)]
; rcx   <- [pb]
mov     dword ptr [rcx],eax
; [rcx] <- eax
mov     rax,qword ptr [PointersAsVariables!pb (00007ff7`4612a220)]
; rax   <- [pb]
mov     eax,dword ptr [rax]
; eax   <- [rax]
shl     eax,1
; eax   <- eax * 2
```

```
mov     rcx,qword ptr [PointersAsVariables!pb (00007ff7`4612a220)]
; rcx   <- [pb]
mov     dword ptr [rcx],eax
; [rcx] <- eax
```

Reconstructing C/C++ Code: Part 2

Now we group pseudo-code together with possible mixed C/C++ and assembly language equivalents:

```
rax   <- address of a          ; int a; int *pa;
[pa]  <- rax                   ; pa = &a;


rax   <- address of b          ; int b; int *pb;
[pb]  <- rax                   ; pb = &b;


rax   <- [pa]                  ; *pa = 1;
[rax] <- 1


rax   <- [pb]                  ; *pb = 1;
[rax] <- 1


rax   <- [pb]                  ; eax = *pb;
eax   <- [rax]


rcx   <- [pa]                  ; eax = eax + *pa;
eax   <- eax + [rcx]


rcx   <- [pb]                  ; *pb = eax;
[rcx] <- eax


rax   <- [pb]                  ; eax = *pb;
eax   <- [rax]


eax   <- eax * 2               ; eax = eax * 2;


rcx   <- [pb]                  ; *pb = eax;
[rcx] <- eax
```

Reconstructing C/C++ Code: Part 3

Next, we combine more mixed statements into C/C++ language code:

```
int a, b;
int *pa, *pb;


pa = &a;
pb = &b;


*pa = 1;
*pb = 1;


eax = *pb;
eax = eax + *pa;
*pb = eax;            ; *pb = *pb + *pa;


eax = *pb;
eax = eax * 2;
*pb = eax;            ; *pb = *pb * 2;
```

Reconstructing C/C++ Code: C/C++ program

Finally, we have something that looks like complete C/C++ code:

```
int a, b;
int *pa, *pb;

pa = &a;
pb = &b;

*pa = 1;
*pb = 1;

*pb = *pb + *pa;
*pb = *pb * 2;
```

If we look at the project source code *PointersAsVariables.cpp*, we see exactly the same code that was compiled into the executable file that we were disassembling.

Example of Disassembly Output: Optimized Program

The fully optimized program from the *Release* project folder contains fewer CPU instructions:

```
0:000> uf main
PointersAsVariables!main [C:\NewWork\WDPF-X64\PointersAsVariables\PointersAsVariables.cpp @ 5]:
00007ff6`ccf81000 lea     rax,[PointersAsVariables!a (00007ff6`ccf9bbf4)]
00007ff6`ccf81007 mov     dword ptr [PointersAsVariables!a (00007ff6`ccf9bbf4)],1
00007ff6`ccf81011 mov     qword ptr [PointersAsVariables!pa (00007ff6`ccf9bbf8)],rax
00007ff6`ccf81018 lea     rax,[PointersAsVariables!b (00007ff6`ccf9bbf0)]
00007ff6`ccf8101f mov     qword ptr [PointersAsVariables!pb (00007ff6`ccf9bc00)],rax
00007ff6`ccf81026 xor     eax,eax
00007ff6`ccf81028 mov     dword ptr [PointersAsVariables!b (00007ff6`ccf9bbf0)],4
00007ff6`ccf81032 ret
```

We see that the Visual C++ compiler was able to figure out the result of computation: a = 1; b = 4; However, one question remains, why did the compiler not optimize away the first two instructions initializing **pa** and **pb** variables? The answer lies in the nature of a separate compilation model in C and C++. We can compile several compilation units (*.c* or *.cpp*) files separately and independently. Therefore, there is no guarantee that another compilation unit would not reference our globally declared and defined pa and pb variables.

We can also see that the compiler reordered instructions. These instructions can be seen in pseudo-code:

```
rax     <- address of a
[a]     <- 1
[pa]    <- rax
rax     <- address of b
[pb]    <- rax
[b]     <- 4
```

It is because **pa** initialization with the address of the variable **a** is independent of assigning 1 to the memory of the variable **a**, and the reordered sequence of instructions could be executed faster on modern processors.

Chapter x64.9: Memory and Stacks

Stack: A Definition

A stack is a simple computational device with two operations, push and pop, that allows us to pile up data to remember it in LIFO (Last In First Out) manner and help in easy retrieval of the last piled data item, as shown in Picture x64.9.1.

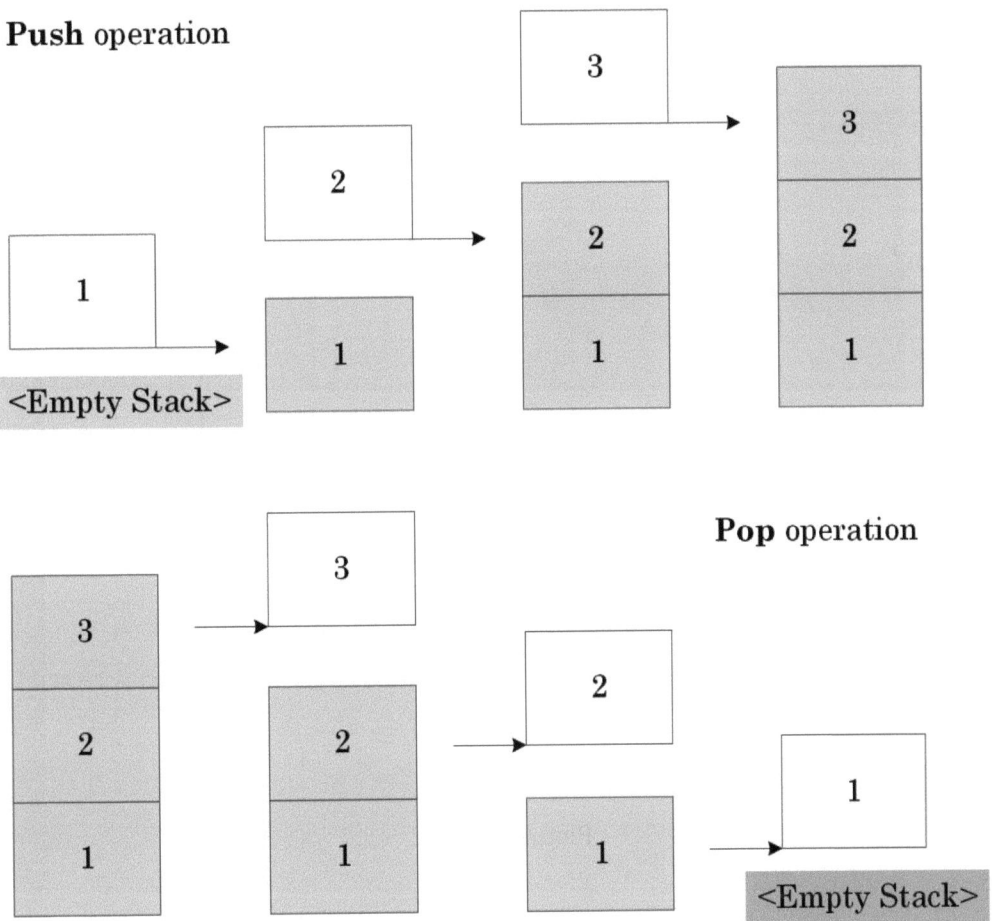

Picture x64.9.1

Stack Implementation in Memory

CPU RSP register (Stack Pointer) points to the top of a stack. As shown in Picture x64.9.2, a stack grows towards lower memory addresses with every push instruction, and this is implemented as the RSP register decrement by 8. We can read the top stack value using the following instruction:

```
mov rax, [rsp]
```

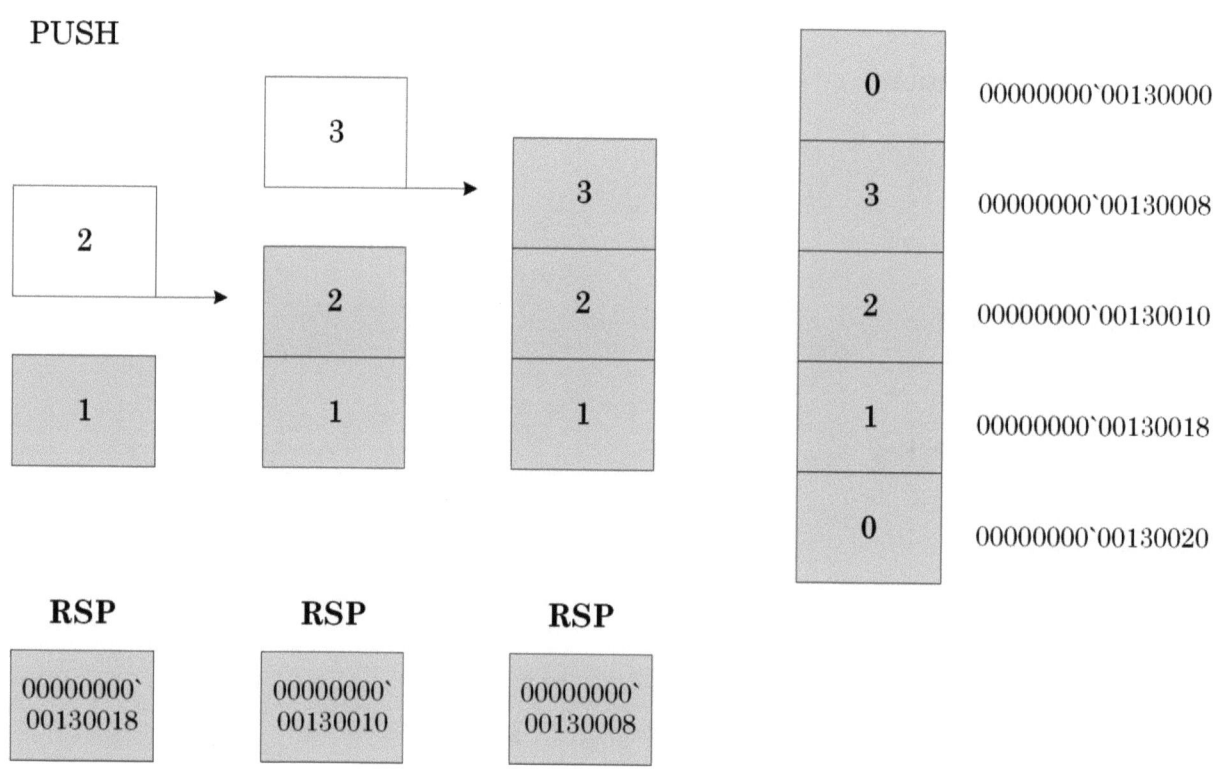

Picture x64.9.2

The opposite POP instruction increments the value of the RSP register, as shown in Picture x64.9.3.

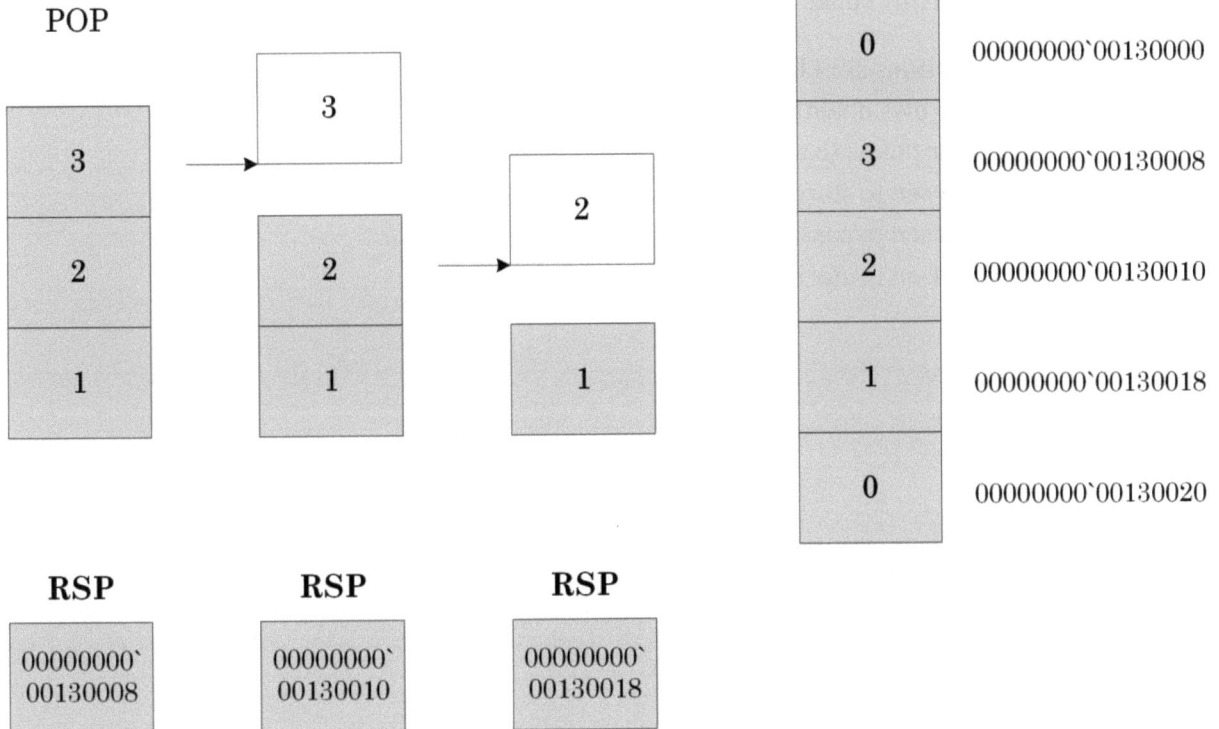

Picture x64.9.3

Things to Remember

Here is the summary of what we have learned about stacks with the last 3 points covered in the subsequent chapters of this book:

- Stack operations are LIFO – Last In First Out
- The stack grows down in memory
- RSP register points to the top of a stack
- Stacks are used to store return addresses for CALL instructions
- Stacks are used to pass additional parameters to functions
- Stacks are used to store local and temporary variables

PUSH Instruction

We can push a value stored in a register, a value stored at a memory address, or a constant (an immediate operand):

PUSH r/mem/imm

Here is PUSH simplified pseudo-code adopted from Intel manual:

```
IF OperandSize = 64
      THEN
            RSP <- RSP - 8
            [RSP] <- OperandValue   ; quad word
      ELSE
            RSP <- RSP - 2
            [RSP] <- OperandValue   ; word
FI
```

Examples:

```
push  rax

push  word ptr [rbx]

push  0
```

POP instruction

We can pop a value stored on the top of a stack to a register or a memory address:

POP   r/mem

Here is POP simplified pseudo-code adopted from Intel manual:

```
IF OperandSize = 64
        THEN
                OperandValue <- [RSP] ; quad word
                RSP <- RSP + 8
        ELSE
                OperandValue <- [RSP] ; word
                RSP <- RSP + 2
FI
```

Examples:

```
pop    rax

pop    word ptr [rbx]
```

Register Review

So far, we have seen and used general-purpose CPU registers:

- RAX (among its specific uses is to contain function return values)
- RBX
- RCX
- RDX

We also have special purpose registers:

- RIP (Instruction Pointer)
- RSP (Stack Pointer)

AMD64 and Intel EM64T architectures introduced additional general-purpose registers: R8, R9, R10, R11, R12, R13, R14, and R15.

These additional registers are used a lot in x64 code. More general-purpose registers allow faster code execution because temporary computation results can be stored there instead of memory locations. Here is a disassembly fragment from the *memmove* function:

```
0:000> uf memmove
ntdll!memmove:
00000000`77654690 mov        r11,rcx
00000000`77654693 sub        rdx,rcx
00000000`77654696 jb         ntdll!memmove+0x1aa (00000000`7765483a)
[...]
ntdll!memmove+0xb0:
00000000`77654740 mov        rax,qword ptr [rdx+rcx]
00000000`77654744 mov        r10,qword ptr [rdx+rcx+8]
00000000`77654749 add        rcx,20h
00000000`7765474d mov        qword ptr [rcx-20h],rax
00000000`77654751 mov        qword ptr [rcx-18h],r10
00000000`77654755 mov        rax,qword ptr [rdx+rcx-10h]
00000000`7765475a mov        r10,qword ptr [rdx+rcx-8]
00000000`7765475f dec        r9
00000000`77654762 mov        qword ptr [rcx-10h],rax
00000000`77654766 mov        qword ptr [rcx-8],r10
00000000`7765476a jne        ntdll!memmove+0xb0 (00000000`77654740)
[...]
```

Application Memory Simplified

When an executable file is loaded into memory, its header and sections are mapped to memory pages. Some data and code are copied unmodified, but some data is initialized and expanded. The first stack is also created at this stage. RIP register is set to point to the first program instruction, and RSP points to the top of the stack. This simplified process is shown in Picture x64.9.4.

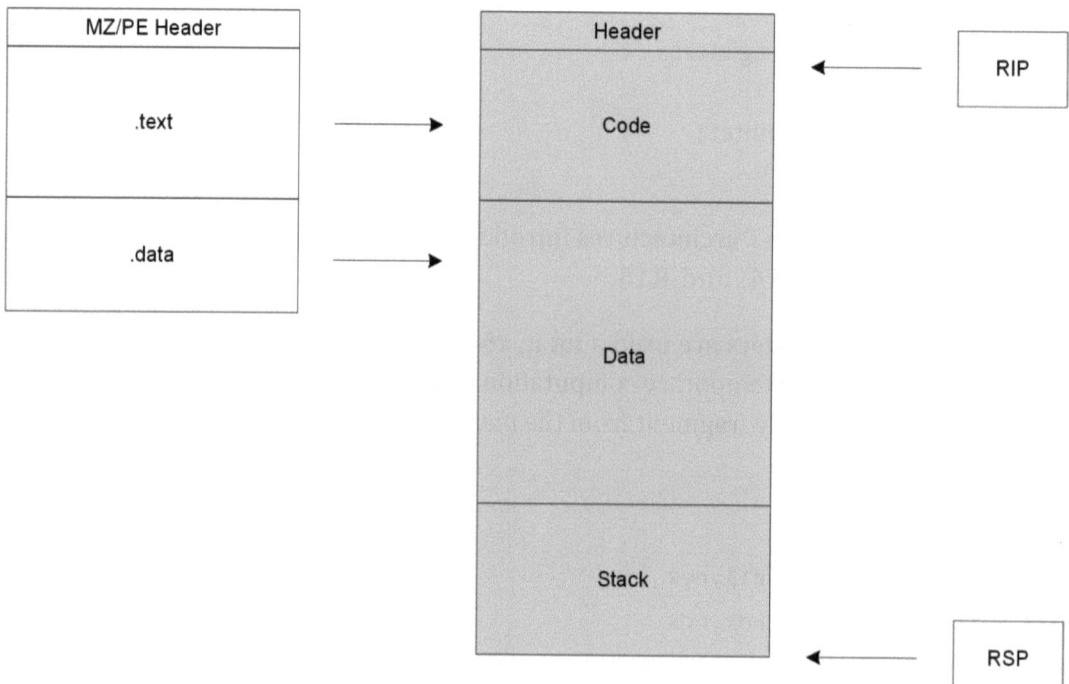

Picture x64.9.4

Stack Overflow

By default, the stack size is 1Mb (compiler dependent). However, this limit can be changed by the linker /STACK option or done via Visual C++ project Linker\System options as shown in Picture x64.9.5.

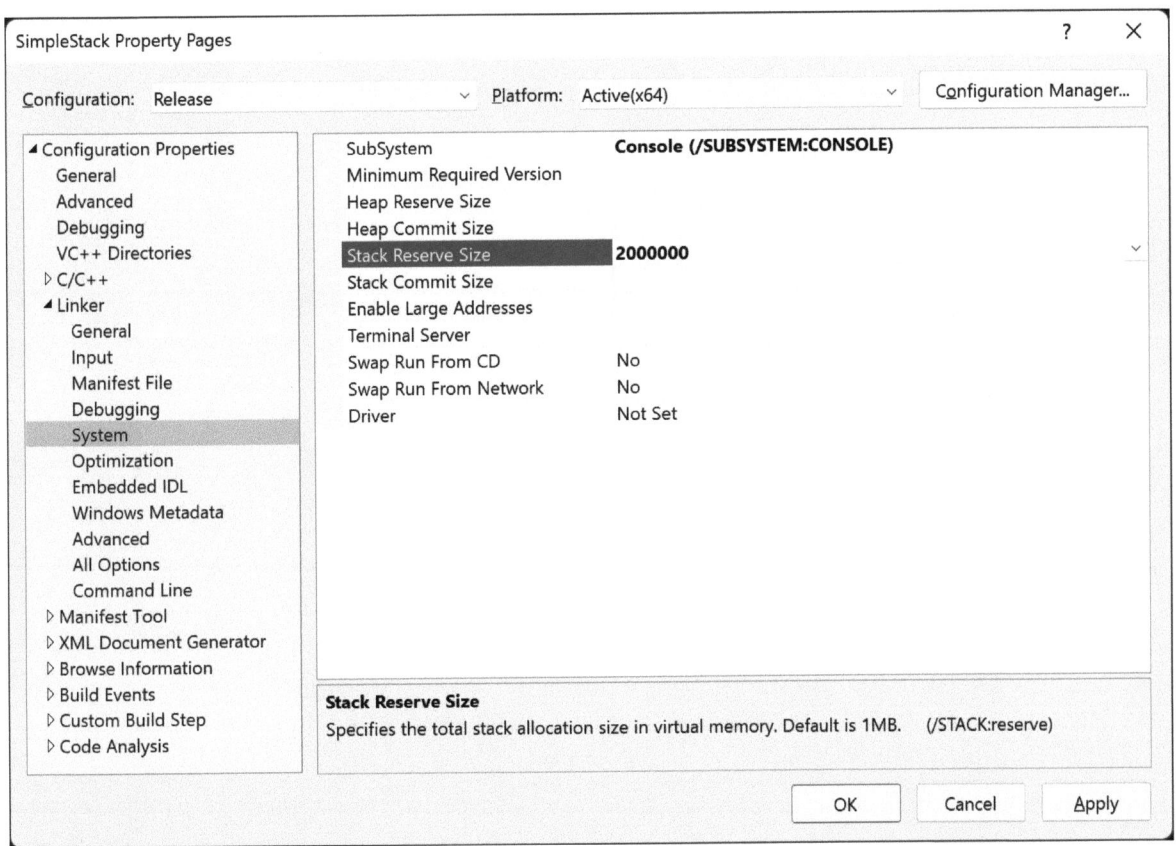

Picture x64.9.5

If a stack grows beyond the reserve limit, then a stack overflow exception occurs (exception code C00000FD). This exception might be caused by an unlimited recursion or very deep recursion:

```
int func()
{
    func();
    return 0;
}
```

Or very large local variables:

```c
int func()
{
    int array[1000000] = { 1 };
    printf("%d", array[1000000-1]);
     // use array to prevent the compiler to optimize it away
}
```

Jumps

Another instruction we need to know and understand before we look deeper into C and C++ functions is called JMP (Jump). Picture x64.9.6 shows instructions in memory and corresponding values of the RIP register.

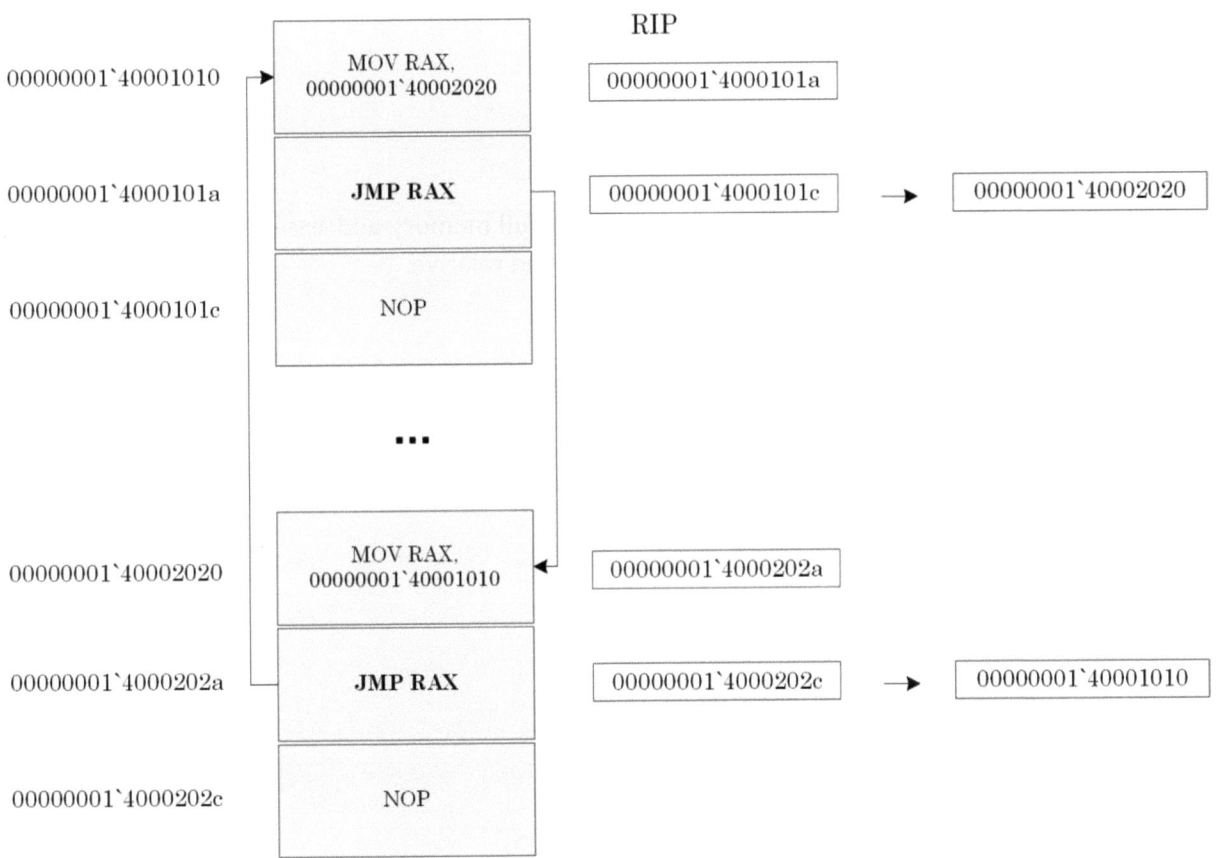

Picture x64.9.6

We see that JMP instruction changes RIP to point to another memory address, and the program execution continues from that location. The code shown in Picture x64.9.6 loops indefinitely: this can be considered a hang and CPU spike.

Here is a pseudo-code for absolute JMP instructions adopted from Intel manuals and some examples:

```
; Format and arguments:
  JMP r/mem64
; Pseudo-code:
  RIP <- DEST ; new destination address for execution
; Examples:
  JMP   RAX
  JMP   [RAX]
```

The jump is called absolute because we specify full memory addresses and not a relative +/- number to the current RIP value. The latter jump is called relative.

Calls

Now we discuss two very important instructions that make the implementation of C and C++ function calls much easier. They are called CALL and RET. Picture x64.9.7 shows instructions in memory and corresponding values of RIP and RSP registers.

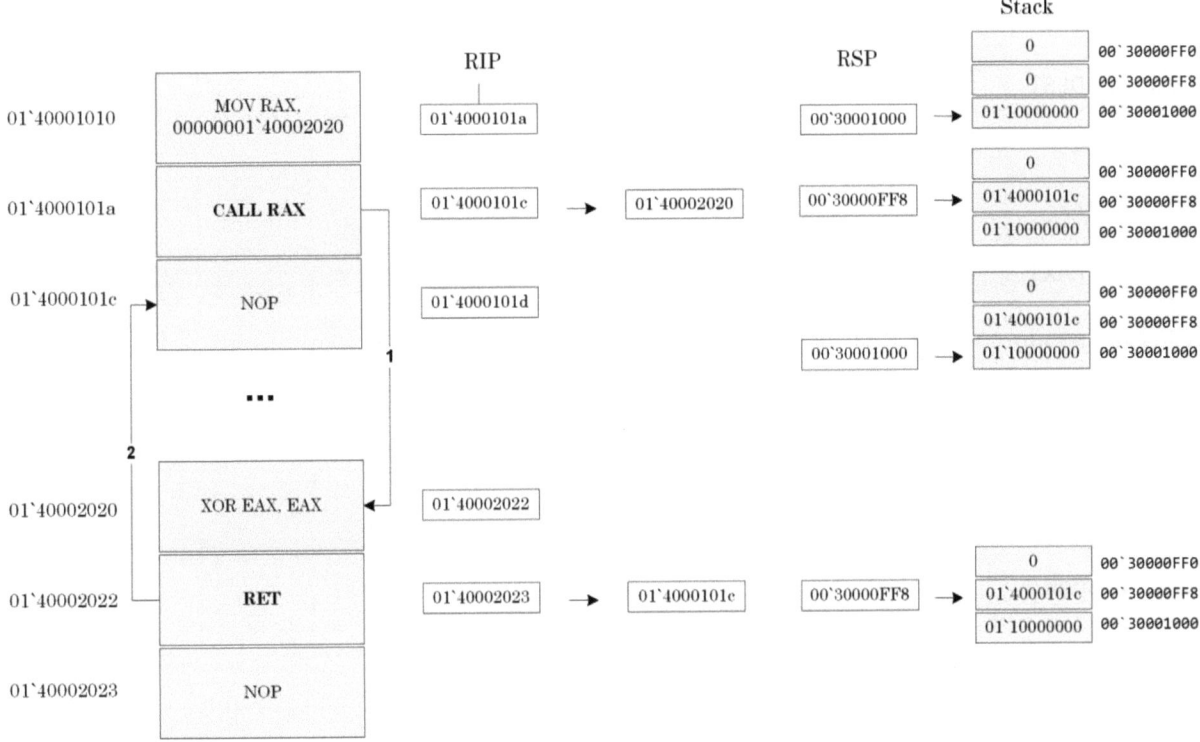

Picture x64.9.7

We see that the CALL instruction pushes the current value of RIP to the stack and changes RIP to point to another memory address. Then the program execution continues from the new location. RET instruction pops the saved RIP value from the stack to the RIP register. Then the program execution resumes at the memory location after the CALL instruction.

Here is a pseudo-code for CALL instructions and some examples adopted from Intel manuals:

```
; Format and arguments:
  CALL r/mem64
; Pseudo-code:
  PUSH (RIP)
  RIP <- DEST
; Examples:
  CALL  RAX
  CALL  [RAX]
```

Here is a pseudo-code for RET instruction adopted from Intel manuals:

```
; Format:
  RET
; Pseudo-code:
  RIP <- POP()
```

Call Stack

If one function (the caller) calls another function (the callee) in C and C++, the resulting code is implemented using CALL instruction, and during its execution, the return address is saved on the stack. If the callee calls another function, the return address is also saved on the stack, and so on. Therefore, we have the so-called call stack of return addresses. Let's see this with a simple but trimmed down example.

Suppose we have 3 functions with their code occupying the following addresses:

```
func    00000001`40001000 - 00000001`40001100
func2   00000001`40001101 - 00000001`40001200
func3   00000001`40001201 - 00000001`40001300
```

We also have the following code where *func* calls *func2*, and *func2* calls *func3*:

```
void func()
{
    func2();
}
void func2()
{
    func3();
}
```

When *func* calls *func2*, the caller return address is pushed to the stack, and RSP points to some value in the 00000001`40001000 – 00000001`40001100 address range, say 00000001`40001020. When *func2* calls *func3*, the caller return address is also pushed to the stack, and RSP points to some value in the 00000001`40001101 – 00000001`40001200 address range, say 00000001` 40001180. If we interrupt *func3* with a debugger and inspect RIP, we would find its value in the range of 00000001`40001201 – 00000001`40001300, say 00000001`40001250. Therefore, we have the following memory and register layout shown in Picture x64.9.8 (the usual function prolog is not shown: we learn about it in the next chapter).

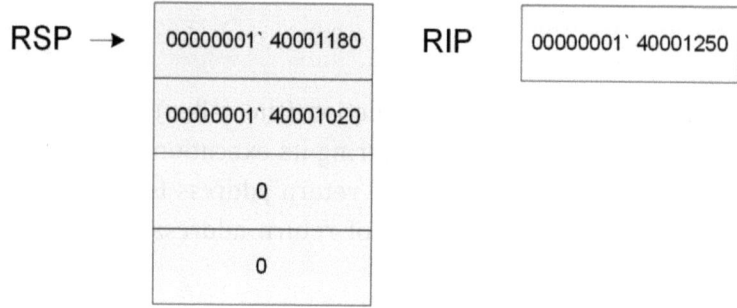

Picture x64.9.8

The debugger examines the value of RIP and the values on top of the stack and reconstructs this call stack:

```
func3
func2
func
```

The debugger gets address ranges corresponding to *func*, *func2*, and *func3* functions from the so-called symbol files (that have the .PDB file extension). Downloaded projects also contain .PDB files corresponding to .EXE files to allow WinDbg debugger to understand the memory location of the *main* function, for example.

Exploring Stack in WinDbg

To see call stack in real action, we have a project called "SimpleStack", and it can be downloaded from:

https://bitbucket.org/softwarediagnostics/pfwddr2/src/master/x64/Chapter9/

The executable is located in the *Release* subfolder. We load *SimpleStack.exe* using File\Open Executable... menu option in WinDbg and get the following output (the output, especially addresses, may differ for your Windows version):

```
Microsoft (R) Windows Debugger Version 10.0.22000.194 AMD64
Copyright (c) Microsoft Corporation. All rights reserved.

CommandLine: C:\PFWDDR2\x64\Chapter9\Release\SimpleStack.exe

************* Path validation summary **************
Response                         Time (ms)      Location
Deferred                                        srv*
Symbol search path is: srv*
Executable search path is:
ModLoad: 00007ff6`21110000 00007ff6`21131000   SimpleStack.exe
ModLoad: 00007ff8`eb5c0000 00007ff8`eb7c9000   ntdll.dll
ModLoad: 00007ff8`ea540000 00007ff8`ea5fd000   C:\WINDOWS\System32\KERNEL32.DLL
ModLoad: 00007ff8`e8b20000 00007ff8`e8e94000   C:\WINDOWS\System32\KERNELBASE.dll
(817c.11c4): Break instruction exception - code 80000003 (first chance)
ntdll!LdrpDoDebuggerBreak+0x30:
00007ff8`eb69cc74 cc              int     3
```

We allow the output of registers:

```
0:000> .prompt_allow +reg
Allow the following information to be displayed at the prompt:
(Other settings can affect whether the information is actually displayed)
    sym - Symbol for current instruction
    dis - Disassembly of current instruction
     ea - Effective address for current instruction
    reg - Register state
    src - Source info for current instruction
Do not allow the following information to be displayed at the prompt:
  None
```

Then we put a breakpoint to the *main* function and run the program until WinDbg breaks in:

```
0:000> bp SimpleStack!main
*** WARNING: Unable to verify checksum for SimpleStack.exe
```

```
0:000> .asm no_code_bytes
Assembly options: no_code_bytes
```

```
0:000> g
Breakpoint 0 hit
rax=00007ff62112b308 rbx=00000255e5ec9c50 rcx=0000000000000001
rdx=00000255e5ec9c50 rsi=0000000000000000 rdi=00000255e5ecd010
rip=00007ff62111f5a0 rsp=0000009cce74fae8 rbp=0000000000000000
 r8=00000255e5ecd010  r9=0000000000000000 r10=0000000000000000
r11=0000009cce74fa80 r12=0000000000000000 r13=0000000000000000
r14=0000000000000000 r15=0000000000000000
iopl=0         nv up ei pl nz na po nc
cs=0033  ss=002b  ds=002b  es=002b  fs=0053  gs=002b             efl=00000206
SimpleStack!main:
00007ff6`2111f5a0 mov     qword ptr [rsp+10h],rdx ss:0000009c`ce74faf8=00007ff621111299
```

The function *func3* has a breakpoint instruction inside that allows a debugger to break in and stop the program execution to inspect its state. We resume our program execution from our breakpoint in *main* function to allow *main* function to call *func*, *func* to call *func2*, *func2* to call *func3*, and inside *func3* to execute the explicit breakpoint:

```
0:000> g
(817c.11c4): Break instruction exception - code 80000003 (first chance)
rax=00007ff62112b308 rbx=00000255e5ec9c50 rcx=0000000000000001
rdx=00000255e5ec9c50 rsi=0000000000000000 rdi=00000255e5ecd010
rip=00007ff62111f592 rsp=0000009cce74fa58 rbp=0000000000000000
 r8=00000255e5ecd010  r9=0000000000000000 r10=0000000000000000
r11=0000009cce74fa80 r12=0000000000000000 r13=0000000000000000
r14=0000000000000000 r15=0000000000000000
iopl=0         nv up ei pl nz na po nc
cs=0033  ss=002b  ds=002b  es=002b  fs=0053  gs=002b             efl=00000206
SimpleStack!func3+0x2:
00007ff6`2111f592 int     3
```

Now we can inspect the top of the stack:

```
0:000> dq rsp
0000009c`ce74fa58  00007ff6`2111f589 00000000`00000fa0
0000009c`ce74fa68  00000000`00000002 00000000`00000000
0000009c`ce74fa78  00000000`00000000 00007ff6`21120298
0000009c`ce74fa88  00007ff6`2111f579 00007ff6`21120290
0000009c`ce74fa98  00000000`00000000 04100800`000806ea
0000009c`ce74faa8  bfebfbff`fffaf387 00007ff6`211202d0
0000009c`ce74fab8  00007ff6`2111f5b2 00000000`0000001f
0000009c`ce74fac8  00000000`00000000 00000000`00000000
```

The data is meaningless for us, and we use another command called **dqs** to dump memory with corresponding symbols from PDB files (we can also use **dps** command instead):

```
0:000> dqs rsp
0000009c`ce74fa58  00007ff6`2111f589 SimpleStack!func2+0x9 [C:\NewWork\WDPF-X64\SimpleStack\func2.c @ 6]
0000009c`ce74fa60  00000000`00000fa0
0000009c`ce74fa68  00000000`00000002
0000009c`ce74fa70  00000000`00000000
0000009c`ce74fa78  00000000`00000000
0000009c`ce74fa80  00007ff6`21120298 SimpleStack!__xc_z
0000009c`ce74fa88  00007ff6`2111f579 SimpleStack!func+0x9 [C:\NewWork\WDPF-X64\SimpleStack\func.c @ 6]
0000009c`ce74fa90  00007ff6`21120290 SimpleStack!pre_cpp_initializer
0000009c`ce74fa98  00000000`00000000
0000009c`ce74faa0  04100800`000806ea
0000009c`ce74faa8  bfebfbff`fffaf387
0000009c`ce74fab0  00007ff6`211202d0 SimpleStack!__acrt_tran_fma3_initializer
0000009c`ce74fab8  00007ff6`2111f5b2 SimpleStack!main+0x12 [C:\NewWork\WDPF-X64\SimpleStack\SimpleStack.c @ 6]
0000009c`ce74fac0  00000000`0000001f
0000009c`ce74fac8  00000000`00000000
0000009c`ce74fad0  00000000`00000000
```

The current value of RIP points to *func3* and return addresses on the stack are shown in bold. WinDbg is able to reconstruct the following call stack or stack trace:

```
0:000> k
# Child-SP          RetAddr               Call Site
00 0000009c`ce74fa58 00007ff6`2111f589    SimpleStack!func3+0x2 [C:\NewWork\WDPF-X64\SimpleStack\func3.c @ 5]
01 0000009c`ce74fa60 00007ff6`2111f579    SimpleStack!func2+0x9 [C:\NewWork\WDPF-X64\SimpleStack\func2.c @ 6]
02 0000009c`ce74fa90 00007ff6`2111f5b2    SimpleStack!func+0x9 [C:\NewWork\WDPF-X64\SimpleStack\func.c @ 6]
03 0000009c`ce74fac0 00007ff6`21111220    SimpleStack!main+0x12 [C:\NewWork\WDPF-X64\SimpleStack\SimpleStack.c @ 6]
04 (Inline Function) --------`--------    SimpleStack!invoke_main+0x22 [d:\a01\_work\43\s\src\vctools\crt\vcstartup\src\startup\exe_common.inl @ 78]
05 0000009c`ce74faf0 00007ff8`ea5554e0    SimpleStack!__scrt_common_main_seh+0x10c [d:\a01\_work\43\s\src\vctools\crt\vcstartup\src\startup\exe_common.inl @ 288]
06 0000009c`ce74fb30 00007ff8`eb5c485b    KERNEL32!BaseThreadInitThunk+0x10
07 0000009c`ce74fb60 00000000`00000000    ntdll!RtlUserThreadStart+0x2b
```

We can use **kL** command to remove source code line output from the stack trace:

```
0:000> kL
# Child-SP          RetAddr               Call Site
00 0000009c`ce74fa58 00007ff6`2111f589    SimpleStack!func3+0x2
01 0000009c`ce74fa60 00007ff6`2111f579    SimpleStack!func2+0x9
02 0000009c`ce74fa90 00007ff6`2111f5b2    SimpleStack!func+0x9
03 0000009c`ce74fac0 00007ff6`21111220    SimpleStack!main+0x12
04 (Inline Function) --------`--------    SimpleStack!invoke_main+0x22
05 0000009c`ce74faf0 00007ff8`ea5554e0    SimpleStack!__scrt_common_main_seh+0x10c
06 0000009c`ce74fb30 00007ff8`eb5c485b    KERNEL32!BaseThreadInitThunk+0x10
07 0000009c`ce74fb60 00000000`00000000    ntdll!RtlUserThreadStart+0x2b
```

Chapter x64.10: Local Variables

Stack Usage

In addition to storage for return addresses of CALL instructions, the stack is used to pass parameters to functions and store local variables. The stack is also used to save and restore values held in registers when we want to preserve them during some computation or across function calls. For example, suppose we want to do multiplication, but at the same time, we have other valuable data in register RAX and RDX. The multiplication result overwrites RAX and RDX values, and we temporarily put their values on stack:

```
mov     rax, 10
mov     rdx, 20
...
...
...                     ; now we want to preserve RAX and RDX
push    rax
push    rdx
imul    rdx             ; RDX and RAX contain the result of RAX*RDX
mov     qword ptr [result], rax
pop     rdx             ; pop in reverse order
pop     rax             ; stack is LIFO
```

Addressing Array Elements

We can also consider stack memory as an array of memory cells, and often RSP **register** is used to address stack memory elements in the way shown in Picture x64.10.1, where it slides into the frame of stack memory called a stack frame. The first diagram depicts 64-bit (qword) memory cells, and the second depicts 32-bit (dword) memory cells.

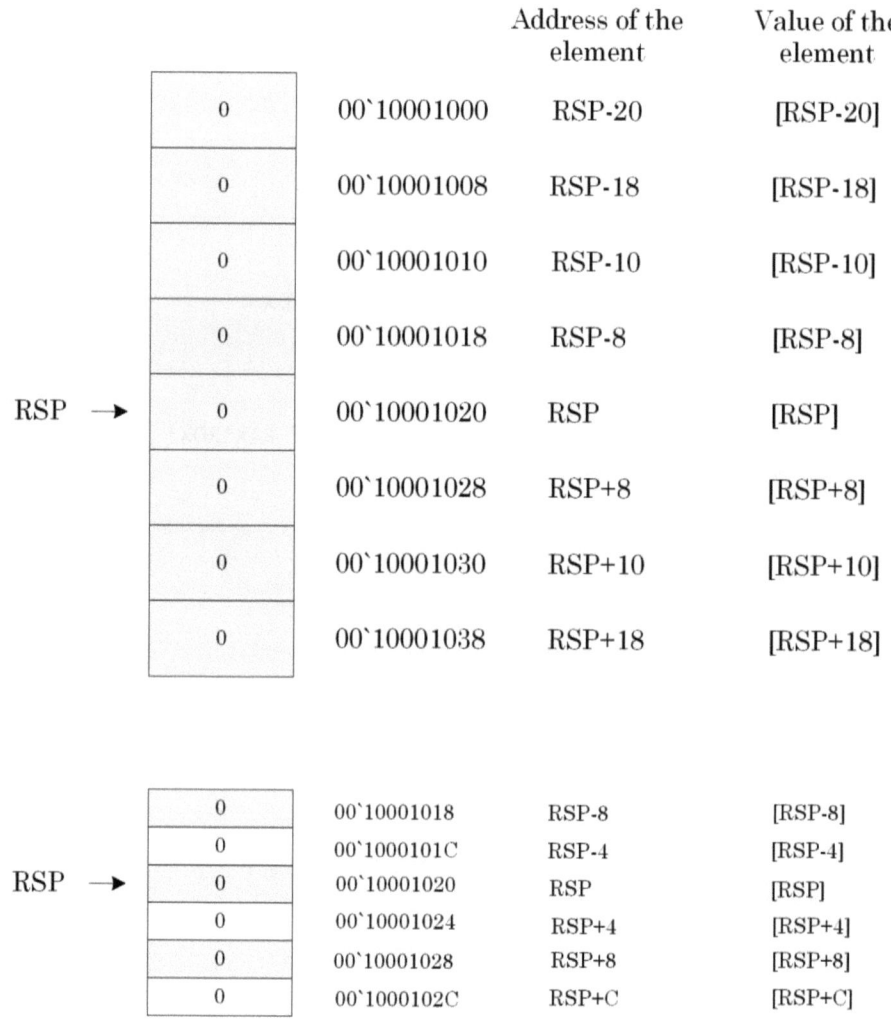

Picture x64.10.1

Stack Structure (No Function Parameters)

Suppose the following function is called:

```
void func()
{
    int var1, var2;
    // Body Code
    // ...
}
```

Before the function body code is executed, the following pointers are set up:

- [RSP] contains local variable var1 (DWORD)
- [RSP+4] contains local variable var2 (DWORD)

This memory layout is illustrated in Picture x64.10.2.

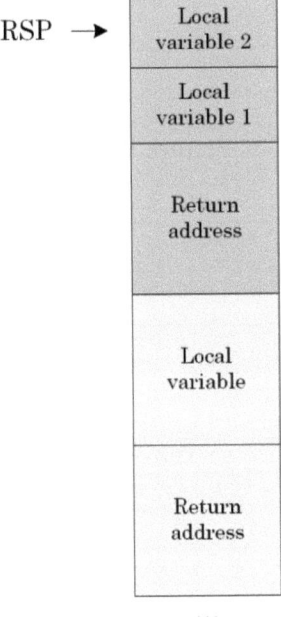

Picture x64.10.2

Function Prolog

The sequence of instructions that makes room for local variables is called a function prolog. One example is in Picture x64.10.3, where *func* calls *func2*, which has one local variable *var*. Sometimes saving necessary registers is also considered as part of a function prolog.

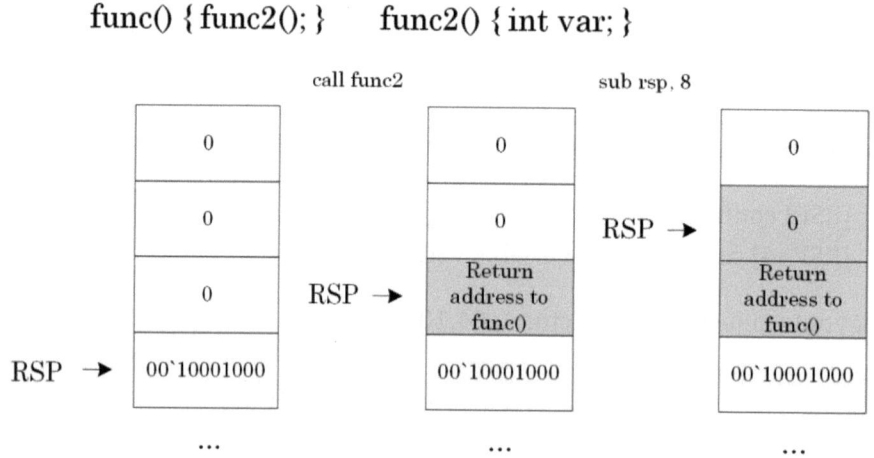

Picture x64.10.3

Function Epilog

Before the function code makes a return to the caller, it must restore the previous value of the RSP register to allow the caller to resume its execution from the correct address previously saved on the stack. This sequence of instructions is called a function epilog, and it is shown in Picture x64.10.4. Sometimes restoring necessary registers is also considered as the part of a function epilog.

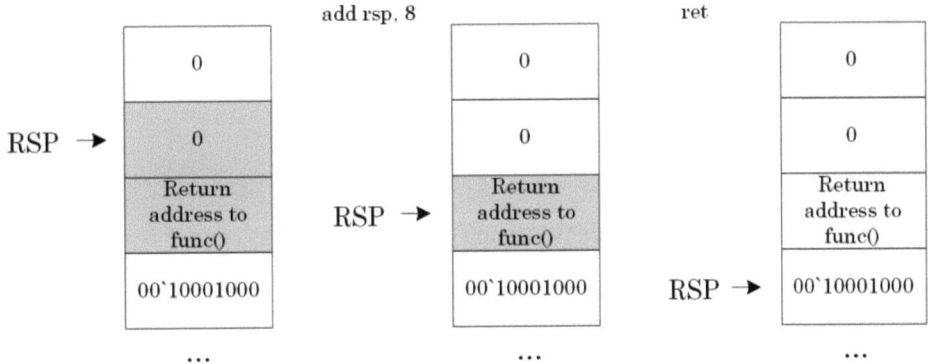

Picture x64.10.4

"Local Variables" Project

The project for this chapter can be downloaded from:

https://bitbucket.org/softwarediagnostics/pfwddr2/src/master/x64/Chapter10/

The executable is located in *Debug* subfolder. We load it into WinDbg and disassemble its *main* function.

First, we load *LocalVariables.exe* using File\Open Executable… menu option in WinDbg and get the following output (the output, especially addresses, may differ for your Windows version):

```
Microsoft (R) Windows Debugger Version 10.0.22000.194 AMD64
Copyright (c) Microsoft Corporation. All rights reserved.

CommandLine: C:\PFWDDR2\x64\Chapter10\Debug\LocalVariables.exe

************* Path validation summary **************
Response                         Time (ms)     Location
Deferred                                       srv*
Symbol search path is: srv*
Executable search path is:
ModLoad: 00007ff6`bf990000 00007ff6`bfabe000   LocalVariables.exe
ModLoad: 00007ff8`eb5c0000 00007ff8`eb7c9000   ntdll.dll
ModLoad: 00007ff8`ea540000 00007ff8`ea5fd000   C:\WINDOWS\System32\KERNEL32.DLL
ModLoad: 00007ff8`e8b20000 00007ff8`e8e94000   C:\WINDOWS\System32\KERNELBASE.dll
(8678.e60): Break instruction exception - code 80000003 (first chance)
ntdll!LdrpDoDebuggerBreak+0x30:
00007ff8`eb69cc74 cc              int     3
```

We allow the output of registers:

```
0:000> .prompt_allow +reg
Allow the following information to be displayed at the prompt:
(Other settings can affect whether the information is actually displayed)
   sym - Symbol for current instruction
   dis - Disassembly of current instruction
    ea - Effective address for current instruction
   reg - Register state
   src - Source info for current instruction
Do not allow the following information to be displayed at the prompt:
  None
```

Then, we put a breakpoint to the *main* function and run the program until WinDbg breaks in:

```
0:000> bp LocalVariables!main
*** WARNING: Unable to verify checksum for LocalVariables.exe
```

```
0:000> .asm no_code_bytes
Assembly options: no_code_bytes
```

```
0:000> g
Breakpoint 0 hit
rax=0000000000000001 rbx=0000000000000000 rcx=0000000000000001
rdx=00000141743d9d80 rsi=0000000000000000 rdi=0000000000000000
rip=00007ff6bf997590 rsp=00000033982ffa48 rbp=0000000000000000
 r8=00000141743dd1b0  r9=0000000000000000 r10=0000000000000000
r11=00000033982ff9f0 r12=0000000000000000 r13=0000000000000000
r14=0000000000000000 r15=0000000000000000
iopl=0         nv up ei pl nz na po nc
cs=0033  ss=002b  ds=002b  es=002b  fs=0053  gs=002b             efl=00000206
LocalVariables!main:
00007ff6`bf997590 mov     qword ptr [rsp+10h],rdx
ss:00000033`982ffa58=00007ff6bf9c3203
```

Next, we disassemble our *main* function:

```
0:000> uf main
LocalVariables!main [C:\NewWork\WDPF-X64\LocalVariables\LocalVariables.cpp @ 2]:
    2 00007ff6`bf997590 mov     qword ptr [rsp+10h],rdx
    2 00007ff6`bf997595 mov     dword ptr [rsp+8],ecx
    2 00007ff6`bf997599 push    rdi
    2 00007ff6`bf99759a sub     rsp,10h
    5 00007ff6`bf99759e mov     dword ptr [rsp],1
    6 00007ff6`bf9975a5 mov     dword ptr [rsp+4],1
    8 00007ff6`bf9975ad mov     eax,dword ptr [rsp]
    8 00007ff6`bf9975b0 mov     ecx,dword ptr [rsp+4]
    8 00007ff6`bf9975b4 add     ecx,eax
    8 00007ff6`bf9975b6 mov     eax,ecx
    8 00007ff6`bf9975b8 mov     dword ptr [rsp+4],eax
    9 00007ff6`bf9975bc mov     eax,dword ptr [rsp]
    9 00007ff6`bf9975bf inc     eax
    9 00007ff6`bf9975c1 mov     dword ptr [rsp],eax
   10 00007ff6`bf9975c4 mov     eax,dword ptr [rsp]
```

```
10 00007ff6`bf9975c7 imul    eax,dword ptr [rsp+4]
10 00007ff6`bf9975cc mov     dword ptr [rsp+4],eax
12 00007ff6`bf9975d0 xor     eax,eax
13 00007ff6`bf9975d2 add     rsp,10h
13 00007ff6`bf9975d6 pop     rdi
13 00007ff6`bf9975d7 ret
```

Its source code is the following:

```
int main(int argc, char* argv[])
{
    int a, b;

    a = 1;
    b = 1;

    b = b + a;
    ++a;
    b = a * b;

    return 0;
}
```

Below is the same assembly language code but with comments showing operations in pseudo-code and highlighting function prolog and epilog:

```
00007ff6`bf997590 mov    qword ptr [rsp+10h],rdx ; saving main parameters
00007ff6`bf997595 mov    dword ptr [rsp+8],ecx   ;   on the stack
00007ff6`bf997599 push   rdi             ; saving registers that might be used outside
00007ff6`bf99759a sub    rsp,10h         ; creating stack frame for local variables
00007ff6`bf99759e mov    dword ptr [rsp],1       ; [a] <- 1
00007ff6`bf9975a5 mov    dword ptr [rsp+4],1     ; [b] <- 1
00007ff6`bf9975ad mov    eax,dword ptr [rsp]     ; eax <- [a]
00007ff6`bf9975b0 mov    ecx,dword ptr [rsp+4]   ; ecx <- [b]
00007ff6`bf9975b4 add    ecx,eax                 ; ecx <- ecx + eax
00007ff6`bf9975b6 mov    eax,ecx                 ; eax <- ecx
00007ff6`bf9975b8 mov    dword ptr [rsp+4],eax   ; [b] <- eax   (b = b + a)
00007ff6`bf9975bc mov    eax,dword ptr [rsp]     ; eax <- [a]
00007ff6`bf9975bf inc    eax                     ; eax <- eax + 1
00007ff6`bf9975c1 mov    dword ptr [rsp],eax     ; [a] <- eax   (++a)
00007ff6`bf9975c4 mov    eax,dword ptr [rsp]     ; eax <- [a]
00007ff6`bf9975c7 imul   eax,dword ptr [rsp+4]   ; eax <- eax * [b]
00007ff6`bf9975cc mov    dword ptr [rsp+4],eax   ; [b] <- eax   (b = a * b)
00007ff6`bf9975d0 xor    eax,eax                 ; eax <- 0     (return value)
00007ff6`bf9975d2 add    rsp,10h                 ; restoring previous stack frame
00007ff6`bf9975d6 pop    rdi                     ; restoring registers
00007ff6`bf9975d7 ret                            ; return 0
```

Disassembly of Optimized Executable (Release Configuration)

If we load *LocalVariables.exe* from the *Release* project folder, we would see very simple code that just returns 0:

```
0:000> uf main
LocalVariables!main [C:\NewWork\WDPF-X64\LocalVariables\LocalVariables.cpp @ 2]:
    2 00007ff7`41fe1000 xor     eax,eax
   13 00007ff7`41fe1002 ret
```

Where is all the code we have seen in *Debug* version? It was optimized away by the Visual C++ compiler because the results of our calculation are never used. Variables **a** and **b** are local to the *main* function, and their values are not accessible outside when we return from the function.

Chapter x64.11: Function Parameters

"FunctionParameters" Project

In this chapter, we learn how a caller function passes its parameters via registers and how a callee (the called function) accesses them. We use the following project that can be downloaded from this link:

https://bitbucket.org/softwarediagnostics/pfwddr2/src/master/x64/Chapter11/

Here is the project source code:

```
// FunctionParameters.cpp
int arithmetic (int a, int b);

int main(int argc, char* argv[])
{
    int result = arithmetic (1, 1);

    return 0;
}


// Arithmetic.cpp
int arithmetic (int a, int b)
{
    b = b + a;
    ++a;
    b = a * b;

    return b;
}
```

Stack Structure

Recall from the previous chapter that the RSP register is used to address stack memory locations. That memory layout was illustrated by Picture x64.10.1. Here we provide a typical example of the stack memory layout for the following function:

```
void func(int Param1, int Param2)
{
    int var1, var2;
    // stack memory layout at this point
    // [RSP]     = var1 (DWORD)
    // [RSP+0x4] = var2 (DWORD)
    // [RSP+0x8] = return address (QWORD)
    // [RSP+0x10]      = Param1 (DWORD stored in QWORD cell)
    // [RSP+0x18]      = Param2 (DWORD stored in QWORD cell)
    // …
}
```

The typical stack frame memory layout for the function with 2 arguments and 2 local variables is illustrated in Picture x64.11.1.

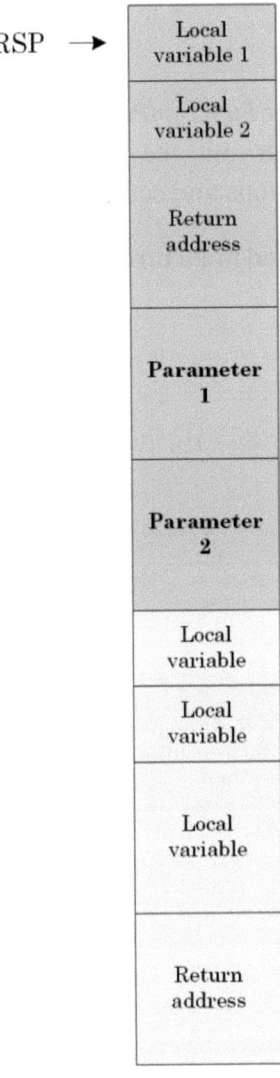

Picture x64.11.1

Function Prolog and Epilog

Now, before we try to make sense of the *FunctionParameters* project disassembly, we look at the very simple case of one function parameter and one local variable to illustrate the standard function prolog and epilog sequence of instructions and corresponding stack memory changes.

The function prolog is illustrated in Picture x64.11.2, and the function epilog is illustrated in Picture x64.11.3.

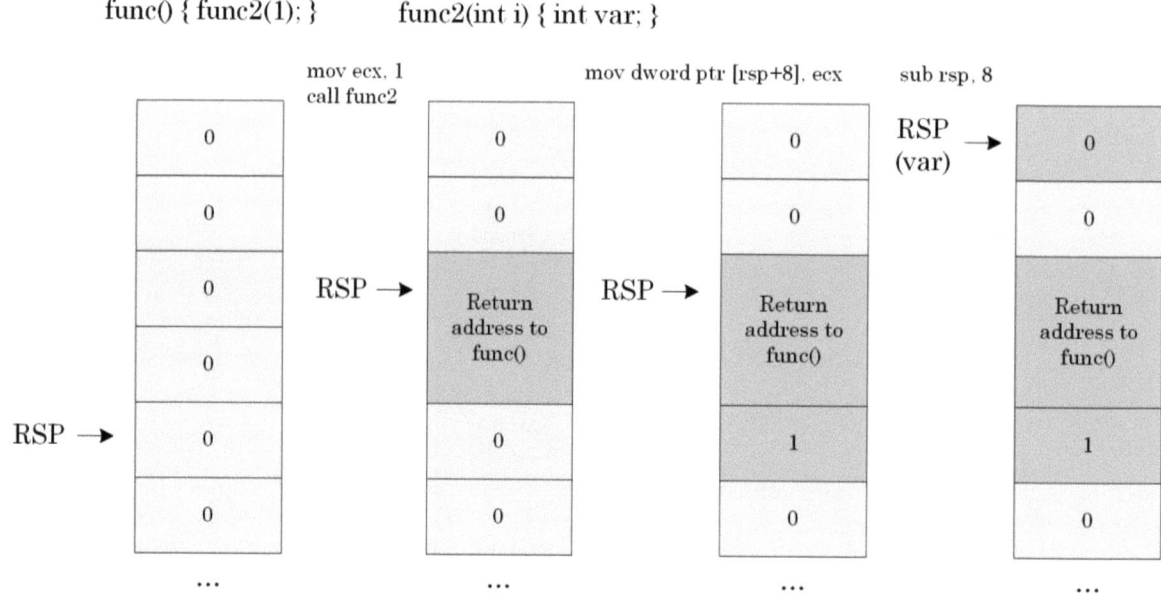

Picture x64.11.2

Here the function parameter is passed via the ECX register (lower double word part of the RCX register). It is saved on the stack nevertheless because RCX is used later in calculations. Generally, the first two function parameters are passed via ECX and EDX registers when parameters are double words like integers and RCX and RDX registers when parameters are quad words like pointers. If a function has the 3rd and 4th parameters, they are passed via R8 and R9 registers. Finally, more parameters are passed via the stack locations using the PUSH instruction.

Chapter x64.11: Function Parameters

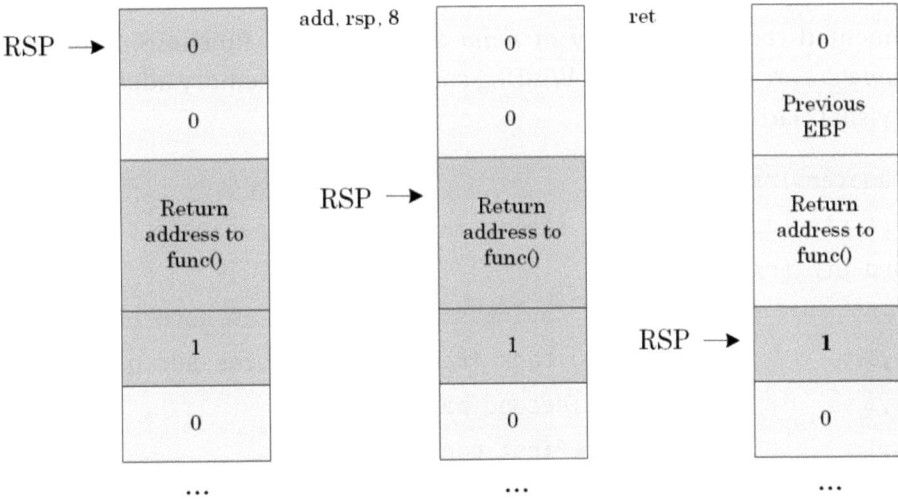

Picture x64.11.3

Project Disassembled Code with Comments

Here is commented code disassembly of *main* and *arithmetic* functions from *Debug* version of *FunctionParameters.exe* done by the **uf** WinDbg command with memory addresses and binary codes removed for visual clarity.

FunctionParameters!main:

mov	qword ptr [rsp+10h],rdx	; saving main function parameters on stack
mov	dword ptr [rsp+8],ecx	;
push	rdi	; saving RDI that might be used outside
sub	rsp,30h	; stack frame for variables and parameters
mov	edx,1	; second parameter
mov	ecx,1	; first parameter
call	FunctionParameters!ILT+10620(?**arithmetic**YAHHHZ) (00007ff6`b2fc3981)	
mov	dword ptr [rsp+20h],eax	; saving result in a local variable
xor	eax,eax	; return value (0)
add	rsp,30h	; restoring previous stack frame
pop	rdi	; restoring RDI register
ret		; return 0

FunctionParameters!arithmetic:

mov	dword ptr [rsp+10h],edx	; saving the second function parameter [b]
mov	dword ptr [rsp+8],ecx	; saving the first function parameter [a]
push	rdi	; saving RDI that might be used outside
mov	eax,dword ptr [rsp+10h]	; eax <- [a] [rsp+8h+8h] shift due to rdi
mov	ecx,dword ptr [rsp+18h]	; ecx <- [b] [rsp+10h+8h] shift due to rdi
add	ecx,eax	; ecx <- ecx + eax
mov	eax,ecx	; eax <- ecx
mov	dword ptr [rsp+18h],eax	; [b] <- eax (b = b + a)
mov	eax,dword ptr [rsp+10h]	; eax <- [a]
inc	eax	; eax <- eax + 1
mov	dword ptr [rsp+10h],eax	; [a] <- eax (++a)
mov	eax,dword ptr [rsp+10h]	; eax <- [a]
imul	eax,dword ptr [rsp+18h]	; eax <- eax * [b]
mov	dword ptr [rsp+18h],eax	; [b] <- eax
mov	eax,dword ptr [rsp+18h]	; eax <- [b] (return result)
pop	rdi	; restoring saved RDI
ret		; return (return value is in eax)

In *arithmetic* code, we see dynamic addressing of local variables and parameters, where rsp+8h was pointing to the first function parameter first, but then we saved the RDI register, and the stack pointer was shifted by 8 bytes towards lower addresses (-8), so next time we use rsp+8h+8h or rsp+10h to compensate for the shift.

We can put a breakpoint on the first arithmetic calculations address and examine raw stack data pointed to by the RSP register (we removed source code references for clarity):

```
0:000> .asm no_code_bytes
Assembly options: no_code_bytes
```

```
0:000> .prompt_allow +reg
Allow the following information to be displayed at the prompt:
(Other settings can affect whether the information is actually displayed)
    sym - Symbol for current instruction
    dis - Disassembly of current instruction
     ea - Effective address for current instruction
    reg - Register state
    src - Source info for current instruction
Do not allow the following information to be displayed at the prompt:
  None
```

```
0:000> uf arithmetic
FunctionParameters!arithmetic [C:\NewWork\WDPF-X64\FunctionParameters\Arithmetic.cpp
@ 2]:
    2 00007ff6`b2fc7590 mov     dword ptr [rsp+10h],edx
    2 00007ff6`b2fc7594 mov     dword ptr [rsp+8],ecx
    2 00007ff6`b2fc7598 push    rdi
    3 00007ff6`b2fc7599 mov     eax,dword ptr [rsp+10h]
    3 00007ff6`b2fc759d mov     ecx,dword ptr [rsp+18h]
    3 00007ff6`b2fc75a1 add     ecx,eax
    3 00007ff6`b2fc75a3 mov     eax,ecx
    3 00007ff6`b2fc75a5 mov     dword ptr [rsp+18h],eax
    4 00007ff6`b2fc75a9 mov     eax,dword ptr [rsp+10h]
    4 00007ff6`b2fc75ad inc     eax
    4 00007ff6`b2fc75af mov     dword ptr [rsp+10h],eax
    5 00007ff6`b2fc75b3 mov     eax,dword ptr [rsp+10h]
    5 00007ff6`b2fc75b7 imul    eax,dword ptr [rsp+18h]
    5 00007ff6`b2fc75bc mov     dword ptr [rsp+18h],eax
    7 00007ff6`b2fc75c0 mov     eax,dword ptr [rsp+18h]
```

```
   8 00007ff6`b2fc75c4 pop     rdi
   8 00007ff6`b2fc75c5 ret
```

`0:000> bp 00007ff6`b2fc7599`

`0:000> g`

```
Breakpoint 0 hit
rax=0000000000000001 rbx=0000000000000000 rcx=0000000000000001
rdx=0000000000000001 rsi=0000000000000000 rdi=0000000000000000
rip=00007ff6b2fc7599 rsp=00000091842ffdc0 rbp=0000000000000000
 r8=00000220c577d1c0  r9=0000000000000000 r10=0000000000000000
r11=00000091842ffdb0 r12=0000000000000000 r13=0000000000000000
r14=0000000000000000 r15=0000000000000000
iopl=0         nv up ei pl nz na pe nc
cs=0033  ss=002b  ds=002b  es=002b  fs=0053  gs=002b             efl=00000202
FunctionParameters!arithmetic+0x9:
00007ff6`b2fc7599 mov     eax,dword ptr [rsp+10h] ss:00000091`842ffdd0=00000001
```

`0:000> dqs rsp L10`

```
00000091`842ffdc0  00000000`00000000 ; saved RDI
00000091`842ffdc8  00007ff6`b2fc75fd FunctionParameters!main+0x1d ; return address
00000091`842ffdd0  00000001`00000001 ; parameter 1 (dword)
00000091`842ffdd8  00007ff6`00000001 ; parameter 2 (dword)
00000091`842ffde0  03100800`000806ea
00000091`842ffde8  00007ff6`b2fc77d5 FunctionParameters!pre_cpp_initialization+0x15
00000091`842ffdf0  0000e669`00000000
00000091`842ffdf8  00007ff6`b2ffb110 FunctionParameters!__acrt_initialize+0x20
00000091`842ffe00  00000000`00000000
00000091`842ffe08  00007ff6`b2fc7a89 FunctionParameters!invoke_main+0x39
00000091`842ffe10  0000e669`00000001
00000091`842ffe18  00000220`c5779d90
00000091`842ffe20  00000000`00000000
00000091`842ffe28  00007ff6`b2fc824d
FunctionParameters!__scrt_release_startup_lock+0xd
00000091`842ffe30  00000000`00000001
00000091`842ffe38  00000220`c577d1c0
```

Parameter Mismatch Problem

To illustrate the importance of understanding stack memory layout, consider this typical interface mismatch problem. The function *main* calls *func* with two parameters:

```
// main.c
int main ()
{
    int locVar;
    func (1, 2);
    return 0;
}
```

The caller is expected the callee function *func* to see this stack memory layout:

```
RSP ->  Return address
        1
        2
        locVar
```

However, the callee expects 3 parameters instead of 2:

```
// func.c
int func (int a, int b, int c)
{
    // code to use parameters
    return 0;
}
```

func code sees this stack memory layout:

```
RSP -> Return address
        a
        b
        c
```

We see that parameter **c** coincides with *locVar* local *main* function variable, and this is clearly a software defect (bug).

Chapter x64.12: More Instructions

CPU Flags Register

In addition to registers, the CPU also contains a special 64-bit RFLAGS register where certain bits are set or cleared in response to arithmetic and other operations. Separate machine instructions can manipulate some bit values, and their values affect code execution.

For example, the DF bit (Direction Flag) determines the direction of memory copy operations and can be set by STD and cleared by CLD instructions. It has the default value of 0, and its location is shown in Picture x64.12.1, where only the first 32 bits of 64-bit RFLAGS are shown.

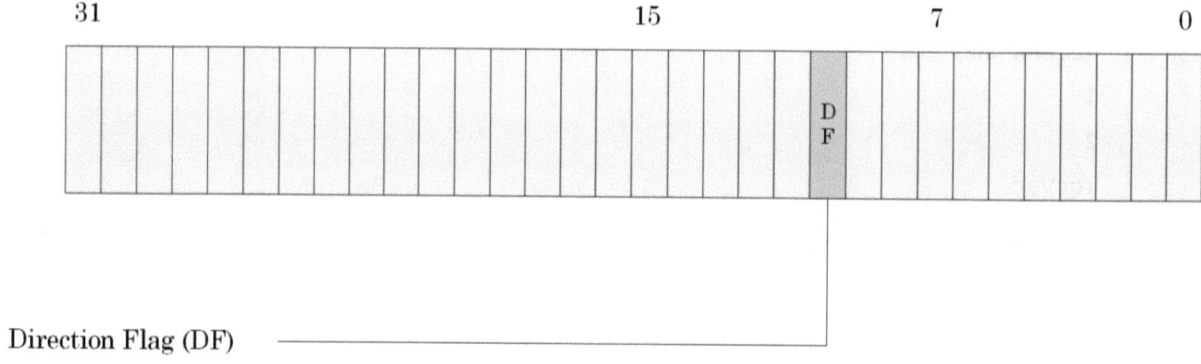

Picture x64.12.1

The Fastest Way to Fill Memory

This way (which may not be fastest on some CPUs) is done by STOSQ instruction that stores a quad value from RAX into a memory location whose address is in the RDI register ("D" means destination). After the value from RAX is transferred to memory, the instruction increments RDI by 8, and RDI register now points to the next QWORD in memory if the DF flag is 0. If the DF flag is 1, the RDI value is decremented by 8, and RDI now points to the previous QWORD in memory. There is an equivalent STOSD instruction that stores double words and increments or decrements RDI by 4.

If we prefix any instruction with the REP prefix, it causes the instruction to be repeated until the value in the RCX register is decremented to 0. For example, we can write very simple code that should theoretically zero "all memory" (practically, it traps because of access violation):

```
xor   rax, rax              ; fill with 0
mov   rdi, 0                ; starting address or xor rdi, rdi
mov   rcx, 0xffffffff / 4   ; 0x1fffffff quad words
rep   stosq
```

Here is REP STOSQ in pseudo-code:

```
WHILE (RCX != 0)
{
      [RDI] <- RAX

      IF DF = 0 THEN
            RDI <- RDI + 8
      ELSE
            RDI <- RDI - 8

      RCX <- RCX - 1
}
```

A simple example of erasing 32 bytes (4x8) is shown in Picture x64.12.2.

316 The Fastest Way to Fill Memory

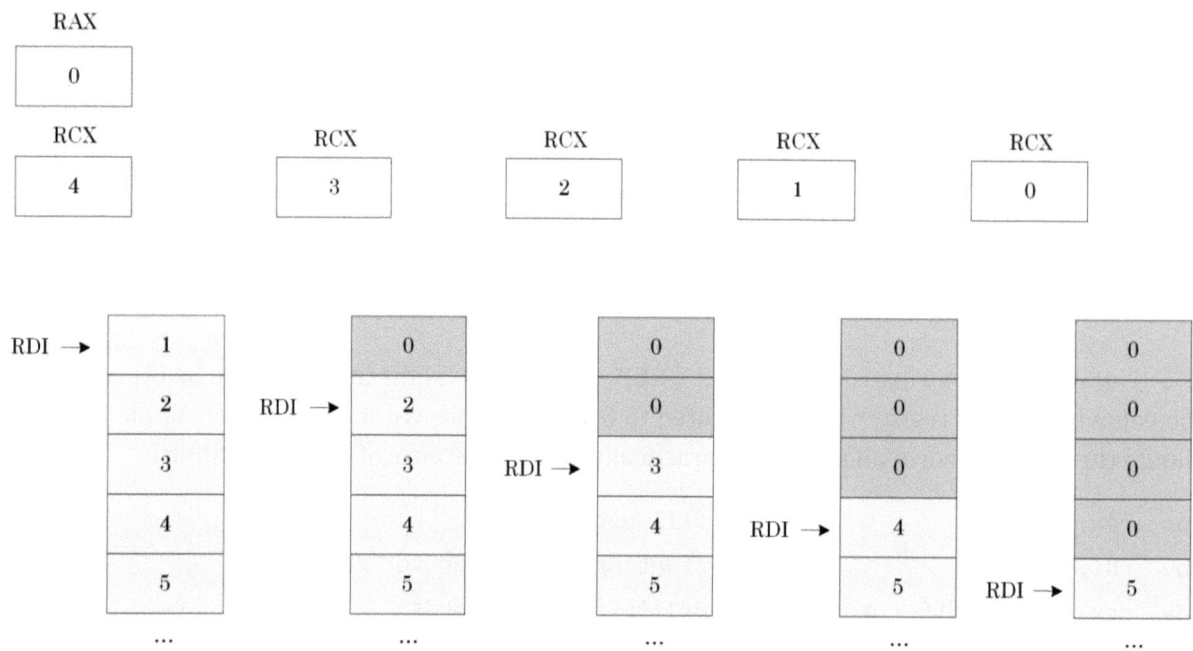

Picture x64.12.2

Testing for 0

ZF bit in the RFLAGS register is set to 1 if the instruction result is 0 and cleared otherwise. This bit is affected by:

- Arithmetic instructions (for example, ADD, SUB, MUL)
- Logical compare instruction (TEST)
- "Arithmetical" compare instruction (CMP)

The location of the ZF bit is shown in Picture x64.12.3.

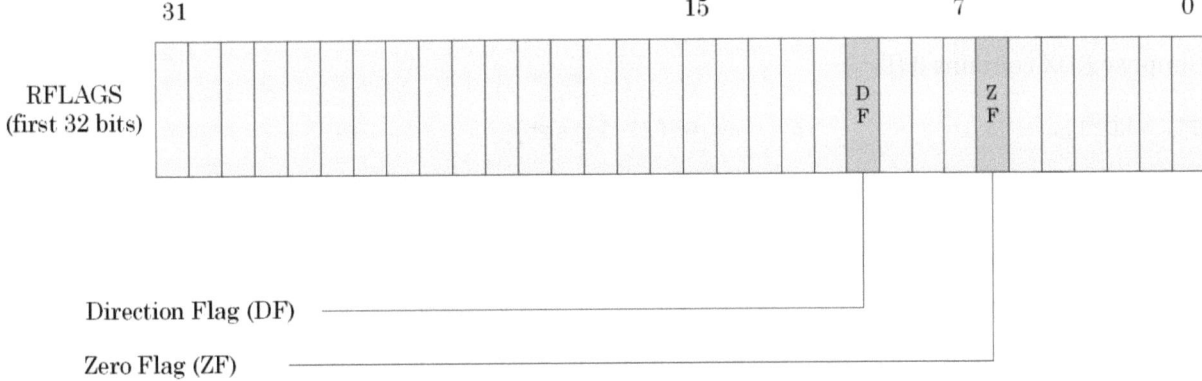

Picture x64.12.3

TEST - Logical Compare

This instruction computes bit-wise logical AND between both operands and sets flags (including ZF) according to the computed result (which is discarded):

```
TEST reg/mem, reg/imm
```

Examples:

```
TEST RDX, RDX
```

Suppose RDX register contains 4 (100_{bin})

```
100bin AND 100bin = 100bin    != 0 (ZF is cleared)
TEST RDX, 1
```

Suppose RDX contains 0 (0_{bin})

```
0bin AND 1bin = 0bin          == 0 (ZF is set)
```

Here is TEST instruction in pseudo-code (details not relevant to ZF bit are omitted):

```
TEMP <- OPERAND1 AND OPERAND2
IF TEMP = 0 THEN
        ZF <- 1
ELSE
        ZF <- 0
```

CMP – Compare Two Operands

This instruction compares the first operand with the second and sets flags (including ZF) according to the computed result (which is discarded). The comparison is performed by subtracting the second operand from the first (like SUB instruction: SUB RAX, 4).

```
CMP    reg/mem, reg/imm

CMP    reg, reg/mem/imm
```

Examples:

```
CMP    RDI, 0
```

Suppose RDI contains 0

```
0 - 0    == 0 (ZF is set)

CMP    RAX, 16
```

Suppose RAX contains 4_{hex}

$4_{hex} - 16_{hex}$ = FFFFFFFF`FFFFFFEE$_{hex}$!= 0 (ZF is cleared)

$4_{dec} - 22_{dec}$ = -18_{dec}

Here is CMP instruction in pseudo-code (details not relevant to ZF bit are omitted):

```
TEMP <- OPERAND1 - OPERAND2
IF TEMP = 0 THEN
       ZF <- 1
ELSE
       ZF <- 0
```

CMP instruction is equivalent to this pseudo-code sequence:

```
TEMP <- OPERAND1
SUB  TEMP, OPERAND2
```

TEST or CMP?

They are equivalent if we want to test for zero, but CMP instruction affects more flags:

TEST RAX, EAX

CMP RAX, 0

CMP instruction is used to compare for inequality (TEST instruction cannot be used here):

CMP RAX, 0   ; > 0 or < 0 ?

TEST instruction is used to see if individual bit is set

TEST RAX, 2   ; 2 == 0010$_{bin}$ or in C language: **if (var & 0x2)**

Examples where RAX has the value of 2:

TEST RAX, 4   ; 0010$_{bin}$ AND 0100$_{bin}$ = 0000$_{bin}$ (ZF is set)

TEST RAX, 6   ; 0010$_{bin}$ AND 0110$_{bin}$ = 0010$_{bin}$ (ZF is cleared)

Conditional Jumps

Consider these two C or C++ code fragments:

```
if (a == 0)                          if (a != 0)
{                                    {
    ++a;                                 ++a;
}                                    }
else                                 else
{                                    {
    --a;                                 --a;
}                                    }
```

CPU fetches instructions sequentially, so we must tell the CPU that we want to skip some instructions if some condition is (not) met, for example, if a != 0.

JNZ (jump if not zero) and JZ (jump if zero) test ZF flag and change RIP if ZF bit is cleared for JZN or set for JZ. The following assembly language code is equivalent to C/C++ code above:

```
        CMP     [A], 0                       MOV     EAX, [A]
        JNZ     label1                       TEST    EAX, EAX
        INC     [A]                          JZ      label1
        JMP     label2                       INC     EAX
label1: DEC     [A]                          JMP     label2
label2:                              label1: DEC     EAX
                                     label2:
```

The Structure of Registers

Some 64-bit registers have a legacy structure that allows us to address their lower 32-bit, 16-bit, and two 8-bit parts, as shown in Picture x64.12.4.

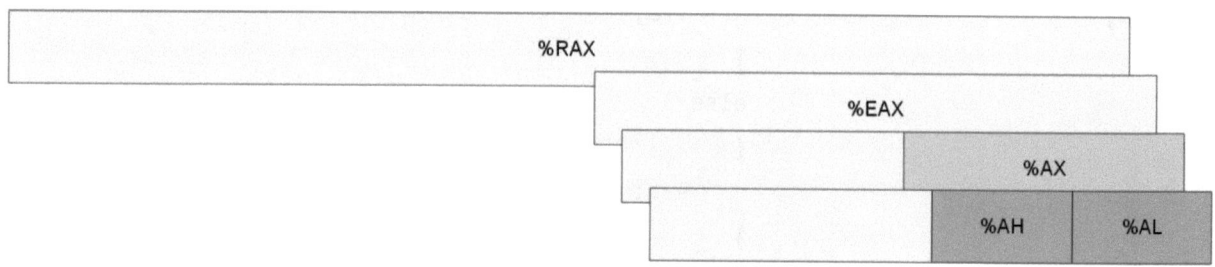

Picture x64.12.4

Function Return Value

Many functions return values via AL, EAX, or RAX register. For example:

`long long func();`

Return value is in RAX.

`int func();`

Return value is in EAX.

`bool func();`

Return value is in AL.

Note: bool values occupy one byte in memory.

Using Byte Registers

Suppose we have a byte value in the AL register, and we want to add this value to the ECX register. However, we don't know what values other parts of the full EAX register contain. We cannot use this instruction, for example:

```
MOV    EBX, AL    ; operand size conflict
```

The proposed solution in pseudo-code:

```
EBX <- AL              or       EAX <- AL

ECX <- ECX + EBX                ECX <- ECX + EAX
```

We can only use MOV instructions that have the same operand size for both source and destination, for example:

```
MOV    BL, AL

MOV    byte ptr [b], AL    ; in C: static bool b = func()
```

For this task, there is a special MOVZX (Move with Zero eXtend) instruction that replaces the contents of the first operand with the contents of the second operand while filling the rest of the bits with zeros:

```
MOVZX reg, reg/mem
```

Therefore our solution for the task becomes very simple:

```
MOVZX EBX, AL
ADD    ECX, EBX
```

We can also reuse the EAX register:

```
MOVZX EAX, AL
ADD    ECX, EAX
```

Chapter x64.13: Function Pointer Parameters

"FunctionPointerParameters" Project

This project is our final project, and it can be downloaded from

https://bitbucket.org/softwarediagnostics/pfwddr2/src/master/x64/Chapter13/

The summary of the project source code:

```cpp
// FunctionPointerParameters.cpp
int main(int argc, char* argv[])
{
    int a, b;

    printf("Enter a and b: ");
    scanf("%d %d", &a, &b);

    if (arithmetic (a, &b))
    {
        printf("Result = %d", b);
    }

    return 0;
}

// Arithmetic.cpp
bool arithmetic (int a, int *b)
{
    if (!b)
    {
        return false;
    }

    *b = *b + a;
    ++a;
    *b = a * *b;

    return true;
}
```

Commented Disassembly

Here is the commented disassembly from *Debug* executable.

```
FunctionParameters!main:
mov     qword ptr [rsp+10h],rdx ; saving main function parameters on stack
mov     dword ptr [rsp+8],ecx   ;
push    rdi                     ; saving RDI that might be used outside
sub     rsp,60h                 ; stack frame for variables and parameters
lea     rdi,[rsp+20h]           ; filling stack frame with 0xCC
mov     ecx,10h                 ;
mov     eax,0CCCCCCCCh          ;
rep     stos dword ptr [rdi]    ;
mov     ecx,dword ptr [rsp+70h] ;
;
; rcx <- address of "Enter a and b: " string (00007ff6`94cd7f20)
; 0:000> da 00007ff6`94cd7f20
; 00007ff6`94cd7f20   "Enter a and b: "
;
lea     rcx,[FunctionPointerParameters!__xt_z+0x110 (00007ff6`94cd7f20)]
call    FunctionPointerParameters!ILT+6565(printf) (00007ff6`94bd29aa)
lea     r8,[rsp+44h]            ; r8  <- address of b (3rd scanf parameter)
lea     rdx,[rsp+24h]           ; rdx <- address of a (2nd scanf parameter)
;
; rcx <- address of "%d %d" (00007ff6`94cd7f30) (1st scanf parameter)
; 0:000> da 00007ff6`94cd7f30
; 00007ff6`94cd7f30   "%d %d"
;
lea     rcx,[FunctionPointerParameters!__xt_z+0x120 (00007ff6`94cd7f30)]
call    FunctionPointerParameters!ILT+2100(scanf) (00007ff6`94bd1839)
lea     rdx,[rsp+44h]           ; rdx <- address of b (2nd arithmetic parameter)
mov     ecx,dword ptr [rsp+24h] ; ecx <- [a] (1st arithmetic parameter)
call    FunctionPointerParameters!ILT+6290(?arithmeticYA_NHPEAHZ) (00007ff6`94bd2897)
movzx   eax,al                  ; bool result from arithmetic
test    eax,eax                 ; testing for zero
je      FunctionPointerParameters!main+0x6a (00007ff6`94bd87fa)
mov     edx,dword ptr [rsp+44h] ; edx <- [b] (2nd printf parameter)
```

```
;
; rcx <- address of "Result = %d" (00007ff6`94cd7f38)
; (1st printf parameter)
; 0:000> da 00007ff6`94cd7f38
; 00007ff6`94cd7f38   "Result = %d"
;
lea    rcx,[FunctionPointerParameters!__xt_z+0x128 (00007ff6`94cd7f38)]
call   FunctionPointerParameters!ILT+6565(printf) (00007ff6`94bd29aa)
00007ff6`94bd87fa:
xor    eax,eax                  ; return result 0
mov    edi,eax                  ; saving return result in edi
mov    rcx,rsp                  ; the lowest stack address
;
; rdx <- possible address of information about stack frame
;
lea    rdx,[FunctionPointerParameters!__xt_z+0x1c0 (00007ff6`94cd7fd0)]
;
; Debug mode compilation usually includes health checks
;
call   FunctionPointerParameters!ILT+11370(_RTC_CheckStackVars) (00007ff6`94bd3c6f)
mov    eax,edi                  ; restoring return result
add    rsp,60h                  ; restoring previous stack frame
pop    rdi                      ; restoring RDI resister
ret                             ; return 0
```

FunctionParameters!arithmetic:

mov	qword ptr [rsp+10h],rdx	; saving the second function parameter &b
mov	dword ptr [rsp+8],ecx	; saving the first function parameter [a]
push	rdi	; saving RDI that might be used outside
cmp	qword ptr [rsp+18h],0	; if (&b==0) [rsp+10h+8h] shift due to rdi
jne	FunctionParameters!arithmetic+0x16 (**00007ff6`94bd8746**) ; non-zero	
xor	al,al	; false return result (0)
jmp	FunctionParameters!arithmetic+0x49 (**00007ff6`94bd8779**) ; return	

00007ff6`94bd8746:

mov	rax,qword ptr [rsp+18h]	; rax <- address of b (in C: &b)
mov	eax,dword ptr [rax]	; eax <- [b] (in C: t = *b)
add	eax,dword ptr [rsp+10h]	; eax <- [a] [rsp+8h+8h] shift due to rdi
		; (in C: t = t + a)
mov	rcx,qword ptr [rsp+18h]	; rcx <- address of b (in C: &b)
mov	dword ptr [rcx],eax	; [b] <- eax (in C: *b = t)
mov	eax,dword ptr [rsp+10h]	; eax <- [a]
inc	eax	; eax <- eax + 1
mov	dword ptr [rsp+10h],eax	; [a] <- eax (++a)
mov	rax,qword ptr [rsp+18h]	; rax <- address of b (in C: &b)
mov	ecx,dword ptr [rsp+10h]	; ecx <- [a] (in C: t = a)
imul	ecx,dword ptr [rax]	; ecx <- ecx * [b] (in C: t = t * *b)
mov	eax,ecx	; saving ecx in eax
mov	rcx,qword ptr [rsp+18h]	; rcx <- address of b (in C: &b)
mov	dword ptr [rcx],eax	; [b] <- eax (in C: *b = t)
mov	al,1	; return result (true, 1)

00007ff6`94bd8779:

pop	rdi	; restoring saved RDI
ret		; return

Chapter x64.14: Summary of Code Disassembly Patterns

This final chapter summarizes various patterns we have encountered during the reading of this book.

Function Prolog/Epilog

Function prolog

```
mov   qword ptr [rsp+XXX], rcx
; can also be dword mov if the function parameter is 32-bit
; mov   dword ptr [rsp+XXX], ecx
;
; save more parameters if necessary from
; RDX, R8 and R9 registers
sub   rsp, YYY
```

Function epilog

```
add   rsp, YYY
ret
```

Knowing prolog can help identify situations when symbol files or function start addresses are not correct. For example, suppose we have the following stack trace:

```
func3+0x5F
func2+0x8F
func+0x20
```

If we disassemble the *func2* function and see that it doesn't start with prolog, we may assume that the stack trace needs more attention:

```
0:000> u func2 func2+0x8F
add   rsp, 10
ret
mov   qword ptr [rsp+XXX], rcx
```

Here is another example of prolog and epilog from the *printf* function:

```
0:000> uf printf
FunctionParameters!printf:
   49 00000001`400013e0 mov     qword ptr [rsp+8],rcx
   49 00000001`400013e5 mov     qword ptr [rsp+10h],rdx
   49 00000001`400013ea mov     qword ptr [rsp+18h],r8
   49 00000001`400013ef mov     qword ptr [rsp+20h],r9
   49 00000001`400013f4 sub     rsp,58h

FunctionParameters!printf+0x13c:
   73 00000001`4000151c add     rsp,58h
   73 00000001`40001520 ret
```

Parameters and Local Variables

Local variable value

```
mov  reg, [rsp+XXX]
```

Local variable address

```
lea  reg, [rsp+XXX]
```

Passing the first 4 function parameters from right to left

RCX, RDX, R8, and R9

Note: Although we haven't seen examples for more than 4 function parameters, they are passed via the stack, for example, via PUSH instruction or by allocating more stack via SUB RSP, XXX, and then using MOV instructions. Here is one example:

```
0:000> uf CreateProcessW
kernel32!CreateProcessW:
00000000`76ceac30 sub     rsp,68h
00000000`76ceac34 mov     rax,qword ptr [rsp+0B8h]
00000000`76ceac3c mov     qword ptr [rsp+58h],0
00000000`76ceac45 mov     qword ptr [rsp+50h],rax
00000000`76ceac4a mov     rax,qword ptr [rsp+0B0h]
00000000`76ceac52 mov     qword ptr [rsp+48h],rax
00000000`76ceac57 mov     rax,qword ptr [rsp+0A8h]
00000000`76ceac5f mov     qword ptr [rsp+40h],rax
00000000`76ceac64 mov     rax,qword ptr [rsp+0A0h]
00000000`76ceac6c mov     qword ptr [rsp+38h],rax
00000000`76ceac71 mov     eax,dword ptr [rsp+98h]
00000000`76ceac78 mov     dword ptr [rsp+30h],eax
00000000`76ceac7c mov     eax,dword ptr [rsp+90h]
00000000`76ceac83 mov     dword ptr [rsp+28h],eax
00000000`76ceac87 mov     qword ptr [rsp+20h],r9
00000000`76ceac8c mov     r9,r8
00000000`76ceac8f mov     r8,rdx
00000000`76ceac92 mov     rdx,rcx
00000000`76ceac95 xor     ecx,ecx
00000000`76ceac97 call    kernel32!CreateProcessInternalW (00000000`76ce8770)
00000000`76ceac9c add     rsp,68h
00000000`76ceaca0 ret
```

Static/global variable address (or string constant)

```
mov   reg, 0x00000001` 0076d10
```

Local variable vs. local variable address

```
mov   reg, [rsp+XXX]          ; local variable
call  func


lea   reg, [rsp+XXX]          ; local variable address
call  func
```

LEA (Load Effective Address)

The following instruction

```
lea   rax, [rsp+0x8]
```

is equivalent to the following arithmetic sequence:

```
mov   rax, rsp
add   rsp, 0x8
```

Accessing Parameters and Local Variables

Accessing DWORD value

```
mov     eax, dword ptr [rsp+0x8]
add     eax, 0x1
```

Accessing QWORD value

```
mov     rax, qword ptr [rsp+0x8]
add     rax, 0x1
```

Accessing and dereferencing a pointer to a DWORD value

```
lea     rax, [rsp+0x8]
mov     eax, dword ptr [rax]
add     eax, 0x1
```

Accessing and dereferencing a pointer to a QWORD value

```
lea     rax, [rsp+0x8]
mov     rax, qword ptr [rax]
add     rax, 0x1
```

Appendix x64: Using Docker Environment

With this edition, it is possible to use a Docker container image containing preinstalled WinDbg x64 with required chapter materials. However, the output may differ due to the absence of OS symbols.

```
D:\WinDbg.Docker.PFWDDR2>docker pull patterndiagnostics/windbg:10.0.22000.194-pfwddr2
```

```
D:\WinDbg.Docker.PFWDDR2>docker run -it patterndiagnostics/windbg:10.0.22000.194-pfwddr2
```

```
Microsoft Windows [Version 10.0.20348.587]
(c) Microsoft Corporation. All rights reserved.
```

```
C:\WinDbg> windbg64 x64\Chapter2\Debug\ArithmeticProjectC.exe
```

```
Microsoft (R) Windows Debugger Version 10.0.22000.194 AMD64
Copyright (c) Microsoft Corporation. All rights reserved.

CommandLine: x64\Chapter2\Debug\ArithmeticProjectC.exe

************* Path validation summary **************
Response                         Time (ms)     Location
Deferred                                       srv*
Symbol search path is: srv*
Executable search path is:
ModLoad: 00007ff7`ec5e0000 00007ff7`ec70e000   ArithmeticProjectC.exe
ModLoad: 00007ff8`43d70000 00007ff8`43f70000   ntdll.dll
ModLoad: 00007ff8`41370000 00007ff8`4142c000   C:\Windows\System32\KERNEL32.DLL
ModLoad: 00007ff8`40c60000 00007ff8`40fbf000   C:\Windows\System32\KERNELBASE.dll
(7e4.7e8): Break instruction exception - code 80000003 (first chance)
ntdll!LdrpDoDebuggerBreak+0x30:
00007ff8`43e44504 cc              int     3
```

```
0:000> .sympath+ x64\Chapter2\Debug\
Symbol search path is: srv*;x64\Chapter2\Debug\
Expanded Symbol search path is:
cache*;SRV*https://msdl.microsoft.com/download/symbols;x64\chapter2\debug\

************* Path validation summary **************
Response                         Time (ms)     Location
Deferred                                       srv*
OK                                             x64\Chapter2\Debug\
```

```
0:000> bp ArithmeticProjectC!main
*** WARNING: Unable to verify checksum for ArithmeticProjectC.exe
```

```
0:000> .prompt_allow +reg
Allow the following information to be displayed at the prompt:
(Other settings can affect whether the information is actually displayed)
   sym - Symbol for current instruction
   dis - Disassembly of current instruction
    ea - Effective address for current instruction
   reg - Register state
```

```
    src - Source info for current instruction
Do not allow the following information to be displayed at the prompt:
  None
```

```
0:000> g
Breakpoint 0 hit
rax=0000000000000001 rbx=0000000000000000 rcx=0000000000000001
rdx=0000018d85be7d60 rsi=0000000000000000 rdi=0000000000000000
rip=00007ff7ec5e7590 rsp=0000008d7f5bf658 rbp=0000000000000000
 r8=0000018d85be7e00  r9=0000018d85be8e10 r10=0000018d85be032c
r11=0000008d7f5bf600 r12=0000000000000000 r13=0000000000000000
r14=0000000000000000 r15=0000000000000000
iopl=0         nv up ei pl nz na pe nc
cs=0033  ss=002b  ds=002b  es=002b  fs=0053  gs=002b             efl=00000202
ArithmeticProjectC!main:
00007ff7`ec5e7590 4889542410      mov     qword ptr [rsp+10h],rdx
ss:0000008d`7f5bf668=00007ff7ec613213
```

```
0:000> .asm no_code_bytes
Assembly options: no_code_bytes
```

```
0:000> uf main
ArithmeticProjectC!main:
00007ff7`ec5e7590 mov     qword ptr [rsp+10h],rdx
00007ff7`ec5e7595 mov     dword ptr [rsp+8],ecx
00007ff7`ec5e7599 push    rdi
00007ff7`ec5e759a mov     dword ptr [ArithmeticProjectC!a (00007ff7`ec6fa210)],1
00007ff7`ec5e75a4 mov     dword ptr [ArithmeticProjectC!b (00007ff7`ec6fa214)],1
00007ff7`ec5e75ae mov     eax,dword ptr [ArithmeticProjectC!a (00007ff7`ec6fa210)]
00007ff7`ec5e75b4 mov     ecx,dword ptr [ArithmeticProjectC!b (00007ff7`ec6fa214)]
00007ff7`ec5e75ba add     ecx,eax
00007ff7`ec5e75bc mov     eax,ecx
00007ff7`ec5e75be mov     dword ptr [ArithmeticProjectC!b (00007ff7`ec6fa214)],eax
00007ff7`ec5e75c4 mov     eax,dword ptr [ArithmeticProjectC!a (00007ff7`ec6fa210)]
00007ff7`ec5e75ca inc     eax
00007ff7`ec5e75cc mov     dword ptr [ArithmeticProjectC!a (00007ff7`ec6fa210)],eax
00007ff7`ec5e75d2 mov     eax,dword ptr [ArithmeticProjectC!a (00007ff7`ec6fa210)]
00007ff7`ec5e75d8 imul    eax,dword ptr [ArithmeticProjectC!b (00007ff7`ec6fa214)]
00007ff7`ec5e75df mov     dword ptr [ArithmeticProjectC!b (00007ff7`ec6fa214)],eax
00007ff7`ec5e75e5 xor     eax,eax
00007ff7`ec5e75e7 pop     rdi
00007ff7`ec5e75e8 ret
```

```
0:000> q
quit:
NatVis script unloaded from 'C:\Program Files\Windows
Kits\10\Debuggers\x64\Visualizers\atlmfc.natvis'
NatVis script unloaded from 'C:\Program Files\Windows
Kits\10\Debuggers\x64\Visualizers\ObjectiveC.natvis'
NatVis script unloaded from 'C:\Program Files\Windows
Kits\10\Debuggers\x64\Visualizers\concurrency.natvis'
NatVis script unloaded from 'C:\Program Files\Windows
Kits\10\Debuggers\x64\Visualizers\cpp_rest.natvis'
NatVis script unloaded from 'C:\Program Files\Windows
Kits\10\Debuggers\x64\Visualizers\stl.natvis'
```

```
NatVis script unloaded from 'C:\Program Files\Windows
Kits\10\Debuggers\x64\Visualizers\Windows.Data.Json.natvis'
NatVis script unloaded from 'C:\Program Files\Windows
Kits\10\Debuggers\x64\Visualizers\Windows.Devices.Geolocation.natvis'
NatVis script unloaded from 'C:\Program Files\Windows
Kits\10\Debuggers\x64\Visualizers\Windows.Devices.Sensors.natvis'
NatVis script unloaded from 'C:\Program Files\Windows
Kits\10\Debuggers\x64\Visualizers\Windows.Media.natvis'
NatVis script unloaded from 'C:\Program Files\Windows
Kits\10\Debuggers\x64\Visualizers\windows.natvis'
NatVis script unloaded from 'C:\Program Files\Windows
Kits\10\Debuggers\x64\Visualizers\winrt.natvis'

C:\WinDbg>exit

D:\WinDbg.Docker.PFWDDR2>
```

Printed by Libri Plureos GmbH in Hamburg, Germany